Family Therapy for Beginners:

A Practical Manual on the Concepts, Skills and Techniques of

Structural and Strategic Family Therapy

Jay Cerio, Ph.D.

ii

ISBN-13: 978-0692095386 (Guidance Resource Associates)
ISBN-10: 0692095381

Copies may be purchased from:
Guidance Resource Associates
P.O. Box 1142
Alfred, NY 14802
johncerio@gmail.com

To my wife, Terry,

our children and their spouses, and

our 11 grandchildren.

Acknowledgements

This book is the product of, literally, decades of counseling parents and families that were struggling with the many issues and stresses that are inherent to the organism that we call "the family," as well as my concomitant efforts to train counseling professionals in the skills and conceptual framework for working with families. I have always held the belief that with clients or students, the learning goes in both directions; that is, while I may be helping them learn about themselves or a particular topic, they "teach" me, and make a better counselor and teacher. So, thanks to all of the families and students with whom I have worked over the years, particularly to my New York City students, whose willingness to share their diverse family experiences helped me refine some of the ideas discussed in this book.

I am blessed to be married to a wonderful woman who helped me expand my concept of "family." A talented and successful family therapist in her own right, my wife, Terry, has been an ongoing source of support and insight in my work, as well as an individual with incredible tolerance and patience. In other words, she put up with the constant distraction of my writing this book when we could have been doing something fun together. Thanks, honey.

I would like to thank the many mentors and colleagues who taught me not only the skills for being an effective counselor, but also the essential values and attitudes that optimize a counselor's effectiveness: the late T.F. "Fritz" Renick and Hugh "Gunner" Gunnison, who taught me all of the "basics;" Lyn Styczynski and Len Greenberg, my original family therapy mentors; Salvador Minuchin, whose "tough" supervision helped me become a better family therapist; and my friends, Ray Holz and Bob Bitting, colleagues who share the same values about counseling and people that I do.

A special shout out to my brother, Jim, Dr. Jim Cerio, psychologist extraordinaire, who provides a great example of our family's obsessive-compulsive patterns by starting out intending to just read this book but ending up doing a beautiful and thorough job of editing it. My sincere thanks for all of his efforts!

Table of Contents

General Systems Theory
What is a system?....Subsystem and suprasystems.... More about boundaries....Open and closed systems....Structure and process....Basic laws of GST...Simplified cybernetics: Feedback and control.

In the Beginning
Precursors....Founding parents....Foster parents....Frieda Fromm-Reichman.... Harry Stack Sullivan....Grandparents....Theodore Lidz....Lyman Wynne.... Parents....John Elderkin Bell....Murray Bowen....The Palo Alto Group....Viginia Satir....Jay Haley....Salvador Minuchin....The Godfather....Carl Whitaker...The Women's Project.

Stuctural/Strategic Concepts
Basic assumptions....Developmental stages....World view....Subsystems and boundaries....Hierarchy....Triangles....Triangulation....Circular patterns.

The Genogram

The DAFFI-DUCC

The Role of the Counselor
Power and responsibility....Have a plan....Respect the family....Multiordinality....Be aware of your position.

Basic Microskills
Joining....Interviewing....Observing....Tracking patterns....Moving in and out....Challenging....Reframing....Blocking....Eliciting enactments.

The Different Animal
Role of power...Role of development....Family of origin patterns.

Counseling Couples
Components of couples counseling....Interventions....The ship is sinking.

Introduction

In previous writings, I have made the statement, "Counseling isn't rocket science;" in other words, we counselor educators tend to overly complicate what is, I believe, the scientific art of helping people. But when it comes to family therapy/counseling, I'm going to contradict myself. In the counseling field, *family therapy is rocket science!* If you think of traditional individual and group counseling as the Newtonian physics of the field, family therapy represents the shift to quantum theory. It is necessarily complex because families are complex. It rejects notions of the individual in favor of the organism that we call the family system. It requires a different level of understanding, different conceptual models, and different skills than individual and group counseling approaches. It is, in essence, a field unto itself.

The Family

THERE ARE NO NORMAL FAMILES! Families are these crazy, complex organisms that often defy logic and reason, yet, for the most part, they somehow survive. And for this reason, *EVERY FAMILY IS NORMAL IN ITS OWN WAY!* Some families' idea of normal deviates significantly from the range of culturally acceptable behavior, but in terms of the family's functioning, it attains some state of equilibrium that keeps the family together in spite of its cultural deviance. However, if the family's deviation from cultural norms is harmful, eventually the institutions of the culture must upset the family's stable state and the family will need to find another, more acceptable and safe state of stability to survive.

Don't worry about normal, because it doesn't really exist. One of my mentors once said, "Mistakes are part of being a parent and being a member of a family. If you are going to be a normal parent, you need to understand that you will make mistakes. And for this reason, the capacity to recognize that you have made a mistake, and the capacity to forgive, is inherent to families (Minuchin, Founders Series Video, 1991).

To my Gramma Cerio, family went well beyond biological connections. Family was open and inclusive, not clannish and exclusive. Unconditional love and acceptance were essential to Gramma's idea of family. The Cerio family that I experienced included not only my father's siblings and our cousins, but also people like our Uncle Larry, Aunt Mellie, and Uncle Ray. None of us were related to them by blood, but they were part of our family because Gramma accepted them into the family. And at every family event—weddings, holidays, funerals, birthdays—there they were, and we never questioned whether or not they were our uncles and aunts. They just were, because in our family, people were included.

A family IS what the family defines itself to be. Some families are closed and clannish and accept only individuals related by blood into the family. Some families are open and accepting and allow many individuals into the family who are not biologically related to the family. Some families have two moms and no dads. Others have two dads and no moms. Some families have mothers, fathers, stepmothers, stepfathers, and many, many grandparents. And in our culture, many, many families have just one parent.

The point is that we are always part of a family, whether we want to be or not. That's one of the differences between families and other social groups. We can choose, say, the religious group we want to belong to, but we can't choose our families. So, when we get disenchanted with a social group, we can just quit. But, *YOU CAN NEVER QUIT YOUR FAMILY.* Our families always influence us, even if that influence leads us to leave the family, physically, or choose to be completely different from our families. The fact that individuals decide to live in a way that is different from the way they were raised is a sign of the strong influence of the family. That is why I love working with families. I know that if I can succeed

in helping a family function better, I will have helped the children in that family have better,

more healthy experiences growing up. If this happens, perhaps they will be happier adults who

will provide better experiences to their children. And, so it goes.

It is important for users of this book to understand that I do not consider myself to be a

family therapist. While I am trained in family therapy and have incorporated it into my work, I

am not exclusively a family therapist. I am a psychologist and counselor who uses family

therapy as a foundation for understanding what I do and as a tool for addressing certain types of

counseling issues. In this same way, I also incorporate individual cognitive-behavioral

techniques and play therapy into my work as a counselor. My perspective is that to be an

effective counselor, I must have many "tools in my box," and family therapy is one of my tools.

It is probably because of this that I have gravitated toward structural and strategic therapy,

relatively flexible, open systems of family therapy.

The Field of Family Therapy

Family therapy as a field is the product of the dysfunctional psychotherapy family. There

would be no field of family therapy if it wasn't for those most dysfunctional of parents, the

Freudians. Out of their bickering, disagreements, and authoritarian parenting style was born a

child who was called family therapy. When family therapy raised its head in the 1950's, the

field of psychotherapy was ripe for rebellion. Various pioneers were disillusioned with the focus

of the psychoanalytic approach on the individual and the disregard for the influence of the family

except for the negative influence of parents. Thus, psychoanalysis would isolate clients from the

Family, in order to "cure" them. With the exception of such neo-Freudians as Adler and

Erikson, the staunch, died-in-the-wool Freudians saw the family as destructive.

It was rebels like Bowen, Minuchin, and Whitaker, who stood up and recognized the powerful influence of the family, both positive and negative, on individuals, and the necessity to understand and harness this power to help clients. They concluded from their own experiences that you can never leave your family, so, instead of trying to fix the individual, they saw their mission as helping the family so the individuals in the family could be more functional. The founders also recognized the importance of the field itself being more functional and collaborative, rather than adversarial and confrontative, as had been the case with psychotherapy. Thus, the early attempts to develop approaches for intervening with families involved a great deal of cross fertilization of ideas, cooperative projects, and sharing. When you study models of family therapy, you see many similarities and common ideas that have been incorporated into various approaches.

Research on the general efficacy of family therapy has been very promising. Reviews of the research have demonstrated the efficacy of this approach concluding that family therapy is equally or more effective than other treatment approaches and produces positive change in a relatively short period of time (less than 20 sessions) compared to other approaches (Gunn & Fisher, 1989). The improvement rate when using family therapy with child behavioral problems is 71 percent, with the overall improvement rate across problems and client groups being 73 percent. Watzlawick, Weakland, and Fisch (1974) report an improvement rate of 72 percent with no reported symptom substitution. Gurman (1983) and Gurman, Kniskern, and Pinsof (1986) in reviews of outcome research, concluded that several different types of family therapy were more effective than individual therapy with family-focused problems.

Becoming a Family Therapist

Can any counselor become a family therapist? My answer is an emphatic, "No." Not everyone who enters the counseling field has the temperament and skills to deal with families effectively, just as not everyone possesses the characteristics and skills to be a good individual counselor. The effective family counselor needs to be an expert in multi-tasking: simultaneously focusing on individual family members, tracking what other members are doing, conceptualizing the dynamics, thinking tactically about how to shift an immediate dynamic, and thinking strategically about where the family needs to arrive at the end of a session and in the future to be more functional. All of these tasks need to be automatic in order to maintain the immediacy of the counseling interaction. There are many, many counselors who are very good individual therapists who just cannot do all of the tasks described above very well. This doesn't mean that they are bad counselors, it just means that they should stay away from working with families.

So, what makes a good family therapist? In addition to the ability to observe, think, and act simultaneously, I think that effective family counselors possess the following backgrounds:

- Solid individual counseling skills and experience.

- The capacity to empathize with individual family members who are presenting very different viewpoints.

- Play therapy skills and experience which helps keep young children engaged during family sessions.

- Comfort with highly charged emotional situations.

- The capacity to join and become part of the family, and

- The capacity to disengage and become a neutral outsider, when necessary.

- Knowledge of the systems conceptual framework.

- A good sense of humor and knowing when to use it.

- A "standard bag of tricks" from which to draw interventions.

- Enough creativity to develop unique interventions for unique family situations.

One comment on the nature of knowledge in a practical field such as counseling and psychotherapy: Real knowledge is not just an accumulation of information. I will steal from my mathematician son's language to illustrate what I mean.

$$K_R = I + E_P + E_L$$

Where K_R = Real Knowledge

I = Information about the area

E_P = Practical Experience in number of clients seen.

E_L = Life Experience in years

In other words, to truly be knowledgeable about counseling, you need both information about counseling theories and techniques, AND professional experience counseling people. The more clients with whom you have been able to use counseling techniques, the greater the pool of practical knowledge from which you can draw in the future. If you add general life experience to the equation, you end up with something that we might call "*wisdom*" related to the practice of counseling. A book like this contributes only to the information component related to family therapy. If you really want to use family therapy, you will need to seek the practical training and experience component.

Using This Book

The purpose of this book is to provide fledging family counselors with a foundation in the knowledge and skills necessary to begin using family therapy techniques. It is not supposed to be a scholarly, comprehensive text. It is designed to be a simple, straightforward guide to getting started, a resource on the basics. There are many good in-depth texts in the field at this very moment, which I will recommend to you throughout the book. But there aren't many books that deal with the "nuts and bolts"—the practical mechanics of working with families. It's my intention that this book will do just that.

I suggest that you read this book in sequence, as each chapter builds on the information provided in previous chapters. The first chapter reviews the foundational concepts that underlie systems approaches to family therapy and provides background on the development of the field. Chapter 2 focuses on understanding and applying the basic ideas of the structural and strategic approaches. Chapter 3 is devoted to a very important activity: examining the dynamics of the reader's family of origin and thinking about how those family experiences will influence his or her work as a family counselor. Chapter 4 provides an overview of the micro-skills involved in counseling interactions with families. Chapter 5 discusses a framework for interventions, while Chapter 6 discusses the application of family approaches in school settings. Chapter 7 presents ideas for dealing with some of the common challenging family situations encountered by counselors. Chapter 8 is a brief introduction to couples counseling, specifically, the aspects of couples counseling that are somewhat different than those related to seeing entire families.

Throughout the book, I will use the terms family therapist and family counselor interchangeably. I do not differentiate between counseling and therapy because I see this as an issue of semantics and professional turf wars rather than actual practice.

Chapter 1

A Brief History of the
Family Therapy Universe

Chapter Overview

In this chapter, you will:

- Learn the basic tenets of General Systems Theory.

- Learn about some of the founders of the family therapy field.

- Examine important foundation theories and constructs of family therapy.

General Systems Theory

Introduction

Family therapy has been one of the fastest growing approaches in the counseling field since the 1970's. While many of the family therapy models have been in use in one form or another since the mid-1950's (Nichols, 1984), it wasn't until the early 1980's that a number of the major figures in the field published works designed to explain their systems (Madanes, 1981; Minuchin & Fishman, 1981; Whitaker, 1988). In particular, the work of Bowen (1978), the members of the Palo Alto group (Haley, 1976; Jackson & Weakland, 1961), Minuchin (1974), and the Milan associates (Selvini Palazzoli, Boscolo, Cecchin, & Prata, 1974), has led to a view of the family as a constellation of subsystems, emphasizing the effect that change in one family member exerts throughout the entire family.

Before discussing the basic concepts of structural/strategic family therapy, it is important for you to understand the underlying ideas on which the various systems approaches are based. This leads us to a very basic discussion of General Systems Theory (GST). GST grew out of the post-World War II work of Norbert Wiener on cybernetics (1948) and was formally expounded by Ludwig von Bertallanfy (1967). Wiener was the force behind the Cybernetic Conferences of the late 1940's that drew together experts from many scientific and engineering fields, and from which early systems ideas developed (Haley, 1991, Founders Series). Von Bertallanfy sought to formalize these ideas, acknowledging how rules and relationships in one scientific field had direct counterparts in other fields. Therefore, certain general principles crossed the lines of specific disciplines. GST is a theory of theories. It is a meta-theory that connects the common patterns and similarities of theories across such disciplines as biology, computer science, social systems, and, in our case, family functioning. The primary goal of GST is to unify science by developing theories which are applicable to most types of systems.

GST is interested with "organized complexity," with phenomena that cannot be adequately analyzed and understood within a linear viewpoint (organized simplicity) or explained statistically due to randomness (disorganized complexity). This lens is particularly suited to understanding families, which are organized and complex, with strong, ongoing interactions among the parts. GST is also concerned with wholes instead of or in addition to parts. That is, it is non-reductionist; it does not try to explain wholes by reducing them to simpler parts. Instead, in GST the understanding of parts depends on how each part's function serves the whole.

As a result of this conceptual framework, the view of causality--cause-and-effect--is also non-linear. While science traditionally identifies the cause of a phenomenon back through a chain of proximal events, GST is concerned with ***circular or mutual causality*** (Constantine, 1986). The *system*, then becomes the explanation for a phenomenon, not the actions of parts. It is the mutual relationships of the parts that is important.

By now, your eyes have glazed over and you are beginning to doze, thinking about food, and becoming increasingly bored with anything related to family therapy. But bear with me. In a few pages, I will be using "potty" talk-- more specifically, talking about toilets--and things will get very, very exciting! So, read on.

Definitions

    What is a System? A system is any set of interrelated parts or components that exhibit a coherent or consistent behavior as a unit within a bounded area (Constantine, 1986). The system is defined by its ***boundary***, the part of the system that separates the internal parts of the system from its surroundings or environment (Constantine, 1986). The "area" does not have to be concretely defined or observable. For instance, a cell has a physical boundary, the cell wall. On the other hand, a family has *psychological* boundaries, rules for who is considered a member of the family. You can't see them, you can't feel them, but they are there. And you can see how these boundaries function when, for example, someone or something threatens the system, such as a social services caseworker investigating an abuse charge who is met with silence or equivocation from family members. The family's boundary to external influences attempts to keep the caseworker outside the family system.

    Subsystems and Suprasystems. A figure-ground relationship exists within and outside of systems. Every system is comprised of *subsystems* that are enclosed within the systems' boundaries and have specific roles in maintaining the functioning of the system. Conversely, every system is a subsystem of a larger *suprasystem* (Constantine, 1986). The figure-ground relationship becomes important when you are trying to understand the role and function of a system. If you are studying cancer cells in terms of their impact on the body, then you are viewing the cancer cells as subsystems of the human body system. But, if you are interested in structures within a cancer cell that are involved in the cell's functioning, then you are viewing the cell as a suprasystem. Human social systems function in much the same way. An individual is a subsystem of a suprasystem of individuals such as siblings, which is a subsystem of the suprasystem, nuclear family; which is a subsystem of the suprasystem, extended family; which is a subsystem of a suprasystem, community; which is a subsystem of a suprasystem, county or state or nation; ad nauseum. Conversely, a human being is comprised of subsystems, such as the cardiovascular system, nervous system, and endocrine system. These are comprised of subsystems called organs, which are made up of subsystems called tissue, which are made up of subsystems called cells, all the way down to the atomic level. And, as a "real" scientist reminded a certain social "scientist," there are even sub-atomic subsystems comprised of quarks and the elusive "god" particle, Higgs' boson (Cerio, fnals09.blogspot.com). How you perceive the system depends on your frame of reference.

More about boundaries. As stated above, the system *boundary* is what defines a system as an entity that is separate from the surrounding environment. All boundaries should be semi-permeable. They need to simultaneously allow and resist passage of material, information and the like, in order to maintain the integrity of the system. (Constantine, 1986). In most systems, it is usually easier for material to pass in one direction than another. For instance, in families, it should be easier for a parent to join the child subsystem for the purpose of playing (an appropriate activity) than for the child to join the parent subsystem to advise a parent how to discipline a sibling (an inappropriate activity). In the former situation, the roles are appropriate and well-defined, while in the latter they are inappropriate and poorly defined. This "region" where the boundaries of two systems meet is called the *interface*.

Open and Closed Systems. Systems are influenced by the external environment to different degrees, depending on whether they are open or closed. An *open system* is one that affects and is affected by its environment. All living systems are open because they have to be impacted by the environment in which they live and vice versa. A *closed system* is completely isolated from its environment, a limited, self-contained entity (Constantine, 1986).

With the development of the computer and communications technology that exist today, it is difficult to find a truly closed social system. The countries that are probably closest to closed social systems are North Korea and Iran, which tightly control the inflow of information, even on the internet. However, even the regimes of these countries cannot completely block outside influences to their systems. Aside from countries, there are a few aboriginal tribes in South America and Oceana, some fundamental religious groups, and cults that function as closed social systems.

Structure and Process. Within systems, there is an interplay between the system structures and the ongoing processes in the system. *Structure* is the static or stable elements of a system, which includes such things as the subsystems and the system boundaries. *Process* is the relatively dynamic or fluid aspects of a system that we are able to identify by observing change or instability in the system. The thing about structure is that there is really no one true structure; it depends on your point of view. It is virtually impossible to distinguish structure and process because *EVERYTHING IS IN PROCESS*. Therefore, the system structure is constantly changing to different degrees at different points of time and depending on the observer's frame of reference (Constantine, 1986).

As you will see later in the book, these ideas are vividly apparent in family therapy. The structures within families influence the dynamics (or process) and the dynamics of families determine structures. For instance, in disciplinary interactions between parents and a child, one parent may feel incompetent in dealing with the child and is unsuccessful in getting the child to conform to limits. The other parent may then have to step in and, in doing so, succeeds in setting limits and begins to feel more competent in dealing with the child. This dynamic, then, creates a hierarchical structure in which the successful parent is more powerful than the unsuccessful parent. If this becomes an ongoing pattern, the child may even rise above the unsuccessful parent in the hierarchy, which will contribute to maintaining the pattern. On the other hand the parent who is less competent at setting limits may be much more competent in nurturing that same child than the competent limit setting parent. Thus, in the nurturing interaction, the frame of reference changes and the incompetent limit setter attains a higher position in the family hierarchy with the child as the competent nurturer.

Basic Laws of GST

Composition Law. *The whole is more than the sum of its parts.* This simple axiom has entered common usage in our culture. But what does it really mean? In simplest terms it means that no system can be understood merely by an examination of its parts or subsystems because of *process*. Process is the dynamics that occur among the parts of the system that, with the parts, are part of the whole. For example, you can't form an understanding of a family system by simply interviewing individual members of the family. You need to see the members *interact* to really understand how the family system functions (Constantine, 1986).

Decomposition Law. *The part is more than a fraction of the whole.* Similarly, one cannot separate the parts of a system and look at its individual characteristics or functions outside of the context of the system. The dynamics are missing. Hence, when you remove an individual from the context of his family, for instance a child who is referred for individual counseling because he is defiant to his parents, you cannot really understand why he is behaving that way, because you are not able to observe the interactions between the child and his parents. The behavior is not a function of the child as an individual; it is a function of the child plus the context of his family (Constantine, 1986).

Generalized Law of Complementarity. The formal statement of this law is, "To the extent that there is a "graininess" or limit to resolution in measurement (which there always is) or the process of observing affects the observed (which it always does), then, within the limits of resolution or interaction, any two measurements or observations will be complementary, that is, interdependent but not reducible to each other" (Weinberg, 1975). Now for the understandable explanation: Your perspective and functioning in a related interaction of two individuals is interdependent to the extent that more of a behavior from one of the individuals leads to less of that behavior from the other (Constantine, 1986). For instance, two individuals who are good cooks start dating and eventually move in together. As the time passes, one of them begins cooking more of the meals and eventually takes over all of their food preparation. The other, then, cooks less and less and eventually stops cooking, and concludes that she's just not a cook. This was not a conscious decision but occurred as a function of their complementary relationship with each other.

Application Activity: The Law of Complementarity

1) Get three containers large enough to submerge your hand in.

2) Fill one container with tepid water. Fill the second container with cold water and ice. Fill the third container with water that is hot to the touch but not hot enough to burn you.

3) Now, submerge your right hand in the ice water for 20 seconds, remove it and immediately submerge it in the tepid water. Note your perception of the temperature of the tepid water.

4) Then, submerge your left hand in the hot water for 20 seconds, remove it and immediately submerge it in the tepid water. Note your perception of the tepid water temperature once again.

5) Which observation of the tepid water was correct? You have now experienced the Generalized Law of Complementarity.

When you are working with families, sometimes you are observing the family as an outsider, but other times you are within the "set" of the family. The same situation, observed from these two reference points will result in different conclusions about what is going on (WIGO) with the family. We will get into this in more depth in the next chapter.

Simplified Cybernetics: Feedback and Control

As I mentioned earlier, we were going to spend part of this chapter potty talking, and the time has arrived. So, pass out the toilets and enjoy. In this section, I am going to attempt to provide a simplified explanation of the component of GST that is called *cybernetics* (Wiener, 1948). Cybernetics is concerned with how a system receives feedback about its functioning and consequently adjusts itself in order to maintain the stability of the system. I borrow my example from Larry Constantine (1986) who, I believe, provided a wonderfully understandable explanation of this process. Before I begin this discussion, I am going to ask you to go to a toilet in the place you call home, take the top off of the toilet tank, flush the toilet, and observe the mechanisms therein. Flush it again…and again. Then, return to the book and read on.

Feedback Loops

Feedback loops provide information to the system that helps the system adjust to internal or external changes. Sometimes, these adjustments are necessary to maintain the stability of the system or *homeostasis*. Other times, the adjustments help the system change in order to search for a different level of stability.

Homeostasis is the stable state of a system, but it is not a static state. Remember, all systems are in process. So, homeostasis is characterized by a dynamic balance that adjusts to the process of a system and is maintained by an *attenuating feedback loop*.

Attenuating (Negative) Feedback Loops function to maintain aspects of a system's performance or behavior within certain limits. Let's go to the toilet now (Figure 1-1). If you remove the top of the toilet tank and look in, you'll see the following: a float connected to the water in-flow valve and a chain or cord running from the float to the cover of the water outflow drain. You will see the water at a certain level in the tank when the toilet is not flushed. BUT you will also see water stains a little bit above and a little bit below the existing water level. The way that the

water level is maintained in a toilet is an example of an attenuating feedback loop.

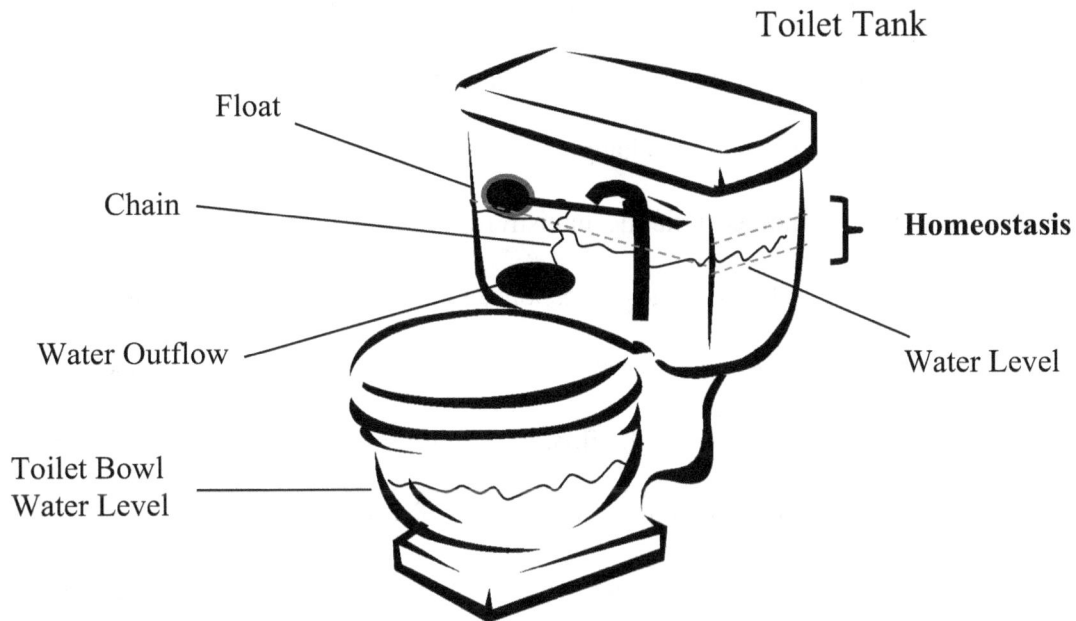

Figure 1-1: The Toilet as a Feedback Mechanism

The float-valve feedback loop functions to keep the tank full, but not too full. You probably

notice every so often that you hear the sound of water trickling into the tank when the toilet is not

being used. This is because a little water has seeped out of the tank through the outflow drain,

causing the float to go down a little and open up the inflow valve. Less water in the tank results in

more water coming in. On the other hand, the outflow valve sometimes opens a little to allow some

water to drain from the tank. This occurs because too much water has been allowed into the tank

through the inflow valve, causing the float to raise enough to pull on the chain that lifts the outflow

cover a little. More water in the tank results in some water having to be released. There are minor

deviations, then, in the water level; deviations are not eliminated, instead they are attenuated (made

smaller). These fluctuations around a reference point such as the average water level in the toilet tank, are called *hunting behavior* (Constantine, 1986).

You see similar hunting behavior in your car's cruise control system. If you set your cruise control for 65 miles per hour, you have probably noticed that the speedometer needle doesn't remain right on 65. The needle may move up to 67 sometimes and down to 63 at other times. This is the way that the cruise system adjusts to changes in grade, wind, and the like. It's the hunting behavior of that system, as the homeostatic mechanism responds to feedback.

The homeostasis of a system changes in response to deviations from the usual feedback received by the system. In our toilet example above, a small crack in toilet tank will cause a more dramatic change in the hunting behavior. The float will drop farther and open the inflow valve more. Water will be allowed into the tank until the volume of water flowing in equals the outflow through the crack. The float will drop no further and the water level will be maintained around this point, establishing a new homeostasis for the system.

The other type of feedback loop that is important to our understanding of systems is the *amplifying feedback loop*. The function of this type of feedback is to increase deviation from some point of reference. In other words, a small input is amplified into a large effect. In the case of our toilet, the small input of pushing the toilet handle triggers an amplifying feedback loop that results in the toilet tank being emptied, the old water in the bowl going down the drain and replaced by the clean water from the tank, and the tank being refilled with new water until the float reaches the required level to close the inflow valve, re-establishing homeostasis. It is like throwing a pebble into the middle of a pond and watching the waves reverberate outward from the first small circle until the pond is covered with larger and larger circles of ripples. A very small event makes big waves (Constantine, 1986).

All homeostatic mechanisms depend on continual input and regulation by active

feedback. For something to remain the same in a family, there must be a mechanism that maintains it that way.

Feedback Loops in a Families

Let's look at how these feedback loops might operate in a family. I like to take a common situation from my family: my primary-school aged grandchildren having an overnight with "MumMum" and "Papa."

My wife and I were preparing dinner in the kitchen, which was located right below the bedroom we reserve for our grandsons. We could hear them playing above us, the noise level remaining tolerable. Then we heard two large bangs above us. My wife asked me to go up and check on the boys and tell them to stop jumping off the bed. I did so and the kids quieted down. After a few minutes, the room above us became very quiet. My wife became curious about the absence of noise and asked me to check on our grandsons to make sure that they were staying out of mischief. I went upstairs again and said, "You are being awfully quiet. I hope you aren't getting into something." The boys giggled but weren't doing anything that they shouldn't. I went back down stairs and the noise level increased above us. Suddenly there was a loud crash. My wife asked me to tell the boys that they had to come downstairs and play in the kitchen where we could see them.

This is an example of the interplay between attenuating and amplifying feedback loops.

- MumMum (my wife) monitored the level of noise and signaled Papa (me) when it was time for a response.

- I then took action intended to reverse deviation from the acceptable. First, the kids were too noisy, so their noise needed to be decreased to the acceptable range.

- Then the kids were too quiet, so the noise level needed to increase to the acceptable range.

- However, when the loud bang occurred, the noise had escalated beyond what could be tolerated, an amplifying feedback loop kicked in, and they were required to join us in the kitchen, sending the family to a new state of homeostasis in this situation.

The system minimizes deviation in either direction. My wife was not comfortable with the kids being too noisy or too quiet, triggering the attenuating feedback loop. I served as the regulator of the hunting behavior, until the grandsons' behavior became intolerable. Then the amplifying loop was triggered and the situation changed completely. Ideally, families are most functional when there is interplay between these two types of feedback. Attenuating loops limit change and variety of behavior in the family supporting stability, while amplifying loops increase change and variety when this is necessary to respond to a change in circumstances (Constantine, 1986).

These basic concepts of GST provide you with a context for understanding the evolution of family therapy discussed in the next section.

In the Beginning

History is not simply a factual collection of past events and individuals. It is a construction of these facts and personalities based on the perceptions of the reporter, nothing of which is absolutely (or even remotely) objective. But, understanding history—of your country, your ethnic group, or your profession—is necessary if you are to understand how you arrived where you are today. With that in mind, I am going to provide you with a very brief history of what I think are the important events and individuals in the development of family therapy. In doing this, you need to understand that this is far from a comprehensive history of the field, and it is definitely a story filtered through my own perceptions of the field. These are the people and developments that are important to me as a practitioner of family therapy. For a more thorough history of the field from the experts, you should consult one of the many comprehensive texts on family therapy that are readily available, some of which are included in the references for this chapter.

Precursors

In the beginning there was Freud (Freud & Brill, 1995). And it should come as no surprise that psychoanalysis specifically, and the psychotherapy field that it spawned, were dysfunctional families. What would you expect from an approach that used as its foundation the most dysfunctional family in mythology, Oedipus's? At any rate, psychoanalysis had all the elements of a truly screwed up family: The powerful patriarch whose affection toward his "children" (i.e., his followers) was predicated on their complete obedience; "sibling" rivalry among the adherents of psychoanalytic theory trying to curry favor with their "parent;" and black sheep who were cast out of the family and "disinherited" for disagreeing with the parent. It should also be no surprise that family therapy was born after the death of the patriarch, at a time when not only some of the "children" were questioning the value and effectiveness of the approach, but so also were the distant relatives, such as Skinner (1974) and Rogers (1942; 1961/1989). And while Freud was no family therapist, he paid attention to family dynamics in his own, psychoanalytic way (thus, the Oedipal complex), which is to say, he was more interested in how parents damaged their children (Freud, 1920/2016). The disinherited children, such as Alfred Adler (Adler, 1920/2011) and Erik Erikson (Erikson, 1950/1963), on the other hand, viewed parents and families in a more positive light as the primary social influence in the healthy development of the individual.

With post-World War II Europe and the United States as the background, and with the first major developmental gathering on General Systems Theory having occurred in the late 1940's (Wiener, 1948), family systems thinking and family therapy were born. The parents were a group of disillusioned acolytes of psychoanalysis and a group of thinkers who originated far outside the field of psychotherapy from such disparate fields as anthropology and communications. This is where the story really begins. Why, then, in the early 1950's did this small group of pioneers begin to stray from traditional ideas concerning psychotherapy? A number of factors were in play at that time, particularly in relation to the treatment of individuals with severe forms of mental illness, such as schizophrenia.

The times they were a-changing. The spirit of the times made the 1950's particularly ripe for change in the psychotherapy field. As noted above, disenchantment with the "holy grail," psychoanalysis, was increasing. Larger numbers of people were in need of mental health services, particularly World War II veterans who were accessing the expanding Veteran's Administration psychiatric care facilities. Connected to this was growing interest in understanding serious mental illness, particularly schizophrenia. More funding was becoming available through federal and private sources for research on the causes and treatment of schizophrenia, and, as you would expect, many early breakthroughs related to family therapy occurred as a result of work that simply "followed the money." In essence, family therapy was born because the right people were in the right place at the right time.

Observations of the effects of families on individual therapy. Traditional psychotherapy, particularly psychoanalytic approaches, isolated clients from families, viewing parents as the source of clients' mental illness. The prevailing wisdom was that clients could not get better if they were exposed to their families, as if family members were the virus or bacteria that were causing the disease. Unfortunately, this led to situations in which clients, having improved enough to be released from a psychiatric hospitalization, returned to a family environment that had not been modified, thus setting up the client for failure, and a return to the hospital setting (Jackson, 1957).

Observations of the effects of hospitalized patients' improvements on their families and effects of family visits on patients.   During the late 1940's and early 1950's, articles began appearing in the clinical literature regarding observations of how non-hospitalized members of families that had a family member hospitalized for mental illness, would begin to become symptomatic when the hospitalized family member showed improvement (Jackson, 1957). A second pattern that was noted was that the symptoms of hospitalized patients tended to get worse after family visits. One of the classic cases described by Jackson (1965) was that of a depressed, married, middle-aged female who he treated in a hospital setting. Jackson noted that as the depressed woman improved, her husband began to complain to Jackson that her behavior was worse. After her discharge from the hospital, the woman continued in outpatient treatment, continued to improve, and was able to return to work and function normally. During this time, her husband began spiralling downward into depression, eventually lost his job, and, tragically, committed suicide. Jackson concluded that the husband's stability was based on having a "sick wife" in a reciprocal relationship. As long as his wife remained sick, he could function normally. But as his wife became more functional, the husband's emotional stability was disrupted, and he became the "sick" spouse (Jackson).

   Increasing influence of the group movement. By the 1950's, a substantial body of literature had been produced related to group dynamics in counseling and other social situations. For instance, it was noted how in counseling, a decentralized therapist position facilitated interactions among group members. Phenomena, such as the tendencies of groups to develop hierarchies, norms, and their own "cultures," as well as, the assigning of roles to group members were discussed in the literature based on clinical observations (Yalom, 2005). There was a realization during this period that family interactions mimic group interactions. For instance, in families, members implicitly assume or are assigned roles; similarly, families develop hierarchies among their members. The big difference between families and therapy groups is that individuals can choose the group to which they want to belong, but they can't choose their families. Families have a much more involved pre-group history and are much more emotionally connected and reactive. So, while you can simply quit a group you don't like, you can never quit your family, although it is not unusual for family members to try.

Influence of the child guidance movement. The child guidance movement was an outgrowth of Alfred Adler's beliefs about the influence of parents on children's emotional wellbeing (Adler, 1925/2011). Beginning in the 1920's, the advocates of this approach emphasized the importance of intervening with both parents and children when a child developed symptoms of emotional distress (Adler). As the movement grew, child guidance clinics were established that provided counseling services to children who were suffering from emotional problems. The standard intervention model used by these clinics was to provide counseling to the child, as the identified client, in order to address the child's issues directly; and to provide parallel psychotherapy to the parents to help them resolve issues that were seen as contributing to the child's problems. The underlying idea behind this was that, if parents successfully resolved their issues, they would not project or transfer them to the child, which would allow the child to "get better." By the 1940's the child guidance approach was well established throughout Western Europe and the United States.

The Tavistock Institute of Human Relations was a pioneering and influential center of the child guidance movement in the United Kingdom. The staff members at Tavistock, which included such giants as William Bowlby, were leaders in the child psychotherapy and group therapy fields. During the late 1940's, Bowlby began deviating from the usual separate therapy sessions with the child and mother. He started seeing families as a unit for isolated sessions during what he perceived to be resistant periods of individual therapy. He used these family sessions to neutralize or eliminate factors that might be contributing to the resistance, and then returned to the traditional, separate child and parent sessions approach (Nichols & Schwartz, 1991). Because of the importance of Tavistock, this type of experimentation provided support for the mavericks who would adopt the family session as the basic therapeutic interaction in family therapy

The Founding Family

The period during which family therapy came into being as a field is analogous to the epoch in which the United States was founded. In the mid-eighteenth century, a remarkable group of individuals, primarily males, came together at the same time and in the same place to lead the group of thirteen colonies to independence from England. Our nation's founding fathers introduced and gave voice to new ideas about freedom, government, and nationhood that diverged from anything that existed at the time, and eventually led to the successful American Revolution. They did this knowing that they risked everything—their livelihoods, positions of power, and, ultimately, their lives. But they persisted because they were certain that the status quo of colonialism was not working (Ellis, 2000; 2015).

The leaders of the family therapy movement emerged during a similar watershed period in the psychotherapy field. Disillusionment with traditional psychiatry and psychoanalysis was growing during the late 1940's and early 1950's. A significant minority of clinicians and thinkers had become fed up with psychoanalysis: it simply did not deliver on its promise of curing mental illness and reorganizing a dysfunctional personality into a healthy one. Psychoanalysis required that clients have a reasonably high level of intellectual functioning and verbal skills to simply participate in therapy sessions. It took a tremendous amount of time and money, in terms of the number of sessions required per week and the number of years that clients needed to be involved in therapy. And there was still no conclusive research that supported that it worked (Eysenck, 1952).

Furthermore, because of the above requirements, it was inaccessible to "the masses;" that is the largest group of people who required mental health interventions could not access it. As a result, a group of maverick psychiatrists, psychologists, social workers, and "thinkers" began to question the validity of the psychoanalytic approach and started looking elsewhere for ideas and approaches that could be more effective. They weren't really sure about what they were looking for or where the search would lead, and they pursued new alternatives at the risk of their reputations and careers as traditional clinicians. But they persisted.

The individuals that I discuss below are those who I feel were the primary seminal thinkers in the development of family therapy. Some are considered "founders" of family therapy and others, the links between traditional psychotherapy and family therapy. The way I think of them is that family therapy had many parents, foster parents, and godparents. Different people in the field view different individuals in this group as the actual founders, but they all had a hand in establishing what we today call family therapy.

Foster Parents

During the 1940's other "greats" in the psychotherapy field were weighing in with their ideas about how the family influenced the emotional functioning of the individual. Frieda Fromm-Reichman in her work with adolescent females who were diagnosed as schizophrenic (based on the criteria of the time) proposed the idea of the "Schizophrenogenic Mother," a parent personality-type that Fromm-Reichman postulated contributed to the development of schizophrenia. She described this type of mother as domineering, aggressive, rejecting and insecure, particularly in combination with an inadequate, passive, and indifferent father (Fromm-Reichman, 1948). While this idea was a valiant effort to explain family factors that were underlying what was called schizophrenia, it was not borne out by subsequent research, although it enjoyed a long life in the conventional wisdom of that era.

Harry Stack Sullivan, the developer of the Interpersonal Theory of personality (Sullivan, 1968), was also a legendary clinician renowned for his treatment of schizophrenic males. Sullivan used what might be called a quasi-family approach to treatment, creating what he termed, "The "Hospital Family" (Sullivan). This surrogate family consisted of physicians, nurses, therapy aids, and other personnel who had regular contact with the patient. Sullivan believed that the Hospital Family needed to assume common family roles for the patient and become the patient's "healthy family," replacing the patient's real family. The Hospital Family then "re-raised" the patient, substituting healthy parenting interactions and relationships for the pathogenic ones that Sullivan believed that the patients experienced as they were growing up (Sullivan). While this approach was based in pre-family system ideas, Sullivan never really utilized family therapy to treat the patient's family.

Grandparents

Theordore Lidz

Lidz was a neurologist and psychiatrist who was interested in Fromm-Reichmann's schizophrenogenic mother construct, specifically in her assertion that passive, incompetent fathers increased the potential for damage to children when a mother exhibited the schizophrenogenic traits. He conducted intensive clinical investigations of a small number of cases over several years, which led to his conclusion that paternal influence was just as damaging as maternal influence (Lidz & Lidz, 1949). In a follow-up study of 16 families, each of which had one member diagnosed with schizophrenia, Lidz described five major types of paternal "deficits."

- ***The father who is constantly in severe conflict with his wife***. In this family constellation, the father is domineering and rigidly authoritarian. The children become the focal point of

Family Therapy for Beginners   22

parental conflict, with the parents undermining each other's value and power as a parent. The schizophrenic members of these families were daughters who rejected their mothers and identified with the father. Lidz saw this as a cause of the daughter's failing to develop a "female identity."

- *The hostile father*. In these families, the father's hostility was directed toward the children, particularly the sons. The fathers belittled their sons and competed with them for the mothers' affection and attention, behaving more like jealous siblings. The schizophrenic member of these families tended to be sons.

- *The paranoid grandiose father*. The fathers in these families were described as aloof and distant, with the sons tending to model the fathers' most bizarre behavior. Not surprisingly, the schizophrenic member of these families tended to be sons.

- *The nonentity father*. These fathers were barely present in the home and did not participate in childrearing. The children essentially grew up fatherless, and witnessed the father being treated with disdain by the mother. The schizophrenic member of these families tended to be either daughters or sons.

- *The passive/submissive father*. These fathers were pleasant and maternal toward children but were married to domineering wives. The fathers were treated more like children by the mothers, leading Lidz to conclude that they were pathologically weak models for children. The schizophrenic member of these families also tended to be either daughters or sons (Lidz & Lidz, 1949).

While Lidz's "research" is interesting, it is qualitative in nature and a product of the standards for the gender and parent roles of the day. If you re-read some of his descriptions, they sound biased and judgmental by current standards. For instance, the "paranoid grandiose" father describes behaviors that we might now associate with individuals with social skills deficits and Asperger's disorder. The "passive/submissive" father sounds like what is now considered desirable traits in contemporary families: a father who is affectionate with and sensitive toward his children. Thus, while Lidz's research has some heuristic value as an attempt at understanding the influence of family dynamics, it provides little useful information. However, it did, at the time, serve to undermine the idea of the schizophrenogenic mother, reducing the blaming of mothers for their children's emotional problems.

A more important contribution of this foster parent is his constructs of marital schism and marital skew, as means of understanding how the dynamics in the couple relationship impact children. *Marital schism* is the failure of spouses to accommodate each other in order to achieve role reciprocity. Each parent undercuts the other's value to children, placing the children between the parents in a "no win" situation (Lidz & Lidz, 1949). This goes beyond a simple situation where one parent allows the children to do something that the other parent forbade them to do. *Marital skew* is more purposeful, consistent, covert behavior designed to sabotage the relationship that the other parent has with the children (Lidz & Lidz, 1949). In this situation, one parent will make damaging remarks to the children about the other parent or directly tell the children that they don't have to listen to the other parent, as a means of securing the children's alliance against the other parent. Lidz is referring to this same type of behavior occurring when the parents are still *together*, which presents the children with an even more problematic dilemma.

Figure 1-2   Marital Schism/Marital Skew

Marital skew is a serious situation in which one parent is overtly dominating the other. The dominated parent tends to be extremely dependent while the dominating parent is a bully who treats the other parent like a child. The submissive spouse becomes an enabler who supports and encourages the bullying, while the children are placed in the position of trying to balance the marital relationship (Lidz & Lidz, 1949). Even though Lidz, in the 1950's, was attempting to explain factors that might contribute to the development of schizophrenia in children (we know today that these don't), this type of dynamic is relevant today because it is very similar to the interactions typically seen in families where domestic violence is occurring. It is extremely damaging and contributes to emotional problems of children who are exposed to such a dynamic and caught between their parents, but it does not cause children to become schizophrenic.

Lyman Wynne

Wynne is a favorite of mine because he spent the last three decades of his career working in the area that I call home. Wynne was a psychiatrist who studied at Tavistock and was influenced by the group approach that was pioneered there. From the early 1950's to the early 70's he was a research associate at the National Institute of Mental Health, working with, and eventually replacing, Murray Bowen as head of family research. In the 1970's, Wynne was named director of a major family research project at the University of Rochester, where he finished out his career in the early 2000's (Becvar & Becvar, 2000).

Wynne was originally interested in extending psychoanalytic concepts to family therapy, particularly to explain interactional patterns in families with schizophrenic members. In doing this, he proposed two seminal constructs related to family dynamics: pseudo-mutuality and the rubber fence. *Pseudo-mutuality* is the facade developed by a family to give the impression that members have good relationships, when in fact they don't. The family members are so concerned about fitting closely together that there is no room for separateness and differentiation, or for recognition and appreciation of different interests. The family cannot tolerant either intimacy or independence. Thus, the family members attempt to quash conflicts and affectionate feelings (Wynne, Ryckoff, Day, & Hirsch, 1958).

Wynne proposed that pseudo-mutual families create a specific type of boundary around themselves that he named *the rubber fence*. This boundary is designed to keep family members in and non-family members out of the family system. It "stretches" like a rubber band, allowing family members to have necessary interactions with outsiders, such as attending school or working, in order to keep the outsiders from interfering with the family. But if a family member drifts too far from the family, the rubber fence contracts and pulls them back into the nucleus of the family, thereby, preventing the member from being contaminated by the family experiences of other individuals. In this way, the rubber fence blocks any "reality testing" by family members of their experiences in the pseudo-mutual family (Wynne et al.).

Pseudo-hostility is the equilibrium mechanism that Wynne proposed that pseudomutual families employ to pull prodigal members back into the family's orbit. Pseudo-hostility is like the charge of an alpha male gorilla or bull elephant. These types of charges serve as warnings in which the aggressor appears to be on the attack, but turns aside at the last moment, as a way of instilling fear into another animal that is perceived to be a threat. With pseudo-hostility, a powerful family member threatens the member who is drifting, usually in an emotional way, as a way to force the drifting member to "rejoin the fold," thereby restoring the equilibrium of the family (Wynne et al.).

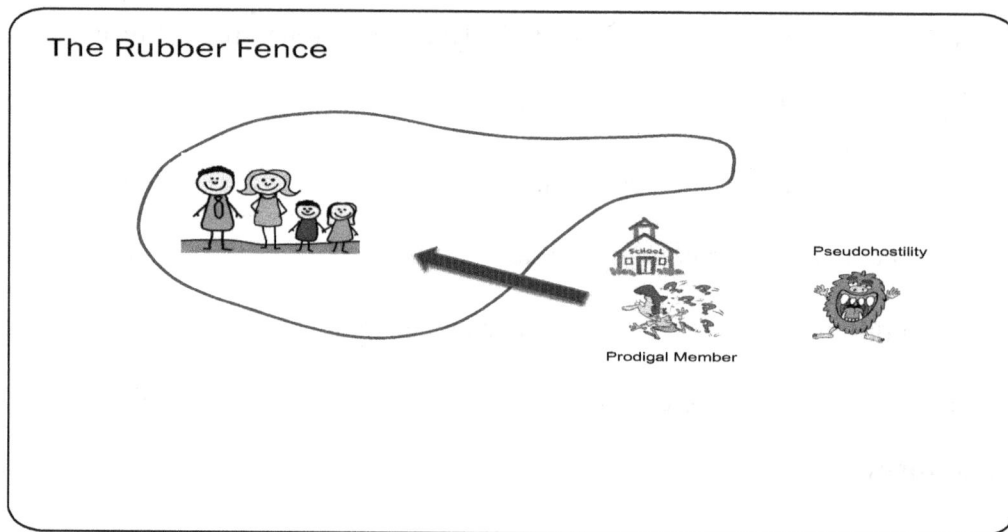

Figure 1-3: The Pseudo-mutual Family

I once saw an adult client who was suffering from depression related to her interactions with her family of origin, a family that turned out to be a classic, pseudo-mutual, rubber fence family. My client hailed from a small town in which her parents had great stature as owners of a successful business. All the children in the family were expected to work in the business and project a façade of the "upstanding," model family. Unfortunately, there was great conflict and a considerable amount of emotional abuse being perpetrated by my client's father in the secrecy of their home. As a child, my client was never allowed to have friends over or go to the houses of classmates. Whenever a friendship became too close for her parents, one of them would begin to make negative comments about the friend and forbid my client from associating with him or her. The same thing would happen with teachers who mentored my client. She also was not allowed to join any typical childhood activities, such as Girl Scouts, or participate in extracurricular activities. When it was

time for her to apply to college, her parents expected her to attend a college to which she would

commute, as had her older siblings. Instead, my client applied and was accepted to a college some

distance away, which required her to be a residential student. When her father heard this, he had a

major emotional explosion, attacking my client verbally, threatening to not pay for her college, and,

eventually telling her that she was "out of the family." My client subsequently took out loans and

enrolled in the college that she had chosen. After the first three weeks of her freshmen year, her

mother called and asked why my client hadn't been coming home for Sunday dinner, as if nothing

had transpired between her and her father. When my client explained that she had been disowned,

her mother simply ignored that and stated that my client was expected home for dinner that

weekend. My client complied, and dinner proceeded as if nothing had happened.

This is a classic example of the rubber fence. My client was allowed just enough freedom to

attend school, but otherwise was home or at the business with her family. When she decided to go

to a college that required her to leave home, there was a huge discharge of anger and rejection by

her father, this pseudo-hostility display serving to pull her back into the family's boundary and

maintain the facade of respectability. When that didn't work, the rubber fence stretched enough to

allow her to attend college away from home, but pulled her back into the family each weekend,

preventing her from developing relationships with individuals outside of the family. This same

pattern was repeated when my client started developing relationships with males and pursuing her

own career goals outside of the family business. Each time, she was "disowned" by her father, only

to be pulled back into the family's powerful boundary. Thus, she became deeply depressed in her

late 30's.

The Parents

John Elderkin Bell

As I mentioned earlier in the chapter, there is some debate over who was the ***first*** family therapist. The two candidates who are usually mentioned are John Elderkin Bell and Murray Bowen (1976). Bell often comes out on top in this debate but is less well known than Bowen because Bell did not publish his ideas until sometime after many of the other founders had risen to prominence. In addition, Bell, unfortunately, developed a form of dementia at a relatively young age and was inactive in the field for the last 20 years of his life. Bell's approach was based on group psychotherapy and was fairly straightforward, incorporating three sequential stages: child-centered, parent-centered, and family-centered stages. The therapy focused on improving communication among family members in each stage. For instance, in the child-centered stage, children were allowed to express their feelings and needs, and in the parent-centered stage, parents responded to their children's issues. This established the foundation for the family-centered stage during which parents and children communicated together and problem-solved (Bell, 1975).

Murray Bowen

A better known "parent," Bowen was a Menninger-trained psychiatrist who learned to view the family, and not the individual, as the unit of dysfunction that needed to be treated. In 1954, Bowen became director of a major federal project on the development and treatment of schizophrenia, based in Washington, DC (Bowen, 2013). It was during the data collection phase of this project, that Bowen became interested in family dynamics. The data collection included meetings with several families and members of the staff during which the staff responded to family members in a non-directive manner. Bowen noticed two things happening as a result of these meetings. The first was that the family dynamics changed, simply due to the interactions that occurred in the data collection meetings. The second was that staff members began adopting the positions of family members with whom they worked and began to act out the family dynamics in staff meetings. Consequently, Bowen decided to develop intentional interventions to help families change dysfunctional patterns, and, thus, family systems therapy was born (Bowen, 1993).

Key Constructs. Bowen's theory is based on the interplay between two forces: fusion and differentiation. Fusion is the force that holds the individual in the family system, much like the gravitational force that maintains planets in their orbits. Differentiation is the force that pulls individuals away from the family so that they may function as independent adults. As children progress into adolescence and adulthood, greater differentiation is desirable. However, when a family functions at a higher level of fusion, that is, extremely close and overly involved with each other's business, differentiation becomes increasingly difficult. Thus, to Bowen, appropriate differentiation was the key to the healthy individual and family (Bowen, 1993; Gilbert, 2004/2006).

One of Bowen's more famous articles involved his own "family of origin crisis." Bowen hailed from a large family that resided in rural Pennsylvania. His parents and siblings tended to be in conflict with each other on a regular basis and, since he was a psychiatrist, would pull him into their conflicts by speaking with him and trying to elicit his support. This is the type of pattern that fused families engaged in, and Bowen felt that, in order for him to be an effective family therapist, he needed to differentiate from his own family. So, he began to implement a consistent method of responding to his parents' and siblings' requests for support in their conflicts with each other. If his mother complained to him about his father, he would end the conversation and ask to speak to his father. Bowen would then inform his father that his "wife" was complaining about him and tell him that he needed to speak with her. If a sibling spoke badly about another sibling, Bowen would write

a letter to the sibling who was the target of the complaint and inform him/her of the name of the

sibling who was complaining, and, again, tell the object of the complaint that he/she needed to

communicate directly with the complainer. This went on for years and came to a climax at a family

reunion at which Bowen externalized many of the conflicts and pulled himself out of interactions,

refusing to become involved in their arguments (Ohlsen, 1982).

This situation is a classic example of one of Bowen's main constructs: *triangulation.*

Triangulation is a pressure-release mechanism for families in which two family members who are in

conflict attempt to draw in a neutral third party as a way to redirect the conflict in their relationship.

In Bowen's family, his parents, for instance, would talk to him about their dissatisfaction with each

other and not speak directly to each other about these issues. By doing this, they drained off their

own stress, BUT they placed Bowen in the unenviable position of taking sides (or, in other words,

forming an *alliance*) with one of them (Bowen, 1993). This is a common pattern that is seen in

families in which the parents are experiencing stress in their "couple" relationship. I will discuss the

idea of triangulation further in the next chapter.

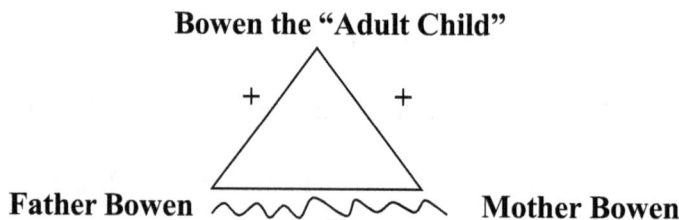

Figure 1-4: Triangulation in the Bowen Family

Bowen thought that individuals tended to "partner" with other individuals from the same

approximate level of differentiation (Bowen, 1993). Therefore, an individual from a highly fused

family will be attracted to a spouse from a highly fused family. The lower the level of differentiation (that is, the greater the degree of fusion), the higher the potential for problems. If nothing happens to disrupt this pattern of fusion, it is then projected onto the children, and they will repeat the pattern in their own relationships. So, parents who are from low differentiation families will keep their children fused in the same manner, as was the case in the rubber fence family I described earlier. The children will be expected to be like the parents and not allowed to develop identities that deviate from what the parents consider "acceptable." When the children grow up and become involved with potential spouses, they will not only be likely to be attracted to individuals from similarly fused families, but their parents probably won't approve of individuals who are more differentiated. The pattern, then, perpetuates itself (Bowen).

The problem with fusion is that it interferes with the normal adolescent developmental task of forming an individual identity separate from one's family. The child is not allowed enough emotional distance to adequately accomplish this task. When this occurs, the child is then placed in the dilemma of wanting and needing to be connected to their family, but at the same time being repulsed by the suffocating emotional environment that prevents them from differentiating. Bowen hypothesized that this situation fuels what he calls "the emotional cutoff" (Bowen, 1993). Faced with few good options for differentiating, the child runs away from the family, either by physically removing themselves or emotionally, by becoming symptomatic. The physical form of cutoff often takes the form of moving away from the family, such as going to college or taking a job that is a long distance from the family home to purposely reduce the possibility that family members will visit or have any knowledge about what the individual is doing. Bowen hypothesized that the emotional form of cutoff took the form of schizophrenic symptoms that allowed the individual to simply escape reality. Since we know now that schizophrenia is biologically based, the latter explanation is incorrect. However, it's important to keep in mind that Bowen was developing this explanation at time when little was known about the causes of schizophrenia, and he was, after all, in charge of a major research project that was trying to explain how schizophrenia developed. Bowen's explanation of the emotional cutoff is more useful in helping us understand how families influence the degree of connection that individual family members maintain with their family of origin, once they reach adulthood.

Therapeutic Approach. Bowen asserted that tension or conflict within the family is manifested in one or more of the following:

- Marital Conflict – Arguing, disagreeing, passively opposing each other.

- One Spouse Develops Symptoms – A husband or wife becomes depressed or anxious to the extent that their functioning is impaired.

- Projection onto the Children – A parent complains to their child about the other parent, seeks comfort from the child, undermines the other parent's discipline, or takes out anger and frustration toward the other parent on the child. Consequently, the child is triangulated into the couple conflict.

Bowen saw these types of family symptoms as reflecting fusion within the family. Therefore, he saw the primary goal of family therapy as facilitating differentiation of individual family members (Bowen, 1993). Bowen experimented with various approaches to family therapy beginning with the large, multi-family meetings described above. He progressed through several adaptations to focusing just on the couple as the primary unit of change (Bowen, 1993). His assumption was that, if the couple (and therefore, the parents) could differentiate effectively from their families of origin, then they would be able to allow their children to differentiate in a healthy fashion, interrupting the pattern of fusion that led to problems.

Bowenian therapy uses more of an educational framework, with the therapist functioning as a neutral consultant to the couple. The genogram is a key tool that the therapist uses to help the couple trace and understand patterns that are symptomatic of fusion within their families of origin. Based on this, the therapist helps the couple identify patterns that they are replicating, redefine their relationship in a more differentiated way, and teach them how their family's emotional system operates. The therapist models differentiation by avoiding and neutralizing attempts by the spouses to triangulate the therapist into their conflicts. As a result, the couple learns alternative ways of interacting with each other and their children that foster differentiation and minimizes the potential for the development of unhealthy alliances among family members (Bowen, 1993).

Bowen has been tremendously influential over the years because he constructed a logical framework through which family dynamics could be understood, and family therapy conducted. Whether or not one agrees with him and knowing that not all of his hypotheses have gained support, one cannot deny that he developed one of the first cohesive systems of family therapy.

The Palo Alto Group

The next parent is actually a group of parents, the legendary Palo Alto Group, that was brought together by Gregory Bateson on the Stanford University campus. The influence of this group in the development of family therapy cannot be underestimated. The ideas that its members generated provided the foundation of family systems approaches in general. From this group, major approaches to family therapy emerged: strategic family therapy, conjoint family therapy, and, eventually, brief solution-focused therapy. The Palo Alto Group was family therapy's version of a rock-and-roll super group.

Bateson was more or less a "Renaissance" man who, while primarily associated with the field of anthropology, dabbled in ethnography, communications, and systems theory. In some sense, he was a pure, generalist scientist, someone who probably could not have done what he did

with the Palo Alto Group today because of the contemporary obsession with specialization and credentialing. It is likely that because he had such a variety of interests and did not emerge from the psychology and psychotherapy fields, he was able to think more divergently about family interactions and to pursue explanations that were outside of what was considered to be "conventional wisdom" (Bateson, 1975).

Bateson initiated his research with a group of relatively disparate thinkers: Jay Haley had a background in communication; John Weakland was a chemical engineer with some background in cultural anthropology; and William Fry was a psychiatrist who conducted research on the function of humor. In 1959, as the group's research morphed into therapy, Don Jackson was asked to join to provide clinical supervision and Virginia Satir was brought on board because of her pioneering work with families in Chicago (Nichols & Schwartz, 1991).

Bateson was involved in a project that focused on understanding closed cultures of the time (such as communist China) through motion pictures produced in those countries. This drew Haley to his doorstep, and Bateson offered him a job as a research assistant in that project. The motion picture project spawned another research project on communication and learning in primates and, later, dolphins, that led to a research project on paradox in various forms of communication. In 1954, Bateson received a two-year grant to study communication patterns in families of schizophrenics. He was interested in developing a communication theory that explained the genesis of schizophrenia in the family context (Haley, 1991).

Haley claimed that Bateson was led to his interest in schizophrenia when his request to extend funding on a project that was looking at

paradox in communication was denied by a private

foundation (Haley, 1991). Haley's story went that

Bateson entered the meeting at which he was

making the request convinced that his request would

be denied and, when it was, Bateson concluded that

he was being punished for expecting to be denied, and therefore, behaved in a way that led to the

denial. He extrapolated from this, the hypothesis that schizophrenics became psychotic because

they were punished by their parents for reacting in fear when they expected punishment. Thus, the

construct of the double-bind came into being (Haley, 1991).

Key Constructs. The Palo Alto Group generated a number of constructs, based on

Bateson's inductive and deductive approaches, and then attempted to study each construct to

examine whether or not it could be supported by the accumulated data. This was very similar to the

method employed by Einstein and theoretical physicists at the turn of the 20th century (Isaacson,

2007), and was an accepted method of inquiry, although it would not meet today's standards for

research.

Levels of Communication. Bateson proposed that communication occurs on two levels.

The *report* level is comprised of the basic message, that is, the verbal content. The *command* level

is comprised of meta-communication that is usually non-verbal and abstract. This level determines

how the message is understood by the receiver, and often is not overtly noticeable. For instance,

depending on the voice intonation and facial expression, the answer to a simple question such as,

"How are you," can be interpreted in many different ways. If the answer, "Fine," is communicated

so that the voice intonation is congruent with feeling "fine," then this answer will most likely mean "fine" to the questioner. However, if the voice intonation is incongruent with "fine," as is the case with sarcastic responses, then "fine" might in fact mean "lousy" (Satir, 1991).

Homeostasis and Complementarity. Jackson introduced the ideas of homeostasis and complementarity from General Systems Theory to explain the schizophrenic family's functioning. He felt that schizophrenic families maintained their homeostasis through the complementary interplay between the patients' functioning in relation to other family members. In simple terms, this operates like a seesaw. That is, the patient's dysfunctional and unstable behavior helps other family members remain stable. Jackson argued that if the patient becomes stable and more functional, the stability of the non-patient family members is threatened. Therefore, the non-patient family members react to restore the family's homeostasis by undermining the patient's stability OR the patient deteriorates to "save" the family (Jackson, 1957).

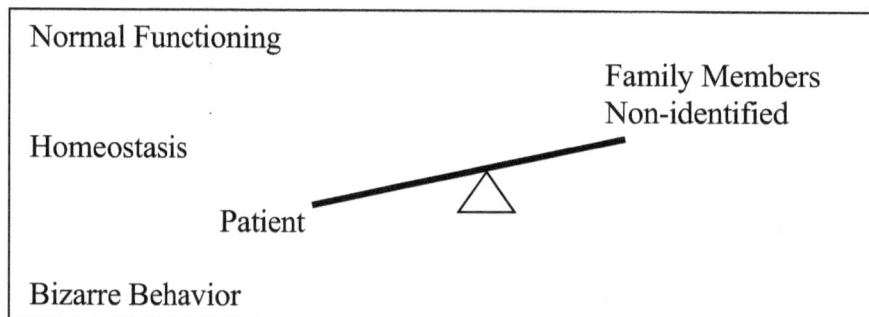

Figure 1-5: Homeostasis and Complementarity

While we now know that this is not an explanation for schizophrenia, it is an idea that has been embraced by the strategic and structural approaches in particular to explain many different types of family interactions.

The double-bind. As I have discussed above, Bateson formulated the double-bind inductively based on his "punishment" experience. As this construct developed, based on clinical observations, it became much more complicated than the simple "mixed message" idea that it has come to mean in popular culture. The double-bind was proposed as an explanation of how

schizophrenics developed psychotic symptoms. The Palo Alto Group viewed these symptoms as

resulting from the stress the patient experienced from dealing with an ongoing reality of distorted

and confusing communication. The basic premise was that the patient was constantly receiving

messages on the two levels of communication (report and command) that contradicted each other,

and that the patient lacked the coping skills to make sense of the contradictions (Bateson, Jackson,

Haley & Weakland, 1956). The components of the double-bind are described in Figure 1-6.

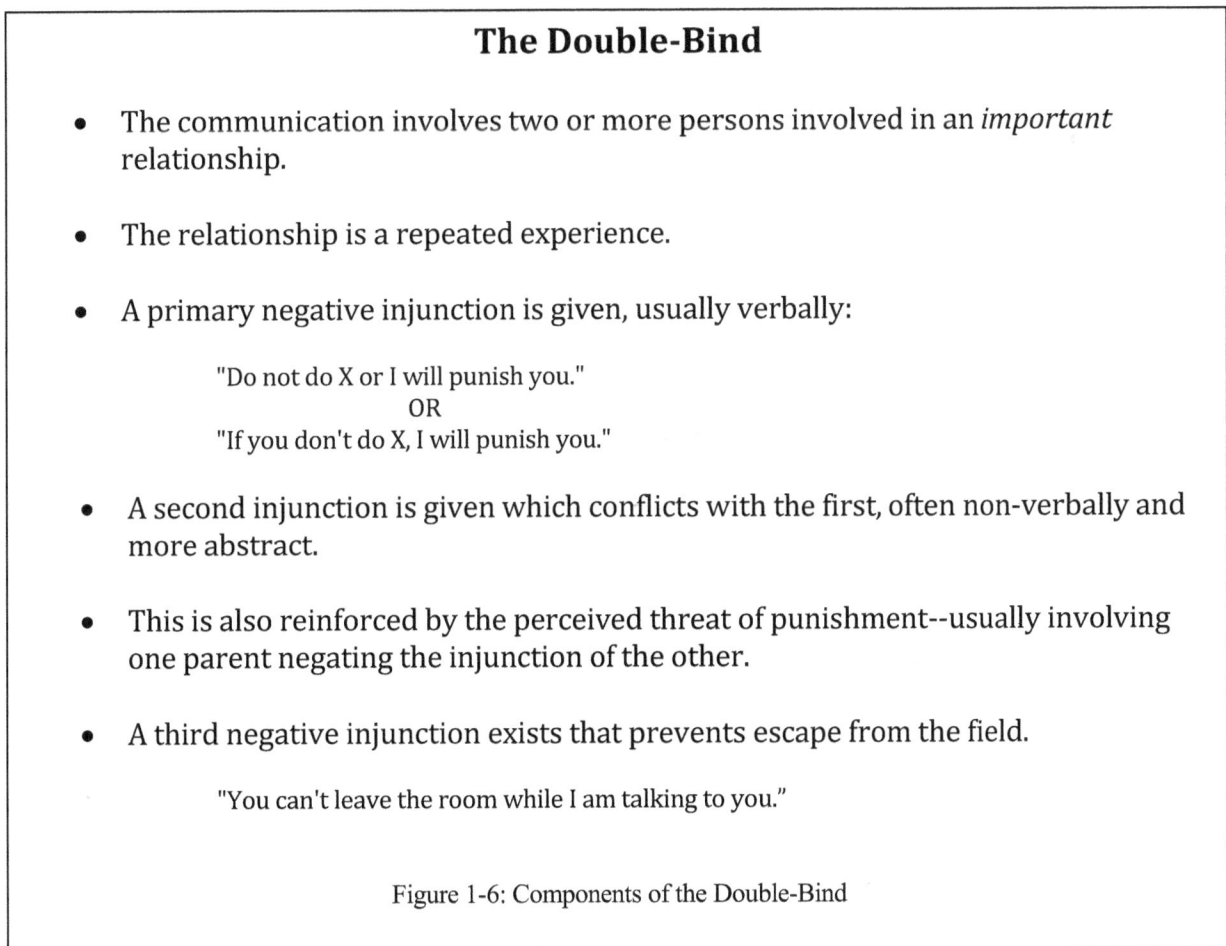

The Double-Bind

- The communication involves two or more persons involved in an *important* relationship.

- The relationship is a repeated experience.

- A primary negative injunction is given, usually verbally:

  "Do not do X or I will punish you."
  OR
  "If you don't do X, I will punish you."

- A second injunction is given which conflicts with the first, often non-verbally and more abstract.

- This is also reinforced by the perceived threat of punishment--usually involving one parent negating the injunction of the other.

- A third negative injunction exists that prevents escape from the field.

  "You can't leave the room while I am talking to you."

Figure 1-6: Components of the Double-Bind

I will use another episode from my rubber fence family client to illustrate this construct. As

I had described in the case material, the children in the family were expected to work in the family business. When my client reached the age of 16, her father required her to work in the sales office of the business. The double-bind she experienced consisted of the following.

- Her father was the source. (Two persons in an important relationship. Relationship was a repeated experience.)

- My client was told by her father, "If you don't understand something, ask me, so you don't make a mistake on an order. (Primary injunction, verbal).

- My client had a question for her father about an order, so she asked him about it. Almost before the question was out of her mouth, her father began screaming at her, "What's the matter with you? Are you stupid? Don't bother me with your stupid questions!" He then continued cursing at her in front of the entire office staff. (A second injunction conflicting with the first, "don't ask.")

- So, my client was afraid to ask her father a question when she was unsure about something, and avoided doing so. Consequently, she did something incorrectly, which her father discovered. He then began yelling at her because she hadn't asked him a question about procedures. (A third injunction, contradicting the second, "I told you to ask.")

- My client wanted to quit working for her father, but he wouldn't allow her to do so. Thus, she was constantly being emotionally abused for doing the wrong thing, by her father. (Final injunction prevented escape.)

We all experience double-binds from time to time as children and adults. The Palo Alto Group saw the problem for schizophrenics as being the pervasiveness and regularity of double-binds in their family communications. Once an individual was conditioned to perceive the world in terms of the double-bind, almost any component of this type of message triggered distress and an escalation episode, because they lacked the coping skills and reality testing required to disqualify the message or the messenger (Bateson et al., 1956).

The double-bind is a historically important construct but has not stood the test of time in research. Studies on the double-bind were difficult in terms of being able to incorporate all components into useful research designs. Analog research using college students could not include the important relationship and repeated experience components. Clinical research could not standardize the double-bind message of patients, and, therefore, lacked treatment integrity. Thus, lacking solid research support, the double-bind simply faded away as a valid explanation for schizophrenia (Dush & Brodsky, 1983; Haley, 1991).

Therapeutic Approach. I am not going to discuss "the" therapeutic approach of the Palo Alto Group, since several approaches emerged from its work, each incorporating different components of the group's ideas. In the next chapter, you will see how these ideas were applied by Jay Haley (1976) in his formulation of strategic therapy. Virginia Satir's (1967) applications are discussed below. The importance of the Palo Alto Group was their emphasis on the critical impact of communication on family dynamics, and how communication between various combinations of family members influences the functioning of each individual.

Virginia Satir

Satir's family therapy work began several years before she joined the Palo Alto Group. She began her career as an elementary school teacher, during which she began focusing on enlisting families' support in her teaching efforts through home visits. She eventually earned her M.S.W. and worked with delinquent teenage girls, again attempting to incorporate families into her therapy with the clients. During this period, she became interested in the humanistic growth orientation to

therapy, partially as a reaction to and rejection of the psychodynamic approach she was exposed to in a clinic setting. In 1951, Satir opened her private practice, specializing in clients who had failed in previous psychotherapy. Her work with families consisted of conjoint sessions with parents and the identified clients. She called this combination the "primary triad," as she saw this particular interactional system as the source of most of the messages to children in the family. Satir was invited to join the Palo Alto Group in 1959 and began working with the Esalon Institute, one of the centers of the humanistic movement, in 1964 (Nichols & Schwartz, 1991).

Key Constructs. By simply reviewing Satir's professional history, it becomes obvious that her approach has a humanistic-growth orientation. She viewed self-esteem as a core curative factor, believing that improving self-esteem would lead to behavioral changes. She focused on non-verbal messages communicated through body language, incorporating family sculpting into her approach. She also developed her idea of the double-level message phenomenon as a way of explaining discrepancies between verbal and non-verbal behavior. She delineated five basic defense mechanisms used by family members: *inhibition* (what one feels but cannot say), *repression* (that which one feels but is not aware), *projection* (what one feels but reacts to when seen in someone else), *suppression* (what one feels but since it does not fit the rules, denies), and *denial* (what one feels but ignores as unimportant) (Satir, 1967).

Therapeutic Approach. Satir defined her approach as a growth-oriented, holistic method that entered the personal system through the affective domain and had an educational focus. She would begin therapy with whichever members of the family attended, but felt that eventually, all the family members had to be physically present at sessions. She believed in making "real contact" with each family member, making sure to physically touch them, give her full attention, actively listen to their perspectives, "value' them as people, and serve as their "companion" in an educational process. The techniques that she used were open to anything that would help the family, but often incorporated sculpting and metaphorical stories. Sculpting involved placing family members in stances that reflected their interactional position in the family, such as blaming, placating, and being super-reasonable. The stories consisted of situations that paralleled those of the family's, as a way of suggesting the possibility of change (Satir, 1967).

Satir was a formidable presence in the therapy room or as a workshop presenter. A tall, robust woman, she would literally raise the feet of a male of average stature off the floor when she gave him a hug of greeting at a workshop. Her personal charisma added to her power when working with families and the dynamic environment of her sessions. Unfortunately, it also made her therapeutic approach less possible to replicate when applied by the average counselor. Thus, while her ideas and methods have been important influences that are incorporated into family therapy work, conjoint family therapy per se, is no longer used as widely in its original form.

Jay Haley

As discussed above, Jay Haley was one of the original members of the Palo Alto Group who helped formulate the idea of the double-bind. From his work there, he developed a brief therapeutic approach that incorporated the group's communication model with Milton Erickson's Utilization approach, which Haley first called "problem-solving therapy" (Haley, 1976). This approach morphed into strategic therapy as Haley refined his ideas and methods between 1967 and 1974, when he worked with Salvador Minuchin at the Philadelphia Child Guidance Clinic. Strategic therapy focused on developing directive interventions that would interrupt the unconstructive patterns that interfered with a family's functioning (Haley). Haley developed his approach further with Cloe Madanes in their work at the Family Therapy Institute of Washington, DC (Madanes, 1981). The specific concepts and techniques of strategic family therapy will be discussed in later chapters of this book.

A prolific writer and brilliant speaker, Haley was an iconoclast and critic of traditional psychotherapy and psychiatry. He was well known for his searing, albeit, witty attacks on the established ideas about mental illness and accepted treatment approaches. Many anecdotes have circulated around the field from individuals who witnessed Haley take many an unsuspecting psychiatrist to task for focusing on diagnosis for diagnosis sake, rather than simply doing something that would provide a client some immediate benefits. Haley died in 2007 at the age of 83.

Salvador Minuchin

Salvador Minuchin started his career as a pediatrician in Argentina, eventually making his way to the U.S. in 1950, after a stint in Israel as an army physician. He studied psychiatry under Loretta Bender at Bellevue Hospital in Manhattan, and then worked with adolescent juvenile delinquents at a Harlem-based agency. He related in his AAMFT "Founders" interview how his

true desire was to be a child psychologist, but that this was not possible in Argentina during the 1940's. So, he took the circuitous route described above to finally be able to work with troubled children (Minuchin, 1991). Minuchin served as director of the Philadelphia Child Guidance Center from 1962 – 1975, a period during which he worked closely with Jay Haley, and established a model family therapy training program with Uvo Montalvo. He went on to work in the metropolitan New York area on projects with psychosomatic families (Minuchin, Rossman & Baker, 1978) and with foster parents and protective workers who he trained to use family interventions to help support reunification of foster children with their biological parents (Minuchin & Nichols, 1993). "Retiring" in 1996, Minuchin continued his interest in training, volunteering his services as a consultant to agencies in Boston and other areas of the country. The concepts and techniques of structural therapy will be discussed in later chapters of this book. He died in 2017 at the ripe old age of 95.

The Godfather

I consider Carl Whitaker to be the godfather of family therapy, in that he was a magnet that drew many of the founders together to share ideas during the infancy of the field. He was yet another maverick psychiatrist who was open to new ways for helping families. Whitaker was born in Northern New York State in 1912 and raised there until the age of 12, when his family moved to Syracuse, then one of the larger industrial centers in the country. He noted many times in workshops and interviews that this move was a major crisis point in his life, the stress of having to deal with the "big city" leading to his first experience of feeling "crazy" (Whitaker, 1991). He felt that this experience helped him empathize with seriously disturbed patients and not fear "craziness."

Whitaker entered the psychotherapy field in a non-traditional manner, starting his career as an obstetrician, switching to psychiatry shortly before World War II, when the federal government was funding intensive short-term residencies in anticipation of the need for psychiatric services that the looming war would generate. During and after the war, Whitaker worked in a number of different psychotherapy treatment settings, including Oakridge National Laboratory. These experiences allowed him to experiment with different and, often novel,

treatment approaches, including traditional play therapy, nursing adult schizophrenics with baby bottles, and rough-and-tumble play with behaviorally disordered boys. He felt that each experience contributed to his eventual focus on working with families (Whitaker, 1991).

Whitaker went on to head the psychiatry department at Emory University School of Medicine in 1946, where he began to emphasize family treatment of schizophrenics as part of the residency program. During this time, he introduced the approach of using a co-therapist as part of his family therapy approach. He worked with a series of co-therapists, the most well-known of who, Augustus "Gus" Napier, teamed with him in 1968. Napier later documented Whitaker's work in the classic book, *The Family Crucible* (1978). Whitaker saw the co-therapist as providing a rational balance to his more symbolic, metaphorical interactions with families, in essence, the "straight man" to Whitaker's "comedian" (Ohlsen, 1982). During his Emory period, Whitaker was also responsible for starting the Sea Island Conferences, a series of gatherings of many of the pioneers in the family therapy field. At these conferences, volunteer families would be seen by several of the participants, who would employ their particular therapeutic approach while being observed by the other participants. This protocol allowed the founders to compare and contrast their various techniques and conceptual frameworks and generated a great deal of cross-fertilization of ideas.

Whitaker left Emory in 1955 to enter private practice, and in 1965 accepted a professorship in psychiatry at the University of Wisconsin, where he retired from the formal phase of his career in 1982. He worked with a few more co-therapists during this period, including David Keith and William Bumberry, the latter co-authoring with Whitaker the one book he wrote about his approach, which he called symbolic-experiential therapy (Whitaker & Bumberry, 1989). He also worked closely with Salvador Minuchin during this time, treating families as co-therapists and presenting training workshops together. In fact, in his later years, Whitaker described Minuchin as his "last co-therapist" (Whitaker, 1991).

After retiring from the University of Wisconsin, Whitaker continued to be active in the field, training family therapists around the world through workshops, and meeting with his former trainees in what he called "cuddle groups" to help them deal with the stress that was a natural result of working intensely with families. Whitaker was finally slowed by a debilitating stroke in 1992, dying three years later at the age of 83.

Key Constructs. Whitaker believed that the family had to be treated as a whole, often making the statement, "I don't believe in individuals" (Whitaker & Bumberry, 1989). He believed that the therapist needed to get intensively involved with the family in order to help the family function in a healthy way. He incorporated elements of psychoanalysis, humanistic approaches, play therapy, and even structural family therapy into his ideas. Whitaker felt that families develop a "symbol world" that is comprised of universal symbols, such as death and sex, and idiographic symbols that are unique to the family's experience, such as a farmer's love of cows. These symbols represented impulses that family members were experiencing, and which became sources of dysfunction because of anxiety that was generated by particular impulses. He felt that part of the purpose of therapy was to help the family raise these impulses to the level of consciousness in order to reduce the potential of their acting on the impulse, and, therefore, reducing their anxiety. If therapy succeeded in doing this, the family members could then experience each other in a real way without being crippled by fear and would have increased tolerance of the normal stresses of life (Minuchin, Lee & Simon, 1996; Whitaker, 1991; Whitaker & Bumberry, 1988).

Therapeutic Approach. There are no real step-by-step procedures of symbolic-experiential therapy, as Whitaker was more focused on the process rather than the product of therapy. Bumberry did succeed in at least getting Whitaker to articulate the components of his approach, based on videotapes of his therapy sessions, that allowed him to explain what he was doing and why he was doing it. Whitaker described these components as the following:

- *The battle for structure* occurs at the beginning of therapy and is the therapist's opportunity to establish the conditions of therapy and his or her needs as a therapist. Whitaker felt that this forced the family to members to respond with a position of loyalty to the family.

- *Joining* allows the therapist to connect with the family, both by communicating understanding and empathy, and by finding common ground with the family.

- By e*stablishing a metaposition*, the therapist clarifies her/his position as being an outsider who will help the family do what it needs to do to function more constructively, but who will not DO FOR the family.

- Whitaker believed that it was critical to *convene the clan*, by which he meant getting all the members of the family involved in the therapy. He felt this was necessary to avoid sabotage by a member who felt "left out" and that it also helped prevent the therapist from becoming overinvolved.

- *Beginning with dad* was intended to engage the father or men of the family in a higher level of involvement with the family's emotional life. This was an area from which, Whitaker believed, men were woefully absent. He felt that if the father, in particular, could become emotionally available, it gave hope to the rest of the family.

- *Expanding the symptom* was Whitaker's way of getting all the family members to "ante up" to help. He did this by suggesting additional possibilities or outcomes of a particular symptom, or by suggesting additional symptoms, in order to complicate or contaminate the family's accepted perspective. His goal was for the family to *disagree* with him, thereby allying with each other and taking the first step toward rejecting the accepted dysfunctional pattern of the family.

- The *battle for initiative* was Whitaker's way of getting the family to take responsibility for its own improvement. He would force this initially by refusing to initiate scheduling of follow up sessions with families. If a family did not initiate this at the end of the session, it would be up to them to call to schedule the next session.

- The *therapeutic alliance* was established when the family identifies the family, not a member of the family, as the patient, and takes initiative for the direction of the therapy. The therapist can then be more responsive to the family and the family has a better sense of itself. It is during this "stage" that the family begins to make changes that help it be more responsive to stress in an adaptive way.

- *Termination* arrives when the family is able to use its own resources constructively and be its own therapist, while seeing the therapist as more human. The family must initiate the decision to terminate, but it is the therapist's job to illuminate the family's cues.

- Whitaker was one of the first psychotherapy pioneers to emphasize the *empty nest*, that is, the family's and therapist's mutual sense of loss at the termination of counseling. Later in his career he emphasized the importance of "cuddle groups," support groups in which therapists could process these feelings (Whitaker & Bumberry, 1988).

The primary problem with Whitaker's approach is that, while it was incredibly attractive to many in the field, it was very difficult to replicate what he actually did with families. He was a charismatic therapist who helped families through the strength of his personality. Many of his ideas and techniques have been incorporated into other approaches and into the personal styles of individual therapists. But only a small group of practitioners employs symbolic-experiential therapy as a cohesive approach. Because of his profound influence on the development of the family therapy field as a whole, however, Whitaker was a revered figure during his lifetime and continues as such today.

The Women's Project: A Feminist Perspective

If you haven't noticed, with the exception of Satir, there are few female names that appear in the lexicon of the founders. This has been attributed to a paternalistic undercurrent in psychotherapy in general, and in the early family therapy pioneers in particular (Minuchin, Lee, & Simon, 1996). It led to the forming of the Women's Project in the 1980's, a group that sought to integrate feminist perspectives into family therapy theory and practice. This group counted among its members Marianne Walters, one of Minuchin's early colleagues, Peggy Papp from the Ackerman Institute, and Betty Carter (Minuchin, Lee, & Simon, 1996).

The feminist perspective focuses on meaning, connectedness (vs. agency), and the politics of power between men and women (Baker Miller, 1987). This is reflected in Papp's idea of tracing the themes that develop in family interactions that impact how family members live their individual lives (Papp & Imber-Black, 1996). Feminist therapists also see exerting power as an important, if not the primary, way to rebalance a scale that is tilted toward men. The way to do this is by using the collective power of women in the family to establish equal footing with the males in the family (Walters, Carter, Papp, & Silverstein, 1988).

Minuchin was a particular "lightening rod" for criticism regarding sexism in his perspective on families (Minuchin, 1991). This was related to his early ideas on hierarchy and power in the family, as well as the early systems perspective that enmeshment was an indication of family dysfunction. In addition, there are many video examples of his work (1979, 1984), in which he was perceived to be particularly critical, if not demeaning, of mothers during therapy sessions. Minuchin eventually responded to this criticism by reviewing his ideas and practices and modifying them to reflect a more "enlightened" way of thinking (Minuchin, 1991). He subsequently worked with members of the Women's Project and produced publications with them that served to modify some of his earlier ideas.

Summary

The birth of family therapy was one of those seminal developments that occurred because the right people were in the right place at the right time. It was a development that gradually changed the field of psychotherapy, an evolution that is still in process today. In this chapter, I attempted to provide a quick overview of the development of the field of family therapy. But, as I cautioned at the beginning, this is history filtered through my frame of reference, so it is my list of "great persons." There are many other founders who I didn't include—Nathan Ackerman (1966), James Framo (Ivan Böszörményi-Nagy & Framo, 1965), Paul Watzlawick (1978), and Ivan Böszörményi-Nagy (1987), to name a few--who were every bit as influential as those who I included. If you are interested in more complete histories, I again encourage you to seek out some of the comprehensive texts of family therapy approaches that are listed in the references.

Chapter 2

Understanding the Family: Structural/Strategic Concepts

Chapter Overview

In this chapter, you will:

- Review the basic concepts of structural and strategic family therapy.

- Apply these concepts to case examples.

Introduction

The strategic (Haley, 1963; Madanes, 1981) and structural (Minuchin & Fishman, 1981) models of family therapy are two overlapping approaches which are highly adaptable to mental health and school settings. These approaches are problem-driven rather than method-driven. That is, they are open systems in which interventions are tailored to the particular problem, resources of the family, and other factors that may be interfering with the family's normal functioning. These approaches are also flexible enough to integrate components of the larger family system (schools, agencies, religious institutions, etc.) into conceptualizations and interventions. They are very "teachable." Unlike other family therapy approaches, the successes of which depend on a charismatic or idiosyncratic developer, strategic and structural counseling methods are relatively standardized and replicable with appropriate training. This chapter is intended to provide basic information about the application of strategic and structural therapy from a practitioner's frame of reference.

Basic Assumptions

- **The whole is greater than the sum of the parts.**

- **Small changes in one component of a system cause changes throughout the entire system.**

- **The presenting problem is simply a symptom for dysfunction within the system.**

- **Interactions among family members are complementary in nature.**

- **The focus of therapy should not be with the WHAT, but rather with the HOW of family interactions.**

- **Therapy should be problem and not method driven.**

- **Problems are viewed in terms of the family's stages of development and the family structure.**

- **The therapist must observe the entire family in action in order to understand the transactional patterns that occur.**

- **The therapist is part of the family system once she/he joins with the family.**

Figure 2-1: Underlying assumptions of structural-strategic therapy.

The whole is greater than the sum of the parts. The structural and strategic approaches incorporate the law of composition from General Systems Theory. Like other systems, families cannot be understood by simply examining the parts comprising the structure. We must also look at the dynamic part of the family since, like most other systems, families are constantly in process and changing. For instance, a counselor may see a child individually who has been referred because of oppositional behaviors and assume that the child is simply being defiant. However, if the counselor sees the child with his mother, it may become apparent that the mother is depressed and the child's defiance is a reaction to her depression. Thus, the part (the child's behavior) was a component of a larger whole (the dynamic around the mother's depression).

Small changes in a system cause changes throughout the entire system. This assumption is based on chaos theory and the GST concept of homeostasis. Chaos theory proposes that tiny changes in circumstances can have large impacts later. These changes are predictable to within a certain range but cannot be predicted precisely to relate a specific cause to an exact effect (Baker, 2009).

The mandate of a system is to maintain stability or homeostasis. When there is a change in one part of the system (such as the leak in the toilet tank) the rest of the system adjusts because of the feedback loop that affects the other parts of the system, establishing a new level of homeostasis. In families, this is seen when a member of the family becomes symptomatic (for example, begins using alcohol excessively) and other members compensate by taking over responsibilities for, taking care of, or covering for the symptomatic member. When the symptomatic member stops drinking, the roles in the family are de-stabilized and everyone has to figure out how they fit in once again. Therefore, change in one member of the family system reverberated through the rest of the family impacting much more than just the recovering member, as chaos theory predicts.

The presenting problem is simply a symptom for dysfunction within the system. Strategic therapists view the identified client as the *symptom bearer* for the rest of the family. Therefore, it becomes important to hypothesize about the meaning of the symptom: that is, how the presenting problem helps the family. Often, the symptom is a way of getting the family to seek help for the identified client. Once the family is involved in counseling, the counselor can then assess what is really going on that might be fueling the client's problem. So, it is important to ***never take the presenting problem at face value*** and to be prepared to test hypotheses about the functioning of other members and subsystems of the family.

Interactions among family members are complementary. Minuchin (Minuchin & Fishman, 1981) believes that family interactions conform to the systems idea of complementarity. That is, in any two person or two subsystem interaction, more of a particular behavior or function of one party leads to less of that behavior from the second party. Thus, as one parent becomes more of the disciplinarian, the other parent functions less and less in this role. If one member of a couple begins to avoid the financial functions of the household, the other member will begin to take over these functions to make sure that they are adequately addressed. As you observe more families, you will see this phenomenon of complementary interactions occur over and over. It is a very powerful force in the family that a family therapist must track in order to understand how the family operates.

The focus of therapy should not be with the WHAT, but rather with the HOW of family interactions. It is common for counseling professionals to obtain information from clients about what is going on (WIGO), because we are used to working with clients individually using talking types of therapy. Structural and strategic therapies are *action* oriented, therefore, in order to really understand how a family functions in problem situations, the counselor needs to see the family in action. That is why *enactments* are a necessary component of counseling sessions. Having members of the family engage in interactions helps the counselor understand *how* the family operates.

The therapeutic approach should be problem and not method driven. Strategic therapy in particular, is one of the precursors of solution-focused approaches. This type of approach does not try to fit the client into the therapeutic approach, as is the case with individual approaches like Reality Therapy. Instead, strategic therapists tailor their approach to the family's specific problem and resources. So, two different families presenting with a similar problem may end up resolving the problem in very different ways.

Problems are viewed in terms of the family's stages of development and the family structure. Families, like individuals, progress through common developmental stages, each of which has its own set of developmental tasks. Strategic therapy stresses the need to assess family problems in terms of transitions from one stage of development to another. For instance, parents often struggle with discipline issues when their child enters adolescence because the type of discipline that used to work when their child was younger simply does not work with a teenager. So, the parents get frustrated when they try to use the same old strategies and their teen no longer responds to their attempts. The counselor's job then becomes one of helping the parents get "unstuck" by recognizing that the old methods no longer work and that they need to try something new to meet the demands of a new developmental stage.

The therapist must observe the entire family in action in order to understand the transactional patterns that occur. If at all possible, it is important to see all members of the family in counseling sessions. This allows the counselor to observe how the various combinations of family members interact. It has often been the case for me that I develop a completely different picture of the family when I simply listen to descriptions of WIGO from a parent versus see the family members interact. It has also been the case that the family functions very differently when one parent comes in with the children versus both parents being present.

The therapist is part of the family system once she/he joins with the family. It is important for counselors to understand that when they begin seeing a family, they influence the dynamics in the family. The counselor, in effect, becomes a subsystem of the family. Individuals will try to draw the counselor into alliances, look for the counselor's support, and use the counselor as a scapegoat during counseling sessions. There's no escaping the fact that the counselor's mere presence changes the family's interactions.

Developmental Stages

Each family passes through a sequence of stages beginning with couple formation (Minuchin & Fishman, 1981), each stage presenting a series of developmental tasks that must be accomplished.   Most of these are resolved implicitly during the evolution of the family. But,

inevitably, some will present obstacles that need to be addressed more openly and directly in

order to be resolved. As a counselor, it is important to have a clear understanding of the stage of

development at which the family is functioning, as well as the developmental tasks that are

presenting challenges.

Stages of Family Development

- Couple Formation

- The First Child

- Families with Young Children

- Families with Tweens and Teen

- Parent Separation from Children

- Middle-Adulthood Parents with Adult Children

- Adult Children with Aging Parents

Figure 2-2: Stages of Family Development

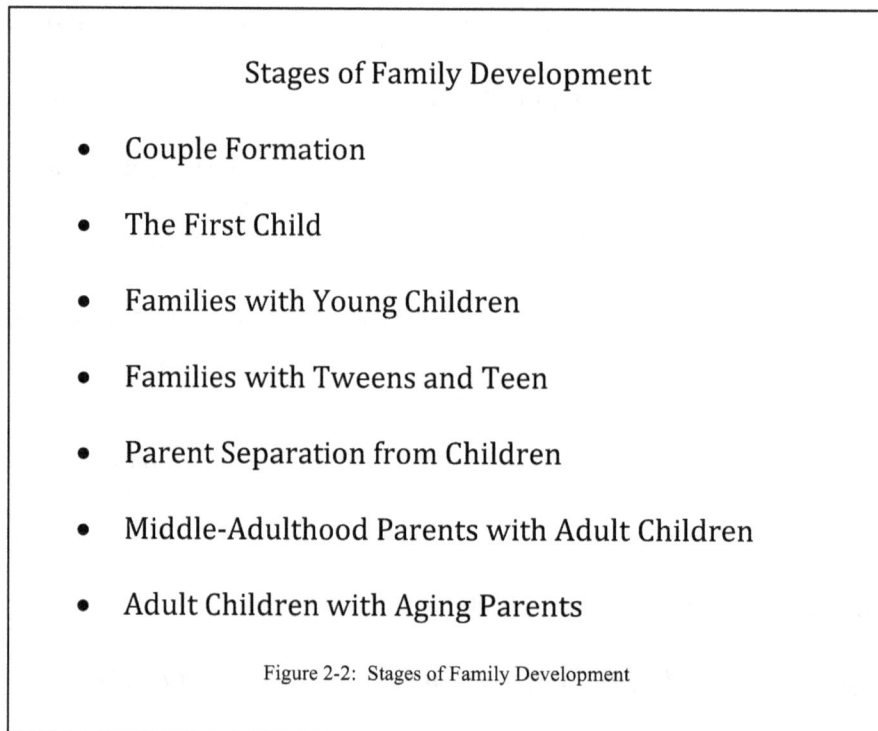

Couple Formation. Family development begins with couple formation, the period during

which the new couple must renegotiate old relationships with members of their families of origin

and with friends. Tasks and issues at this stage include establishing roles for normal tasks, such

as housework and bill paying; parameters for displays of affection and intimacy; relationships

with each partner's families of origin; and, most importantly, distribution of power, which is

typically played out through financial decisions.

The First Child. With the birth of the first child, all bets are off. Conflicts and developmental tasks that had been resolved in the previous stage need to be revisited and renegotiated. Changes in the couple's rules for intimacy, relationships with extended family, and friends again must be revised to meet the demands of the new nuclear family constellation. The focus of the couple now shifts from their relationship with each other to their roles as parents, creating a new subsystem in the family. Decisions need to be made regarding care giving (Who changes diapers? Who gets up at night to feed the baby?); work and finances (Will one parent stay home to raise the child? How will this impact the family financially?); and child care, if both parents continue working. The couple has less time and energy for each other: the best form of birth control is having a child. If there were previous problems in the couple relationship, they often surface in this stage, fueled by the added stress of having a child.

Families with Young Children. Whether or not more children are born, the family eventually progresses to the stage of "families with young children," as their child or children become toddlers and elementary aged. This stage is characterized by a realignment of subsystems within the family, and a reordering of the family hierarchy, particularly in regard to the sibling subsystem. Parents must begin providing flexible boundaries between the family and new subsystems with which it must interact, such as school, church, families of children's friends, and youth organizations. Discipline practices become important as children become more independent and able to make choices. Parents have to make decisions about such things as, family rituals (Which parent's holiday traditions will they adopt?) and religious practices (Will they follow a particular religious belief; if so, which one?) Last but not least, what about the couple? Is there any time for the parents to be a couple?

Families with Tweens and Teens. The aging and maturing of children moves the family on to the stage of families with pre-adolescent children. This is a more recent development in our culture. As kids are exposed to more information and technology at younger ages, some of the issues that used to be characteristic of adolescents now appear at younger ages. Specifically, this stage is characterized by a redefinition of disciplinary procedures and family rules: the parenting approaches which may have been useful with a seven-year-old are no longer appropriate with an eleven-year-old. Children begin the process of separating from their parents and challenging their values and rules. Awareness of peers, particularly differences between the families of peer's and a child's own family helps to fuel some of the challenges of this stage.

The family moves on to its "teenage" stage, as children enter fully into adolescence. While the primary task of the child during this stage is to establish a sense of identity, the task of the family is to establish boundaries flexible enough to allow the adolescent to become his or her own person while still having a sense of connectedness to the family. This is the stage in which many parents make the mistake of thinking that their kids don't need their guidance anymore, withdrawing from the responsibilities of parenting. Frustration and confusion with the things their teenagers are doing often contributes to this. However, it is more important than ever that parents serve as a safety net for their teenagers. The teen's job is to become independent. The family's job is to encourage this without rejecting the teen for some of the inappropriate ways that independence is sought.

Parents Separating from Children. As teenagers become young adults, the family enters the stage of parents separating from children, the main task being "leaving home" (Haley, 1980). This is again a time when parents must support and encourage their children's independence while at the same time working through their own sense of loss and confusion regarding their roles. The focus of the parents moves back to the couple, often requiring redefinition of the couple subsystem's rules for intimacy. Thus, the dyad that was the parents must now go through a period of "couple *re-formation*." Successful resolution of this task in particular hinges on the stability of the couple subsystem before children entered the picture and the degree to which the parents maintained a sense of "couple-hood" during their child rearing. If there were unresolved conflicts, these commonly resurface during this stage. This is a stage in which the future of the couple is particularly at risk, when "couple dissolution" (i.e., divorce) is a common outcome.

There are a number of other ways the family system adjusts if the couple has difficulty "re-forming" and re-establishing intimacy in a satisfying manner. With younger couples, it is not unusual to see them simply maintain their parent roles by having more children. Other couples establish a state of peaceful co-existence, living as "roommates" and pursuing their own interests separate from one another. Still others live together as friends who have common interests, but not as lovers per se. And the fact of the matter is that many couples just stay together for religious, financial, personal, or other reasons, and are miserable.

Middle-Adulthood Parents with Adult Children. In addition to changes in the couple subsystems, relationships with children evolve. Parents and children wrestle with and establish patterns for relating to one another as peers…or not, depending on the level of differentiation in the family. This is the primary task at this stage.

Families with Aging Parents. Finally, the family enters the stage of families with aging parents, a time during which adult children often find themselves fulfilling caregiver roles for elderly parents. This is a stage in which elderly spouses must deal with the loss of their partner, and when children find themselves reversing roles with their parents. Issues such as moving a parent into a nursing home, selling the family home or business, and end-of-life dilemmas disrupt the family's stability, fueling conflicts among siblings.

Developmental Stages and Family Dysfunction

Both Haley (1976) and Minuchin (Minuchin & Fishman, 1981) view one aspect of family dysfunction as the family being "stuck" in a transition from one stage to another. Thus, the family engages in behaviors which may have been effective during an earlier stage, but which no longer work. In addition, it is common for today's families to be functioning in multiple stages at the same time. The phenomenon of the "sandwich generation," in which parents find themselves raising a young child, dealing with a teenager, and taking care of an elderly parent, is one example of this. The recent proliferation of grandparents raising their grandchildren is another. One of the tasks of the counselor is to mobilize the family's resources--to get the family "unstuck" and thereby move it to a higher level of development by adapting to the demands of a new stage or balancing multiple stages of development (Madanes, 1981). Hence, it is important for the counselor to enter the therapy room with at least a working hypothesis about the family constellation, interactions, and developmental stages.

Application Activity: Identifying Developmental Stages

Read each family description and identify the developmental stage or stages of the family.

1) Mr. and Mrs. Casparelli dropped off their youngest daughter for her first year at Ivy University three weeks ago. Mrs C. has dreaded this day for many months. She misses her daughter terribly and doesn't know what to do with her time on the weekends. Mr. C. has been going golfing every Saturday morning and is always busy working on projects at other times.

Family Stage: _____

What are the potential issues? _____

_____

2)   Bob and Jane taught at the same elementary for years before they started dating last May. The two of them became close when they were both going through conflicted divorces and used to talk to each other for support. This eventually led to their current relationship and plan to be married next year. Bob has a nine-year-old son and three-year-old daughter from his marriage and Jane has a 13-year-old daughter from her marriage.

Family Stage(s): _____

What are the potential the issues? _____

_____

Lois is a 78-year-old mother of four and grandmother to 11 children. Her husband, who died a year ago, was her caretaker, since Lois had been exhibiting symptoms of Alzheimer's disease for approximately 4 years. She has been living with her oldest daughter, Emily, since his death. Emily has a son who is a junior in college and two daughters, one in fifth grade and one in eighth grade. Since she has been Lois's caregiver, Emily had to cut back on her hours as a real estate agent.

Family Stage(s): _____

What are the potential the issues? _____

_____

Answers in Appendix A

World Views

A family's world view is another important aspect of the family system which a counselor must understand when working within a family framework. The world view is the family's filter system; that is, it is the family's construction of reality. This filter system consists of the family's culture, basic assumptions, beliefs, and experiences, some of which may be shared by all family members, while others are unique to specific individuals in the family. World views determine how family members see the family fitting into the world at large, as well as how specific family members view themselves and other family members. For instance, in my own work with families, I have found it common for parents to view the child who is symptomatic as the "bad" kid, while viewing other children in the family, who often are also misbehaving, as the "good" kids. These roles harden on the children like egg shells, making it very difficult for parents to notice instances of good behavior by the bad kid, and instances of bad behavior by the good kids. Conversely, the children understand what their roles are supposed to be and behave in a manner that confirms their parents' world views. The world view provides the counselor with another piece of the map for understanding how a particular family sees itself and how it deals with those within and outside of the family. In addition, it provides a clue about how to enter the family system through a path of least resistance.

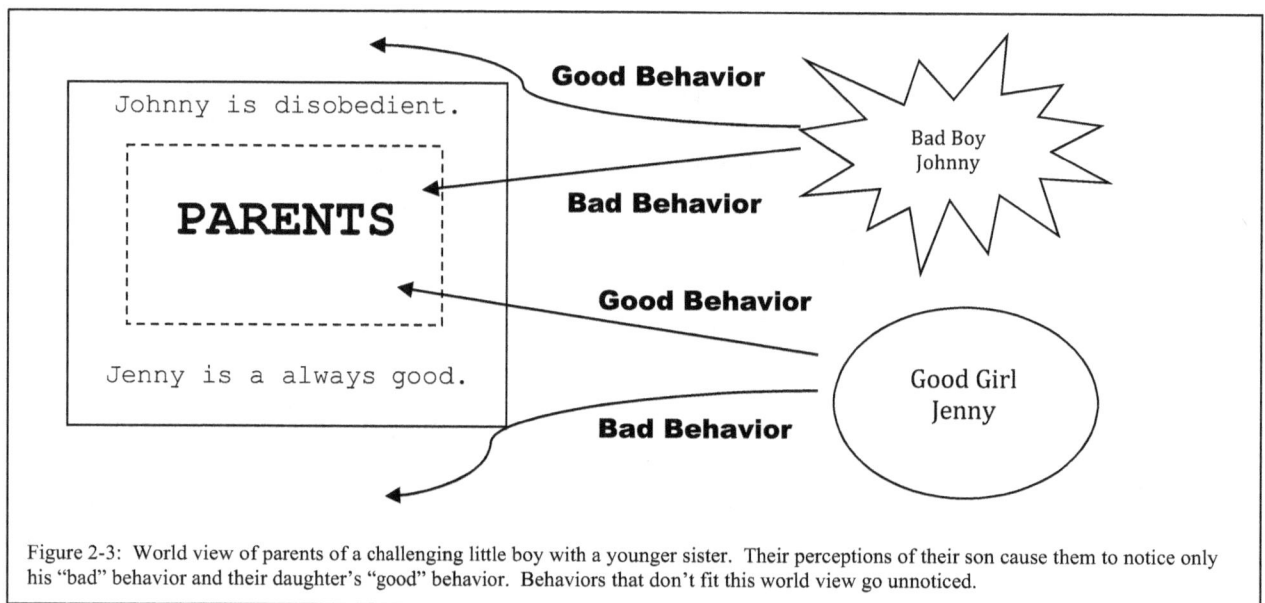

Figure 2-3: World view of parents of a challenging little boy with a younger sister. Their perceptions of their son cause them to notice only his "bad" behavior and their daughter's "good" behavior. Behaviors that don't fit this world view go unnoticed.

I often try to sum up family world views in common adages as a simple code for myself. Some of the common world views I have run into include: "spare the rod and spoil the child" (overly punitive parents); "children are to be seen and not heard" (families where communication between parents and children is problematic); "circle the wagons" (families that are closed about their activities, particularly in cases of social services involvement); "boys will be boys" (families in which there is an acting out male who the parents insulate from consequences); and "she's her mother's daughter (or father's son)" (families in which parents blame each other for a child's problems, families in which there are rigidly enforced role expectations, enmeshed families).

Application Activity: World Views

Read each family description and list the world views of the family.

1)   Tricia Smith finds it impossible to get her three sons to listen to her. She had been in an abusive relationship with their father for 15 years before finally taking the boys and moving to a shelter for domestic violence victims two years ago. She has been living in a rented house with them for about a year. Tricia has tried everything, but the boys simply refuse to follow any directions she gives them. Sometimes, she feels like they are just like their father.

Family Member	World View

2)   The Smith family has a long history with the Department of Social Services in Mohawk County over the past 8 years. During this time period, there have been five reports of child abuse and neglect, two of which led to charges in family court. Several agencies have worked with the Smiths on parenting skills, household management, and work skills. Recently, there was a small fire in the family's house when Mrs. Smith left her 10-year-old daughter home to watch the two younger children while Mrs. Smith went to a convenience store to get cigarettes. She arrived home in time to put out the fire without having to call the fire department. Mrs. Smith told the kids that they would be severely punished if they told anyone about the fire, especially, "those big mouths at school."

Family Member	World View

3)   Tom Crosby was brought up at a time when kids listened to their parents and knew what would happen if they didn't. He expects the same from his own kids. If they don't do what they are supposed to, then they get "the strap." It really ticks him off that do-gooders say you can't hit your kids.

Family Member	World View

Examples in Appendix A

Subsystems and Boundaries

The strategic and structural models are also concerned with subsystems within the family, viewing the family as a network of interconnecting and/or overlapping subsystems (Madanes, 1981; Minuchin & Fishman, 1981). The most common of these are the parent subsystem (mother-father), the sibling subsystem (brothers-sisters), and subsystems which include combinations of extended family members (maternal grandmother-grandfather). With school-aged children, these subsystems often extend outside the nuclear and extended families to include peers, teachers, parents of peers, religious groups, and, social service agencies.

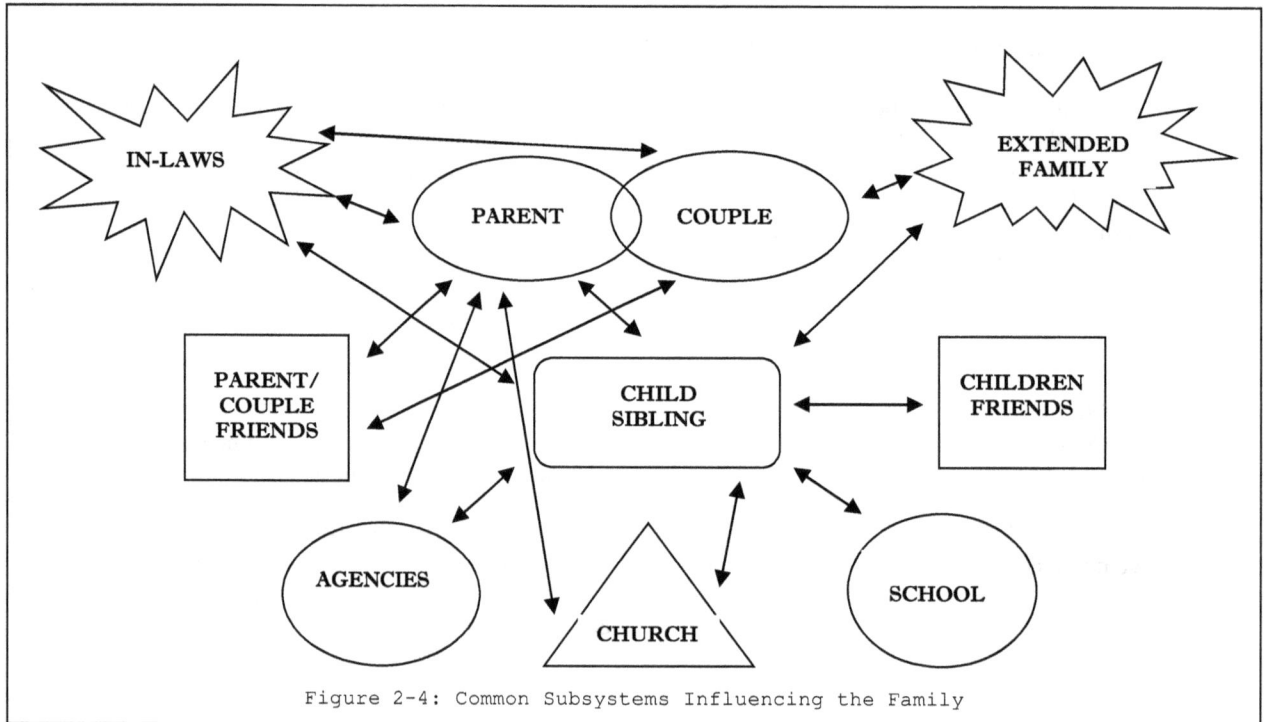

Figure 2-4: Common Subsystems Influencing the Family

The aspect to consider when conceptualizing the subsystems of a specific family is the clarity and flexibility of boundaries. Subsystems are separated from other subsystems within a family by invisible boundaries--that is, the implicit rules for membership, functions, and interactions among members of different subsystems. For instance, the rules for membership in the parent subsystem are that members must be involved in *raising at least one child*, not necessarily that a member be the biological parent of the child being raised. The function of the parent subsystem is *childrearing*. The rule for membership in the sibling subsystem is that a child must have *at least one brother or sister* (again, not necessarily biologically related). The function of the sibling subsystem is *to drive the parent subsystem crazy*.

Boundaries are the way subsystems are defined by their members, and need to be firm enough to clearly differentiate one subsystem from another, yet flexible enough to allow

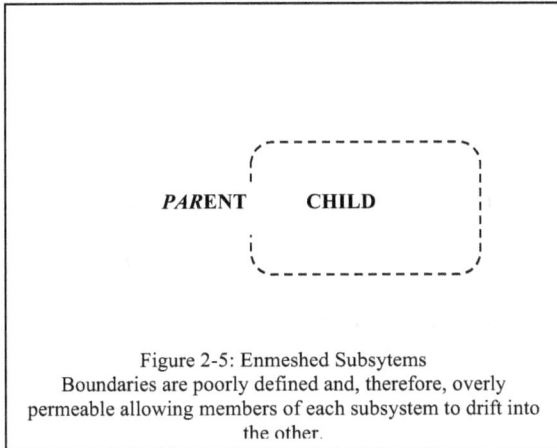

Figure 2-5: Enmeshed Subsytems
Boundaries are poorly defined and, therefore, overly
permeable allowing members of each subsystem to drift into
the other.

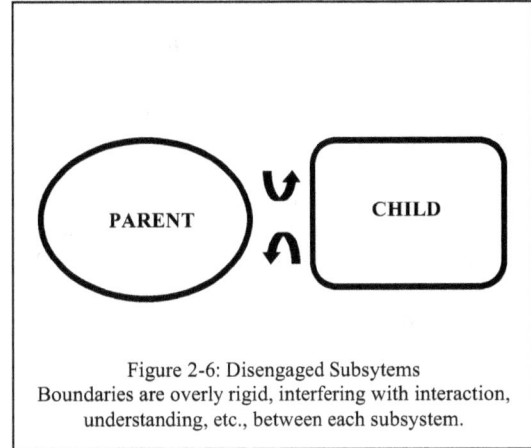

Figure 2-6: Disengaged Subsystems
Boundaries are overly rigid, interfering with interaction,
understanding, etc., between each subsystem.

interactions among members of different subsystems. Overly rigid (*disengaged*) or poorly

defined (*enmeshed*) boundaries may be both a symptom and contributory factor to family

dysfunction (Minuchin & Fishman, 1981). For example, a family consisting of two overly

protective parents and an eleven-year-old son who is not allowed to play with other children

exhibits rather fuzzy boundaries between the parent and child subsystems, while having overly

rigid boundaries between the child and peer subsystems. A family in which a mother constantly

interrupts and speaks for her children is an example of enmeshment, where the parent and child

subsystem boundaries are not well-defined.

Application Activity: Subsystems and Boundaries

Read the family situations below and identify the subsystems involved and whether they are enmeshed or disengaged.

1) Mom is upset because dad is never at home these days. He works late, stops for drinks with his friends after work and spends all of his time at home surfing the net. Mom complains about dad regularly to their 12-year-old son and sometimes even keeps him home from school so that she doesn't get lonely.

   Subsystems _____   Enmeshed   Normal   Disengaged

   Why? _____

2) Dad likes to go out for a few drinks at night, even when he has his 4-year-old and 6-year-old daughters for their overnight visits. So, he piles them in the car and has them wait there while he goes into his favorite bars for a couple of beers. He's careful about locking the car doors, of course.

   Subsystems _____   Enmeshed   Normal   Disengaged

   Why? _____

3) The Chandlers had always been a tight knit family. So, it made sense that when their oldest son was applying to colleges, mom and dad narrowed down the list of possible choices and even told him what his major should be. When he started college, mom had him send his dirty clothes home every two weeks, and would wash and send them back to him. Dad read all of his written assignments and revised them so that they were "college quality."

   Subsystems _____   Enmeshed   Normal   Disengaged

   Why? _____

4) Bill and Jennifer McCarthy truly enjoy spending time together as a couple. But, with four kids, that isn't often possible. Now that there oldest daughter is 15, they have been able to establish a "date night" once per week. Their daughter is very responsible, and when her parents return home, she provides them with a rundown of the night, and then goes to her room to work on homework.

   Subsystems _____   Enmeshed   Normal   Disengaged

   Why? _____

5) A recent news story reported that the parents of a five-year-old left their child home for a week with plenty of food and children's videos while they flew to Mexico for a vacation.

   Subsystems _____   Enmeshed   Normal   Disengaged

   Why? _____

Answers in Appendix A

Hierarchy

The structural concept of the family hierarchy follows along with the idea of subsystems. Minuchin believes that each family establishes a hierarchy which can facilitate or impede its functioning. The typical "normal" hierarchy is one in which the parents are on top, preferably in lateral positions, followed by the oldest child, second oldest, and so forth. Structural and strategic therapy clearly places the parents in the *executive* position in the family. No matter how democratic or authoritative parents in a particular family want to be, they are ultimately accountable for decisions and actions that affect their children. Thus, it is important that they assume the highest position in the family hierarchy.

A hierarchy becomes dysfunctional when a family member assumes or is relegated to an inappropriate position, either higher or lower than the position in which he or she is supposed to be. An example of this is when the youngest child exerts power over his parents by making unreasonable demands on them to which they accede (special dinners, being able to stay up later than the other children). The resulting hierarchy would place the youngest child in the highest position, *above the parents*. The parents and older children in the family would then be relegated inappropriately to lower positions. Mapping the family hierarchy is a way of understanding

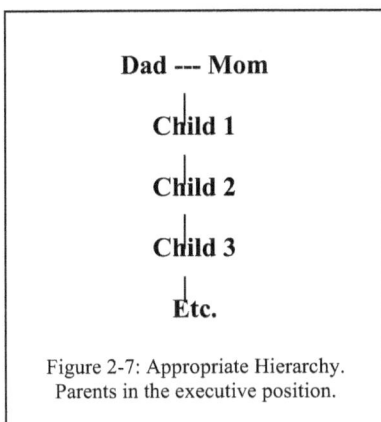

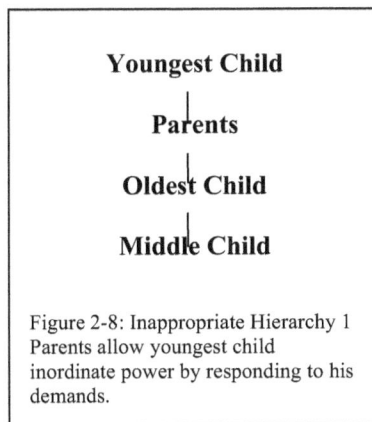

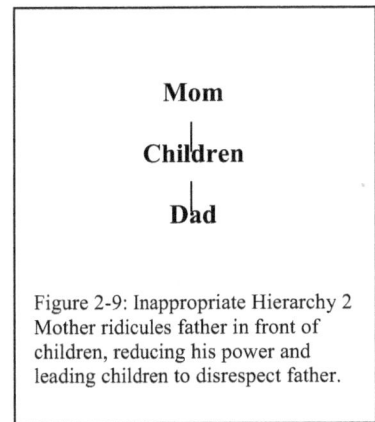

Dad --- Mom

Child 1

Child 2

Child 3

Etc.

Figure 2-7: Appropriate Hierarchy. Parents in the executive position.

Youngest Child

Parents

Oldest Child

Middle Child

Figure 2-8: Inappropriate Hierarchy 1 Parents allow youngest child inordinate power by responding to his demands.

Mom

Children

Dad

Figure 2-9: Inappropriate Hierarchy 2 Mother ridicules father in front of children, reducing his power and leading children to disrespect father.

power in the family. When a child attains a position in the family above one parent, she has more power than that parent in the family, making it difficult for that parent to carry out normal parenting tasks effectively, such as discipline. One parent assuming a position above the other parent can undermine the less powerful parent's authority and respect.

One of the primary goals of the counselor who is operating within a structural framework is to help the family re-establish an appropriate and functional hierarchy. The counselor might make comments about what is "adult" business and what is "child" business during the course of discussions in the family sessions. Homework might be assigned which would clearly place the parents in the caretaking and decision-making roles. Or the family might be taught a "pretend" (Madanes, 1981), a game or role play which metaphorically communicates the appropriate hierarchy.

Application Activity: Family Hierarchy

Hypothesize about the hierarchies in the families below.

1) Dad wears the pants in this family. That is, except, when mom tells him he can't. Mom organizes everything, makes all the plans, pays the bills, and is the primary decision maker with the kids. Dad works hard, gives his paycheck to mom for depositing, and looks to mom for directions about what he needs to do.

    Hierarchy   How might this affect the family?

    _____
    _____
    _____
    _____

2) Emma is a seven-year-old child with severe asthma. In fact, her illness pretty much determines what the family can do and where they can go. They have to avoid places where animal hair might be present, can't go outside much during pollen season, and have to constantly watch for signs that an asthma attack might be starting. Even her older brother and sister have to keep watch and be prepared to call 911 if their parents aren't around to help.

    Hierarchy   How might this affect the family?

    _____
    _____
    _____
    _____
    _____

3) Ron and Don are 13-year-old identical twins who are "holy terrors." Ron has been expelled from school for trying to sell his ADHD medication, and Don becomes physically abusive toward his mother when she tries to enforce rules at home. Mom is afraid of both boys and both parents don't know what to do.

    Hierarchy   How might this affect the family?

    _____
    _____
    _____
    _____

Answers in Appendix A

Triangles

The strategic model emphasizes understanding interactions within the family in terms of triads or triangles--transactional patterns which involve three family members or subsystems (Madanes, 1981). Included in this idea is a conceptualization of the valence of each interaction within the triangle, either positive or negative, the sum of which determines the stability or instability of a triangle. A triangle consisting of father-mother-son, where the interactions are all positive is very stable, in that every relationship is basically equal with no one individual feeling threatened by the relationship between the other two individuals within the triangle. However, the same triangle in which the father-mother valence is negative, and the father-son, and mother-son valences are both positive, constitutes an unstable triangle because there is competition for the son's alliance. The cause of this competition is the need of each parent to strengthen his and her position against the other parent because of a problematic relationship between mother and father. On the other hand, a triangle in which the mother-father and father-daughter valences are negative, and the mother-daughter valence is positive is a stable triangle, as father's "outsider" status actually strengthens the mother-daughter alliance. Examples of stable and unstable triangles are shown below.

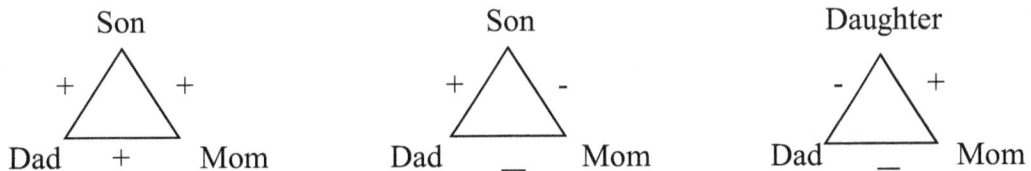

Figured 2-10: Stable Triangles. Firm alliances decrease impetus for change.

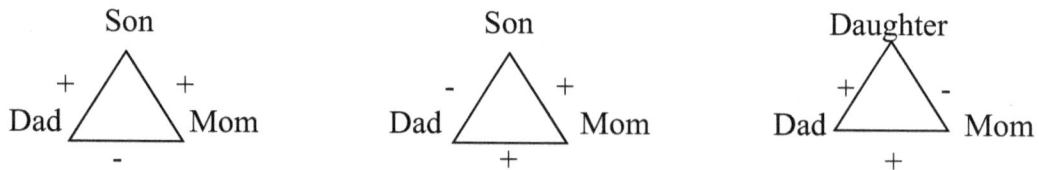

Figured 2-11: Unstable Triangles. Shifting. alliances increase impetus for change.

Triangulation

While the strategic construct of triangles is different from the Bowenian concept of the same name, Bowen's idea of triangulation in family relationships (Singleton, 1982) is also an important frame of reference for the school-based family counselor. Bowen's observation is that as tension increases within the family, for instance, the husband and wife (the individuals involved) seek to relieve tension by involving a third party (their children) and win the third party's support for his or her side of the conflict. Thus, the mother may complain to the child about her husband's lack of affection or infidelities, eventually using the child as an emotional substitute for her spouse. Bowen sees as a goal of his therapeutic approach, the de-triangulation of family members from conflict between individuals (Bowen, 1978). He, in fact, sees his own success at de-triangulating himself from the conflicts within his family of origin, as one of his greatest accomplishments as a family therapist (Nichols, 1984).

Triangulation does not only occur within families, but also on an institutional level. That is, many times, families become skilled at triangulating an institution into their conflicts in order to reduce the tension within the family. This usually results in the feuding parties within the family uniting to battle the institution, thus removing the focus from the real conflict. Schools are one of the primary institutions that become triangulated into family conflicts. One of the primary examples of this is custody battles, in which the non-custodial parent will make demands on the school (e.g., visiting the child during the school day) that are denied to him or her by the custodial parent. When representatives of the school enforce the legal stipulations of the custody agreement as it pertains to school, the non-custodial parent becomes enraged at the school, rather than at his or her ex-spouse. The custodial parent also may become angry, the mere presence of his or her spouse leading him or her to conclude that the school is not doing its "duty." In the end, both parents make demands on the school which they should be directing toward each other through their attorneys.

Application Activity: Family Triangles

Read the following family interaction descriptions and determine the triangles and valances.

1) A family of four with a teenage daughter who constantly teases her younger sister. Mom is always stepping in to defend the younger sister and dad thinks that the older daughter is just being a normal teenager.

2) The wife in a newly married couple in their late 20's is upset about her husband's mother constantly calling him to help her with things at her house. He is an only child, and his father died when he was 12. The wife complains to her own mother, who thinks that the husband's behavior is odd.

3) A divorced mom asks her nine-year-old son's school counselor to see him because he has been upset and defiant on Sundays that he returned from his weekend visits to his father's house. Mom wants her son to have an opportunity to talk about his feelings with someone who is neutral. After the counselor has seen the boy twice, the counselor receives a call from the boy's irate father demanding to know why the counselor is seeing the child and stating that since the couple has joint legal custody, the boy cannot be seen by the counselor without the father's permission.

Examples in Appendix A

Circular (Isomorphic) Patterns

The strategic model does not view family interactions as simple cause-effect or stimulus-response relationships. Rather, the behavior of various family members is seen as part of a rather complicated cycle of events, reactions, and reality constructs which are called isomorphic or circular patterns. These patterns typically provide the map of dysfunctional interactions, including various family members' efforts at triangulating others into family conflicts. Isomorphic patterns are actually closer to the cybernetic concept of feedback mechanisms, each component interaction leading to a subsequent interaction between individuals or sub-systems, at some point resulting in the presenting symptom in the identified patient that brought the family into counseling in the first place. We call these patterns isomorphic because each overt or observable component of the pattern is driven by a corresponding underlying, covert issue or purpose.

Take for example a family of three (father, mother, adolescent son) in which the father recently died from a long terminal illness. The presenting complaint of the mother's is the son's lack of any emotional reaction to his father's death. In discussing the period which led up to her husband's death, mother expresses much anger and resentment toward her husband because of the demands made on her to care for him during his illness. In addition, she reveals a longstanding general lack of intimacy in their relationship which was evident to her shortly after they were married. The hypothesized isomorphic pattern which was used with this family is diagrammed below.

The portions of this pattern which I chose to interrupt were the enmeshed and unnaturally spouse-like relationship between mother and son, and mom's "double-bind" (Weakland, 1960) message to son to simultaneously "be angry at your father for me," but "it's not normal to be angry at your dead father." Through use of a reframe, the son's distancing of himself from mother was re-labeled as normal behavior, as was the present delay between his father's death and the outward expression of his grief. In addition, a proscribed, regular period of mother-son intimacy was scheduled each night via a one-hour ritual of playing games that mother, father, and son used to enjoy playing together. This allowed mother and son to experience a normal level of parent-child intimacy while simultaneously mitigating mother's feelings of abandonment (by the father). At the same time, by making Mom feel less abandoned, it was hoped that she would also allow the boy the opportunity to engage in more age-appropriate teenage activities. This would include separating from his mother.

Circular patterns are one of the most complex constructs for beginning family counselors to understand and apply. It goes against our tendency to reduce or simplify family interactions to simple causes, something that has become ingrained in our culture through the influence of behaviorism. While behavioral explanations might be useful in understanding discreet behaviors, there's nothing simple about how families operate because of the numerous individuals and subsystems that affect a child. Thus, it is necessary to recognize this complexity within the context of the more complicated circular relationships of family interactions.

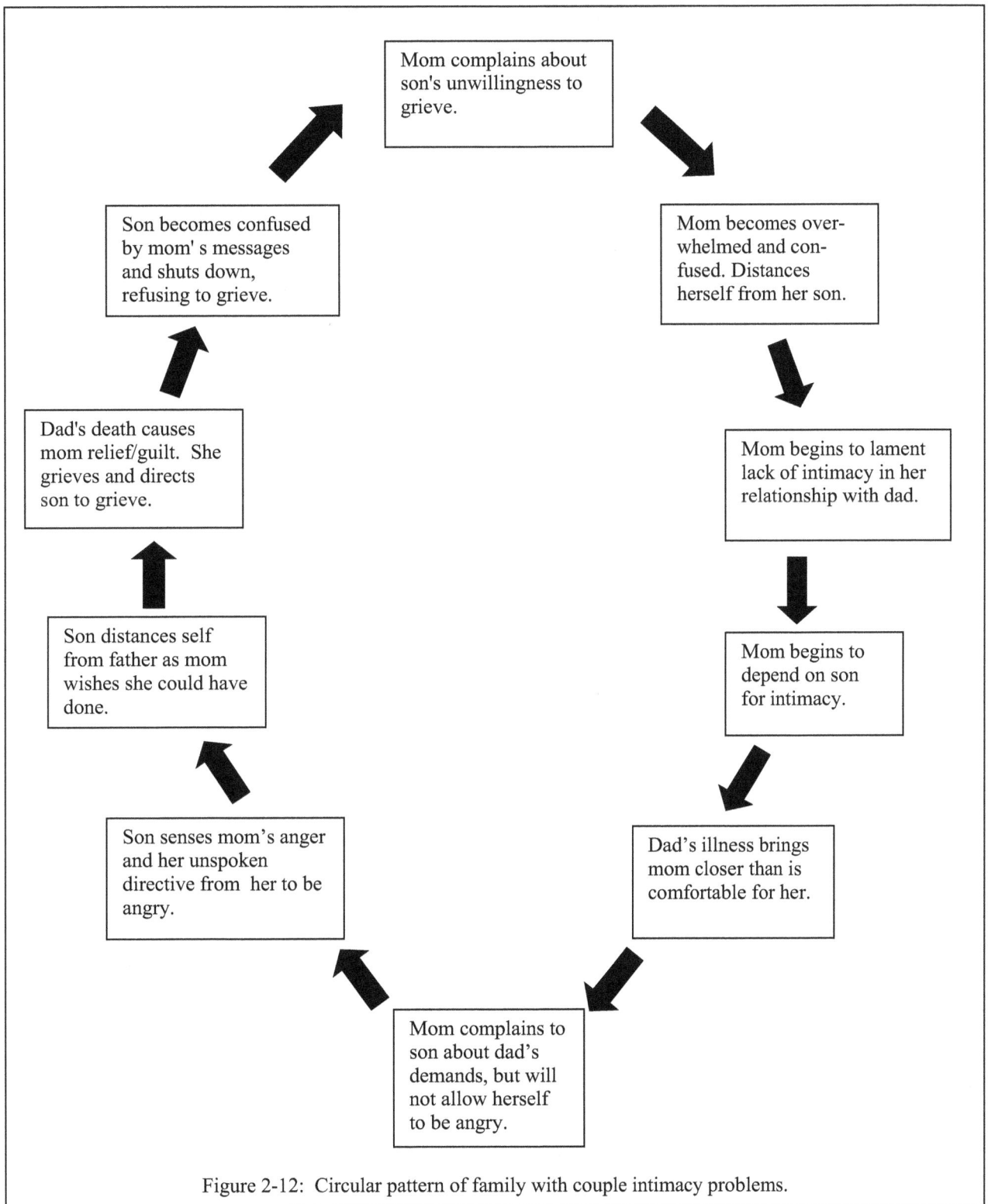

Figure 2-12: Circular pattern of family with couple intimacy problems.

Application Activity: Circular Patterns

Diagram the circular patterns in the families described below.

1) Ben and Sarah have been married for three years and became new parents four months ago. Sarah's time has been predictably occupied with taking care of their daughter.   When Ben has tried to help, Sarah constantly corrects him or takes over and repeats a task he has done, like changing the baby. So, Ben has given up trying to help. For the past month, Ben has been trying to be intimate with Sarah, but she has shown no interest, saying that she's too tired or that they will wake the baby. Feeling increasingly rejected, Ben has begun working overtime several nights a week and coming home just before Sarah goes to bed. Before the baby was born, Ben was more of the "cuddly," emotionally-expressive spouse, and Sarah was more reserved, not liking things like "PDA's" (public displays of affection).

2) The Jones family consists of Tim and Mary and their two children, Bethany (7) and Josh (11). Tim and Mary have had an somewhat rocky relationship, separating for several months when Josh was three. Recently, Tim has been working late and Mary suspects that he may be having an affair. During this time, Mary has spent her evenings playing board games with Josh after Bethany goes to bed. She has occasionally slipped and complained to Josh about Tim's late hours. About a month after Tim began working late, Mary received a note from Josh's teacher requesting that she and Tim come in for a conference. Josh had become uncharacteristically defiant during the past two weeks, culminating with an incident in which he tore up an assignment and refused to do it. Mary showed Tim the letter and the two of them met with Josh's teacher the next day. After the meeting, Tim agreed to Mary's demand that he adjust his work hours so that he could spend more time with Josh. Tim did this and began coming home before dinner, and spent time specifically helping Josh with homework and playing sports with him. Josh's teacher sent progress notes home every school day to keep the parents informed about Josh's school behavior. Four weeks went by with no incidents and good reports on Josh's academics. During the fifth week, Tim began working late again.

Examples in Appendix A

Summary

The purpose of this chapter was to introduce you to the basic concepts that you will be using to understand the functioning of families that you counsel. As you progressed through the chapter, you had the opportunity to apply each concept to examples of family interactions. In Chapter 3, you will move on to conducting an analysis of the dynamics that are present in your own family of origin.

Chapter 3

Analyzing Your Family of Origin

Chapter Overview

In this chapter, you will:

- Learn how to construct a genogram.

- Tell your "family story" by providing examples of important experiences that informed the construction of your genogram.

- Apply your knowledge of structural/strategic concepts by analyzing your family of origin within this framework.

- Identify blindspots and softspots that may potentially influence your work with families as a counselor.

The Genogram

The genogram is a clinical tool that provides the counselor with *some* insight into clients' perceptions of their family relationships. The genogram diagrams the client's family, showing not only the generational relationships, but also the dynamics and quality of relationships (who's close to who, who is estranged, etc.). Typically, genograms focus on three generations of family patterns. If the client has children, the genogram will be constructed starting with the client's nuclear family (spouse/partner and children) and then move back to his/her family of origin (parents and siblings). If the client has no children, the genogram will include information on the client's parents and their siblings, and the client's grandparents. Basic guidelines, adapted from McGoldrick and Gerson (1985), for constructing a simple genogram are provided in Figure 3-1. An example of this activity is provided below.

The nice thing about the genogram is its flexibility. It can be constructed casually during the course of an initial interview or counseling session, the counselor simply filling in relevant

Age
Name — Female

Age
Name — Male

Identified Client or Index Person

Pregnancy   ● Uncompleted Pregnancy

m. 2012 — Marital Relationship

R/b 2017 — Unmarried Couple

s. 2/18 — Separation

dv. 3/08 — Divorce

OR   Biological children/siblings

Oldest ——→ Youngest   Oldest ——→ Youngest

Death
Date of Death
& Cause   Twins   Adopted child

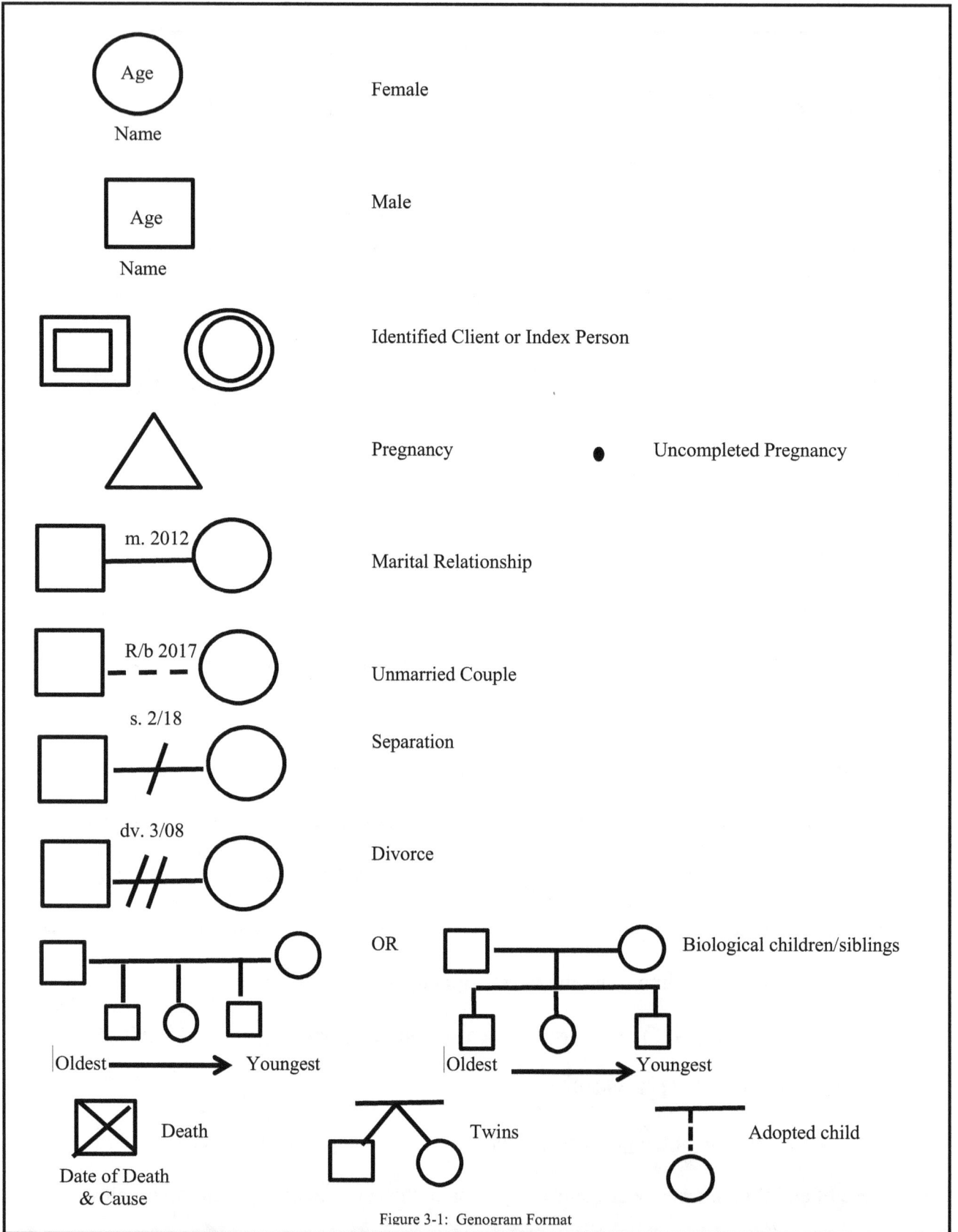

Figure 3-1: Genogram Format

information as it comes up during the session. On the other hand, some approaches, such as Bowenian therapists, employ the genogram as an intentional, structured component of the therapeutic process. In this case, the family information is methodically collected and incorporated into the counseling sessions. Typically used with couples, the genogram helps clients identify dysfunctional patterns that have been transmitted across generations in their families of origin as a means of changing their own interactional patterns to more adaptive ones.

However, the information is collected, there is some standard data that family counselors need to include in constructing a genogram.

- Biological/heredity information, such as each family member's health and psychiatric history.

- World views held by various family members.

- Relationships between children and their siblings, parents and their siblings, and children and family members outside of the nuclear family.

- Marital/divorce patterns throughout the extended family.

- Major events that impacted the family (deaths, child abuse, illnesses, etc.)

As information is obtained about each family member, the counselor records the information under the symbol for that member. That means that you need to leave ample space for the information. You also have to plan for the possibility that the client has had multiple marital relationships, which requires adequate space for recording the information accurately. An example of a partially completed genogram is provided below.

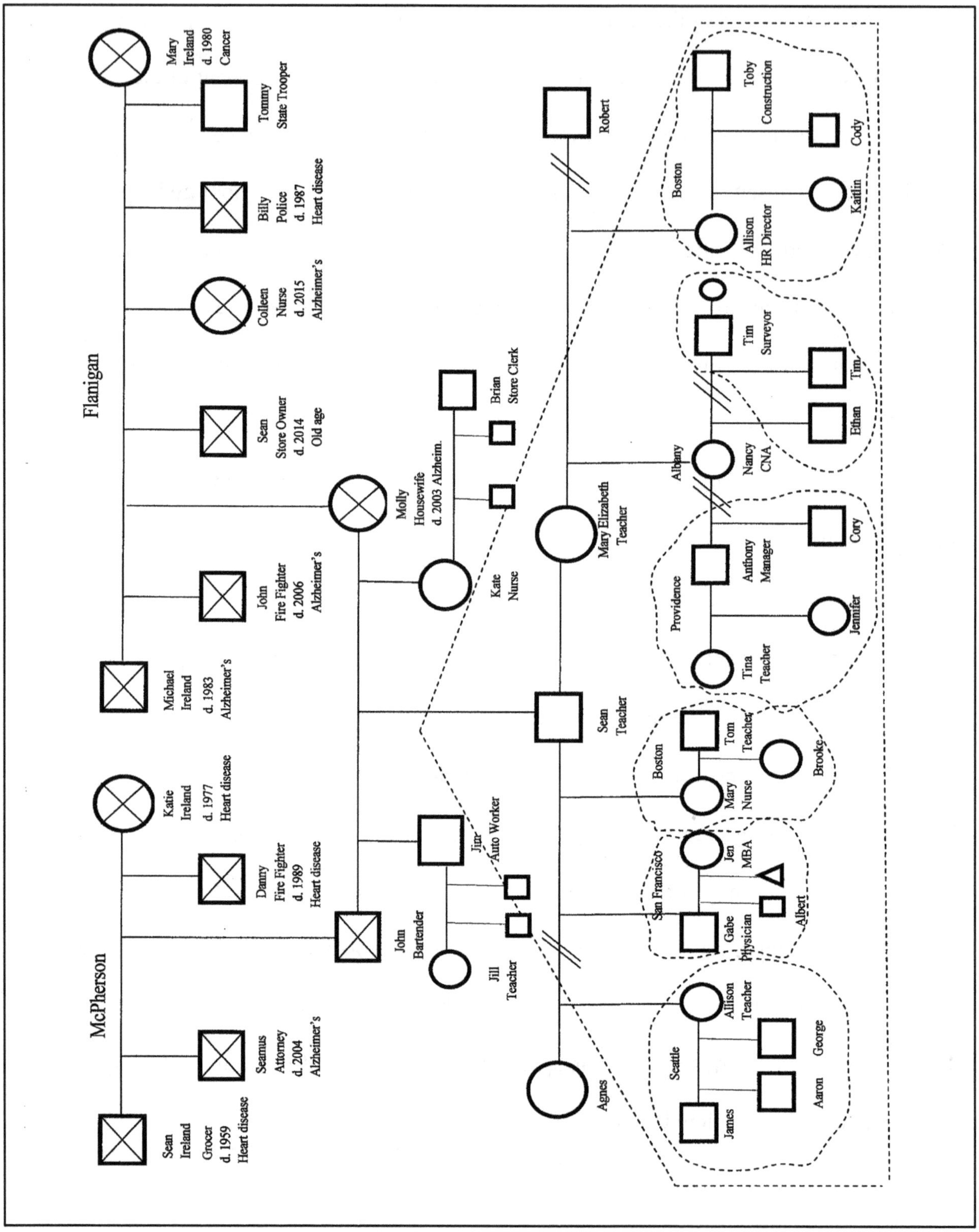

Figure 3.2 Sample of a Four Generation Genogram

Application Activity: Reading the Genogram

Review the sample genogram in Figure 3.2 above and use the information to answer the questions below.

1) What health patterns do you see?

   McPhersons:

   Flanigans:

2) What employment or education patterns are evident?

   McPhersons:

   Flanigans:

3) Which individuals are divorced?

4) List 4 pairs of step-siblings.

5) How many biological children does Nancy in the third generation have?

   How of them reside with her?

6) Are there any pregnancies shown?

   If so, which couple(s) are expecting?

Answers in Appendix B.

Application Activity: Family of Origin Genogram

Now it's time for you to practice constructing a genogram AND begin your analysis of your own family of origin (FoO). You will be drawing a three-generation genogram according to the guidelines provided above. You should take time to interview a parent, grandparent, or other older family member who can provide you with in-depth information about your parents' families. If you have children, you will also include them in this genogram. Your goal is to begin exploring the patterns of interactions in your family, not to portray yourself as the model of the "perfect family." Remember, there are no normal families, only families that are more functional and adapted to their circumstances. Be honest and thorough in order to maximize the usefulness of this activity for your development as a family counselor. When you are done, go on to the next section to begin mapping the dynamics of your family within the structural/strategic framework.

The Dynamic Assessment of Family Functioning Inventory Derived Under Clinical Conditions (DAFFI-DUCC)

Now it's time to introduce you to the DAFFI-DUCC. I developed this tool to help my family therapy students conceptualize the families that they were seeing and to plan sessions. Over the years, it has evolved into a clinical instrument that I am now researching as a family assessment instrument. The difference between the DAFFI-DUCC and other family assessments is that it is completed by the counselor who is seeing a family, rather than family members. So, rather than being an assessment of family members' perceptions of family functioning, it is a way for the counselor, a more objective observer, to think about the family within the structural/strategic framework.

The DAFFI-DUCC is divided into subscales that represent the primary constructs of structural and strategic therapy: symptom function, developmental stages, subsystems and boundaries, hierarchy, triangles, world views and circular patterns. For each of these areas, the clinician can list multiple observations of family interactions that reflect each construct and then rate the observed behavior on the degree that the interaction interferes with the family's functioning. The rating scale is a 10-point (0 – 10) Likert-type scale, with lower ratings indicating a higher degree of dysfunction, and higher ratings indicating a lower degree of dysfunction. A composite score reflecting overall degree of family problems is derived from the lowest ratings on each subscale. A copy of the DAFFI-DUCC is provided at the end of the chapter.

The DAFFI-DUCC is an attempt to quantify constructs that are typically examined qualitatively. That is, we are trying to put a number on something that in reality can't be measured: theoretical concepts. These are the ideas we use to interpret the behaviors that comprise the interactions among family members. In order to do this, clinicians need to rely on their understanding of the concepts, experience with families, and cultural standards for what constitutes functional family interactions. The clinician bases his or her ratings of function on these factors. The procedure for completing the DAFFI-DUCC is outlined below.

Step 1. The first step in completing the instrument is to identify a behavior or situation that reflects one of the constructs. Since every family is different, the specific behaviors and situations will also be different. Write the description of the behavior on the line that's provided. This constitutes an item that will be rated. For any particular construct, you may have one item, two items, or more. It all depends on the family, and the DAFFI-DUCC is designed to be flexible enough to allow for these differences.

Step 2. The next step is to rate the item on the degree it interferes with the family's functioning. As stated above, the rating scale is designed for lower scores to indicate poorer functioning and higher scores, more adaptive functioning. For each individual rating, then, the rater needs to make a subjective judgment regarding how much that particular behavior is interfering with or supporting the family's functioning. Examples are provided below, using the case of an intact family of four in which the youngest child, Nancy, has developed school phobia.

Symptom Function Example:

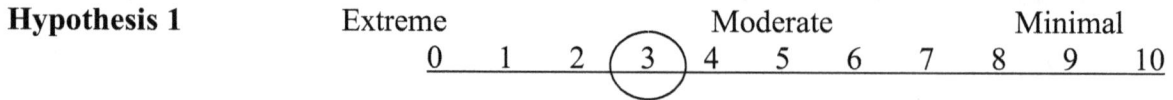

Hypothesis 1

Extreme   Moderate   Minimal

0   1   2 (3) 4   5   6   7   8   9   10

Nancy is refusing to go to school because she is trying to protect her mother.

[Basis for rating: Rater is basing on observation of parent's and child's emotional distress.]

Developmental Stage Example:

Developmental Stage 1 :   Families with younger children

	Minimal	**Moderate**	**Extreme**
Task/Issue Parents agreeing on discipline	0 (1) 2 3	4 5 6 7	8 9 10
Task/Issue Parents having time as couple	0 1 2 (3)	4 5 6 7	8 9 10

Hierarchy Example:

Degree of Interference

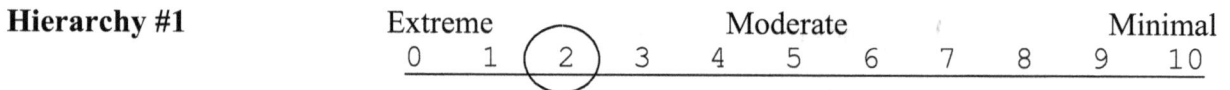

Hierarchy #1

Extreme   Moderate   Minimal

0   1 (2) 3   4   5   6   7   8   9   10

Nancy –   Youngest child assumes more power through anxiety symptoms and refusing to go to school.

Dad –   Takes over discipline when mom is ineffective.

Mom –   Feels like she can't handle Nancy.

Eddy –   Oldest child gets ignored because of all the attention going to Nancy.

Subsystems Example:

Degree of Cohesiveness

	Disengaged	Appropriate	Enmeshed
Hypothesis 1	0 1 2 3 4 5 6 7	8 9 10 9 8 7 6 5 4	(3) 2 1 0

In the above scenario, Mom seeks Dad's help when Nancy throws a tantrum, then defends Nancy when Dad disciplines her.

Subsystem Map

Parent Subsystem   Child Subsystem

The intersecting broken lines around Mom and Nancy indicate the region of enmeshment of the two subsystems. Dad and Eddy are in their respective subsystem positions.

Some other general examples of subsystem mapping:

Mother and son are enmeshed; father is disengaged from mother.

Parent Subsystem   Child Subsystem

Normal subsystems and boundaries.

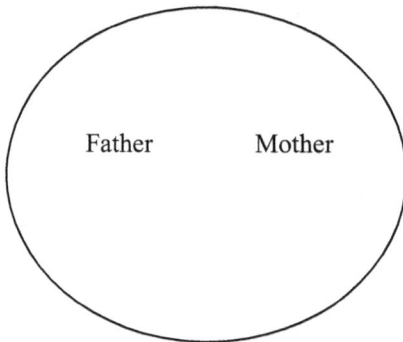

Father   Mother

Daughter

Son

Parent Subsystem   **Child Subsystem**

Parent subsystem disengaged from child subsystem.

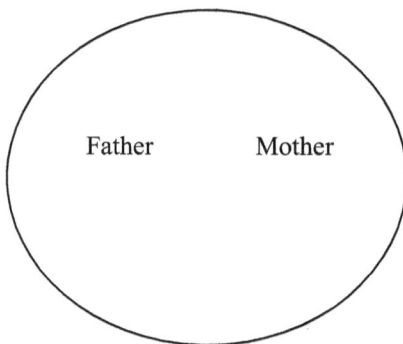

Father   Mother

Daughter

Son

Parent Subsystem   **Child Subsystem**

Wife and husband are disengaged; husband and daughter are enmeshed.

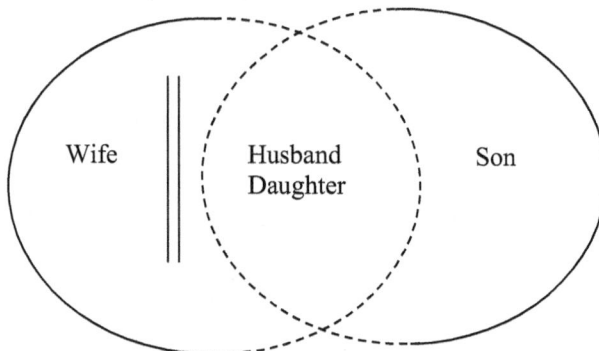

Wife   Husband
Daughter   Son

Couple Subsystem   Child Subsystem

World Views Example:

Family Member	World View	Degree of Interference		

Family Member	World View	Extreme	Moderate	Minimal
Dad	Spare the rod…	0 ①2 3	4 5 6 7	8 9 10

Family Member	World View	Extreme	Moderate	Minimal
Mom	Kids need to be understood	0 1 2 3	④ 5 6 7	8 9 10

....

Triangles Example:

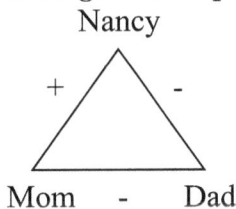

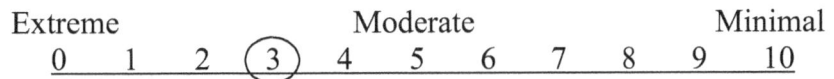

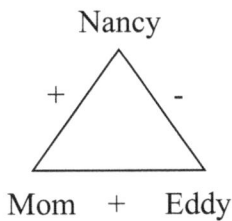

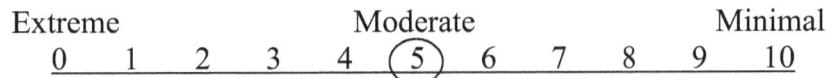

Nancy

+ /\ -
Mom - Dad

Extreme   Moderate   Minimal
0   1   2   ③   4   5   6   7   8   9   10

Nancy

+ /\ -
Mom + Eddy

Extreme   Moderate   Minimal
0   1   2   3   4   ⑤   6   7   8   9   10

Continuing the family scenario from above, two of the triangles that have developed in the family are illustrated. In triangle #1, the mother and father are in conflict over how to deal with Nancy's school refusal. The mother is the parent who is dealing with Nancy's distress and the task of getting her to school, while the father is criticizing both Nancy and the mother for their behavior. In triangle #2, a close, unconflicted relationship is indicated between the mother and both children, but conflict has developed between the children related to the attention that Nancy draws away from Eddy.

Circular Patterns Example:

Degree of Interference

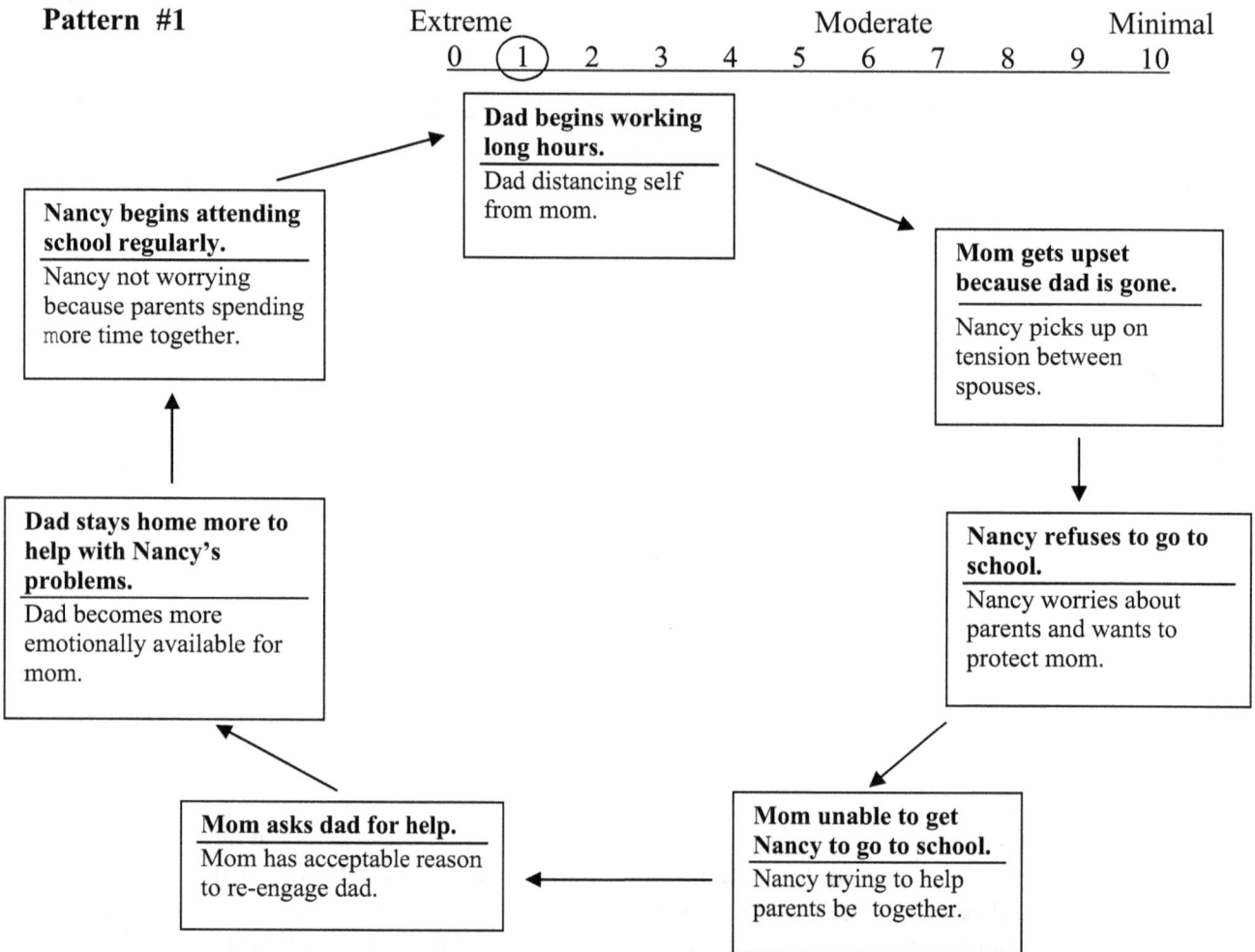

Pattern #1

Extreme					Moderate			Minimal
0 ① 2 3 4		5 6 7			8 9 10			

Dad begins working long hours.
Dad distancing self from mom.

Nancy begins attending school regularly.
Nancy not worrying because parents spending more time together.

Mom gets upset because dad is gone.
Nancy picks up on tension between spouses.

Dad stays home more to help with Nancy's problems.
Dad becomes more emotionally available for mom.

Nancy refuses to go to school.
Nancy worries about parents and wants to protect mom.

Mom asks dad for help.
Mom has acceptable reason to re-engage dad.

Mom unable to get Nancy to go to school.
Nancy trying to help parents be together.

In this scenario, the overt circular pattern is in bold and the isomorphic pattern in un-bolded font.

....

Step 3. After listing and rating all the items in a particular area, for example, subsystems, then write the lowest rating (numerically) in the box at the bottom of the page for that area. Remember, the scale is set up so that the lower the number the more a particular behavior, interaction, or situation contributes to dysfunction in the family.

Believe it or not, you have already had training on how to use the DAFFI-DUCC, since it incorporates all the conceptualizations discussed in Chapter 2. A copy of the instrument is provided at the end of this chapter. What you are going to do now is use an adapted form of the DAFFI-DUCC to analyze your own family. You can copy the following pages or just work in th book as you complete this analysis. It's time to take out your genogram and the information you obtained from your family and go to work.

Your Family of Origin Analysis

Family Developmental Stage

Make a check to indicate the developmental stage(s) in which your family is functioning (one check per stage). For each stage, describe developmental tasks and issues that are confronting the family. Remember, your family can be functioning in multiple stages at any one time.

Developmental Stage 1:
___ Couple Formation   ___First Child (Birth-2)   ___One or More Young Children (2-9)   ___Tweens (10-12)
___ Adolescents   ___Parent Separation from Young Adult Children   ___Middle-Age Parents with Adult Children
___Aging Parents

- **Task/Issue** _____
- **Task/Issue** _____
- **Task/Issue** _____
- **Task/Issue** _____

Developmental Stage 2:
___ Couple Formation   ___First Child (Birth-2)   ___One or More Young Children (2-9)   ___Tweens (10-12)
___ Adolescents   ___Parent Separation from Young Adult Children   ___Middle-Age Parents with Adult Children
___Aging Parents

- **Task/Issue** _____
- **Task/Issue** _____
- **Task/Issue** _____
- **Task/Issue** _____

Developmental Stage 3:
___ Couple Formation   ___First Child (Birth-2)   ___One or More Young Children (2-9)   ___Tweens (10-12)
___ Adolescents   ___Parent Separation from Young Adult Children   ___Middle-Age Parents with Adult Children
___Aging Parents

- **Task/Issue** _____
- **Task/Issue** _____
- **Task/Issue** _____
- **Task/Issue** _____

Your Nuclear Family (If you are married/coupled and/or have children.)

Developmental Stage 1:
___ Couple Formation ___First Child (Birth-2) ___One or More Young Children (2-9) ___Tweens (10-12) ___ Adolescents ___ arent Separation from Young Adult Children ___Middle-Age Parents with Adult Children ___Aging Parents

- **Task/Issue** _____
- **Task/Issue** _____
- **Task/Issue** _____

Developmental Stage 2:
___ Couple Formation ___First Child (Birth-2) ___One or More Young Children (2-9) ___Tweens (10-12) ___ Adolescents ___Parent Separation from Young Adult Children ___Middle-Age Parents with Adult Children ___Aging Parents

- **Task/Issue** _____
- **Task/Issue** _____
- **Task/Issue** _____

Subsystems

Draw the subsystems in your family that are evident, and who comprises these subsystems. Then indicate the clarity of boundaries between subsystems. Use the following symbols for boundaries:

Appropriate ————   Enmeshed --------   Disengaged ═══════

Degree of Cohesiveness

Your Family of Origin now.   ___Disengaged   ___Appropriate   ___Enmeshed

Your Family of Origin as you were growing up.   ___Disengaged   ___Appropriate   ___Enmeshed

Your Nuclear Family now.   ___Disengaged   ___Appropriate   ___Enmeshed

Hierarchy

Provide your perception of the hierarchies among your family members from most (top) to least (bottom) powerful.

Family of Origin now.   **Rationale**

_____
_____
_____
_____
_____
_____
_____

**Family of Origin as
 you were growing up.**   **Rationale**

_____
_____
_____
_____
_____
_____
_____

Nuclear Family now.   **Rationale**

_____
_____
_____
_____
_____
_____
_____

Triangles

Diagram the triangles in your family by listing one family member at each point of a triangle. Then, determine the valance in each dyad:

Positive Relationship = "+"   Conflicted Relationship = "-"   Neutral = o

Family of Origin now:

Triangle #1   **Rationale**   **Triangle #2**   **Rationale**

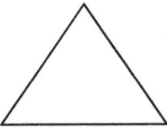   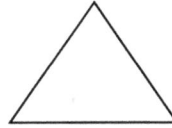

Triangle #3   **Rationale**   **Triangle #4**   **Rationale**

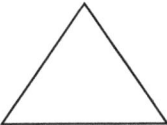   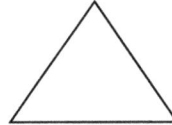

Family of Origin growing up:

Triangle #1   **Rationale**   **Triangle #2**   **Rationale**

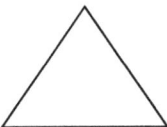   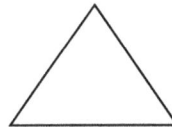

Triangle #3   **Rationale**   **Triangle #4**   **Rationale**

   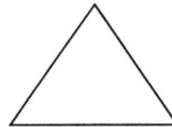

Your Nuclear Family now:

Triangle #1   **Rationale**   **Triangle #2**   **Rationale**

World Views

List the world views of family members.

Family Member   **World View**

_____   _____

_____   _____

_____   _____

_____   _____

_____   _____

_____   _____

_____   _____

_____   _____

_____   _____

World Views of the Entire Family

_____

_____

_____

_____

_____

Circular Patterns

List your hypotheses regarding the overt circular patterns in your family and the underlying causes for these patterns.

Pattern #1

Pattern #2

Summary

1) What did you learn about the dynamics of your family of origin?

2) Blindspots and softspots are the "buttons" that get pushed when you are dealing with clients. When dealing with families, these are dynamics and issues from your own family experiences that may interfere with your work with client families when you observe similar dynamics in those families. What would you consider blindspots and softspots that you need to be aware of when you are working with families?

Family Surname _____   **Date** _____

Identified Client _____ **Age** _____

Other Family Members/Ages _____

_____

Person Completing Form _____

DAFFI-DUCC
Dynamic Assessment of Family Functioning Inventory
Demonstrated Under Clinical Conditions

by

Jay Cerio, Ph.D.

Directions:

- Complete this assessment after the second session with the family. Experienced family clinicians may be able to complete the instrument after one session.
- Follow the directions for each section, which include identifying specific family patterns and rating the pattern on a scale from 0 to 10.
- Compute the average rating for each section and enter that rating on the scoring summary form.
- Plot the average rating on the profile on the last page.

Genogram

Construct a three-generation genogram for the family that illustrates family membership as accurately as possible. You may turn the form sideways if necessary to fit all members.

Symptom Function

List some hypotheses on how the symptom of the identified client helps the family. Consider the metaphor represented by the symptom.

Hypothesis 1

Hypothesis 2

Hypothesis 3

Now estimate the ***Degree of Interference*** that the symptom is causing in the family's functioning.

Extreme   Moderate   Minimal

0	1	2	3	4	5	6	7	8	9	10

SF Estimated Degree of Interference

Family Developmental Stage

List the developmental stage(s) in which the family is functioning. For each stage, describe developmental tasks and issues that are confronting the family and rate the degree of stress that the family is experiencing related to each task or issue.

Developmental Stage 1:

___ Couple Formation ___First Child (Birth-2) ___One or More Young Children (2-9) ___Tweens (10-12)
___ Adolescents ___ Parent Separation from Young Adult Children ___ Middle-Age Parents with Adult Children
___Aging Parents

- **Task/Issue** _____
- **Task/Issue** _____
- **Task/Issue** _____

	Extreme				Moderate				Minimal	
Degree of Stress	0	1	2	3	4	5	6	7	8	9	10

Developmental Stage 2:

___ Couple Formation ___First Child (Birth-2) ___One or More Young Children (2-9) ___Tweens (10-12)
___ Adolescents ___ Parent Separation from Young Adult Children ___ Middle-Age Parents with Adult Children
___Aging Parents

- **Task/Issue** _____
- **Task/Issue** _____
- **Task/Issue** _____

	Extreme				Moderate				Minimal	
Degree of Stress	0	1	2	3	4	5	6	7	8	9	10

Developmental Stage 3:

___ Couple Formation ___First Child (Birth-2) ___One or More Young Children (2-9) ___Tweens (10-12)
___ Adolescents ___ Parent Separation from Young Adult Children ___ Middle-Age Parents with Adult Children
___Aging Parents

- **Task/Issue** _____
- **Task/Issue** _____
- **Task/Issue** _____

	Extreme				Moderate				Minimal	
Degree of Stress	0	1	2	3	4	5	6	7	8	9	10

Developmental Stress (DS) Lowest Rating

Subsystems

List the subsystems in the family that are evident, and who comprises these subsystems. Then list the various subsystems and rate the clarity of boundaries between subsystems.

Degree of Cohesiveness

Hypothesis 1

Disengaged   Appropriate   Enmeshed

0 1 2 3 4 5 6 7 8 .9 10 9 8 7 6 5 4 3 2 1 0

Hypothesis 2

Disengaged   Appropriate   Enmeshed

0 1 2 3 4 5 6 7 8 9 10 9 8 7 6 5 4 3 2 1 0

Hypothesis 3

Disengaged   Appropriate   Enmeshed

0 1 2 3 4 5 6 7 8 9 10 9 8 7 6 5 4 3 2 1 0

Subsystems (SS) Lowest Cohesiveness Rating

Hierarchy

Provide your perception of the family members from most (top) to least (bottom) powerful.
Space is provided for two possible hypotheses.

Degree of Interference

Hierarchy #1   Extreme   Moderate   Minimal

0   1   2   3   4   5   6   7   8   9   10

Rationale

_____

_____

_____

_____

_____

_____

Degree of Interference

Hierarchy #2   Extreme   Moderate   Minimal

0   1   2   3   4   5   6   7   8   9   10

Rationale

_____

_____

_____

_____

_____

_____

Degree of Interference

Hierarchy #3   Extreme   Moderate   Minimal

0   1   2   3   4   5   6   7   8   9   10

Rationale

_____

_____

_____

_____

_____

_____

_____

Degree of Interference

Hierarchy #4   Extreme   Moderate   Minimal

0   1   2   3   4   5   6   7   8   9   10

Rationale

_____

_____

_____

_____

_____

_____

_____

Hierarchy (H) Lowest Interference Rating

Triangles

Diagram the triangles in the family by listing one family member at each point of a triangle. Then, determine the valance in each dyad (positive relationship = "+"; conflicted relationship = "-").

Triangle	**Degree of Interference**

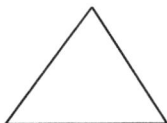

Extreme   Moderate   Minimal
0   1   2   3   4   5   6   7   8   9   10

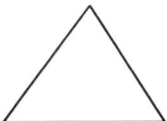

Extreme   Moderate   Minimal
0   1   2   3   4   5   6   7   8   9   10

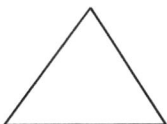

Extreme   Moderate   Minimal
0   1   2   3   4   5   6   7   8   9   10

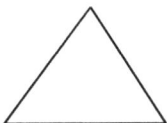

Extreme   Moderate   Minimal
0   1   2   3   4   5   6   7   8   9   10

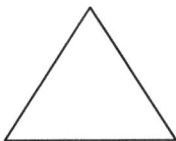

Extreme   Moderate   Minimal
0   1   2   3   4   5   6   7   8   9   10

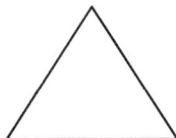

Extreme   Moderate   Minimal
0   1   2   3   4   5   6   7   8   9   10

Triangle (T) Lowest Interference Rating

World Views

List the world views, that is, the beliefs of family members, related to other family members and the family in relation to the world outside of the family. Then rate the degree to which each view interferes with family functioning.

Family Member	**World View**	**Degree of Interference**
_____	_____	Extreme Moderate Minimal 0 1 2 3 4 5 6 7 8 9 10
_____	_____	Extreme Moderate Minimal 0 1 2 3 4 5 6 7 8 9 10
_____	_____	Extreme Moderate Minimal 0 1 2 3 4 5 6 7 8 9 10
_____	_____	Extreme Moderate Minimal 0 1 2 3 4 5 6 7 8 9 10
_____	_____	Extreme Moderate Minimal 0 1 2 3 4 5 6 7 8 9 10
_____	_____	Extreme Moderate Minimal 0 1 2 3 4 5 6 7 8 9 10
_____	_____	Extreme Moderate Minimal 0 1 2 3 4 5 6 7 8 9 10
_____	_____	Extreme Moderate Minimal 0 1 2 3 4 5 6 7 8 9 10
_____	_____	Extreme Moderate Minimal 0 1 2 3 4 5 6 7 8 9 10
_____	_____	Extreme Moderate Minimal 0 1 2 3 4 5 6 7 8 9 10
_____	_____	Extreme Moderate Minimal 0 1 2 3 4 5 6 7 8 9 10
_____	_____	Extreme Moderate Minimal 0 1 2 3 4 5 6 7 8 9 10

Triangles

Diagram the triangles in the family by listing one family member at each point of a triangle. Then, determine the valance in each dyad (positive relationship = "+"; conflicted relationship = "-").

Triangle	**Degree of Interference**

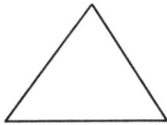

Extreme   Moderate   Minimal
0   1   2   3   4   5   6   7   8   9   10

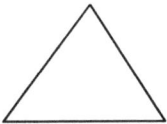

Extreme   Moderate   Minimal
0   1   2   3   4   5   6   7   8   9   10

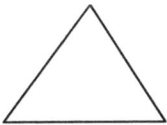

Extreme   Moderate   Minimal
0   1   2   3   4   5   6   7   8   9   10

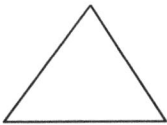

Extreme   Moderate   Minimal
0   1   2   3   4   5   6   7   8   9   10

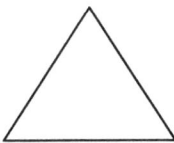

Extreme   Moderate   Minimal
0   1   2   3   4   5   6   7   8   9   10

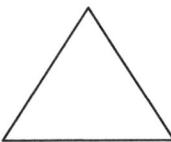

Extreme   Moderate   Minimal
0   1   2   3   4   5   6   7   8   9   10

Triangle (T) Lowest Interference Rating

World Views

List the world views, that is, the beliefs of family members, related to other family members and the family in relation to the world outside of the family. Then rate the degree to which each view interferes with family functioning.

Family Member	**World View**	**Degree of Interference**
_____	_____	Extreme　　　Moderate　　　Minimal 0　1　2　3　4　5　6　7　8　9　10
_____	_____	Extreme　　　Moderate　　　Minimal 0　1　2　3　4　5　6　7　8　9　10
_____	_____	Extreme　　　Moderate　　　Minimal 0　1　2　3　4　5　6　7　8　9　10
_____	_____	Extreme　　　Moderate　　　Minimal 0　1　2　3　4　5　6　7　8　9　10
_____	_____	Extreme　　　Moderate　　　Minimal 0　1　2　3　4　5　6　7　8　9　10
_____	_____	Extreme　　　Moderate　　　Minimal 0　1　2　3　4　5　6　7　8　9　10
_____	_____	Extreme　　　Moderate　　　Minimal 0　1　2　3　4　5　6　7　8　9　10
_____	_____	Extreme　　　Moderate　　　Minimal 0　1　2　3　4　5　6　7　8　9　10
_____	_____	Extreme　　　Moderate　　　Minimal 0　1　2　3　4　5　6　7　8　9　10
_____	_____	Extreme　　　Moderate　　　Minimal 0　1　2　3　4　5　6　7　8　9　10
_____	_____	Extreme　　　Moderate　　　Minimal 0　1　2　3　4　5　6　7　8　9　10
_____	_____	Extreme　　　Moderate　　　Minimal 0　1　2　3　4　5　6　7　8　9　10

World Views of the Entire Family

World View	Degree of Interference

World View   **Degree of Interference**

	Extreme	Moderate	Minimal
	0 1 2 3	4 5 6 7	8 9 10

	Extreme	Moderate	Minimal
	0 1 2 3	4 5 6 7	8 9 10

	Extreme	Moderate	Minimal
	0 1 2 3	4 5 6 7	8 9 10

	Extreme	Moderate	Minimal
	0 1 2 3	4 5 6 7	8 9 10

	Extreme	Moderate	Minimal
	0 1 2 3	4 5 6 7	8 9 10

	Extreme	Moderate	Minimal
	0 1 2 3	4 5 6 7	8 9 10

	Extreme	Moderate	Minimal
	0 1 2 3	4 5 6 7	8 9 10

	Extreme	Moderate	Minimal
	0 1 2 3	4 5 6 7	8 9 10

World Views (WV) Lowest Interference Rating

Chapter 4

The Basic Skills

Chapter Overview

In this chapter you will:

- Familiarize yourself with the basic microskills for conducting family therapy.

- Understand the role of the structural/strategic family therapist.

- Learn how to organize family sessions.

The Role of the Counselor

Power and Responsibility

Structural and strategic family therapy places the counselor in a directive role in which he or she orchestrates many of the interactions during therapy. The counselor is in charge of helping the family change, and any failures in doing so rest squarely on the counselor's shoulders, not the family's. This places a considerable amount of responsibility on the counselor, which also opens up the possibility for abusing what can be a relatively powerful position. The counselor must, then, balance the need to lead the family toward more functional patterns with the need to have the family take control of its destiny.

Have a Plan

You can't "shoot from the hip" when you are seeing families. While in individual counseling, the client sets the agenda as a session progresses, in structural/strategic therapy, the counselor has to determine what needs to be done to help the family function better. Minuchin likens family therapy to chess: a skilled chess player enters a game with a strategy in mind for attaining checkmate against his opponent. Similarly, an effective family counselor has to have a tentative map for what needs to be done to help the family arrive at the destination of better functioning. This map may change based on what the family introduces across the counseling process, but the destination remains the same. Minuchin used to say that in order to get from A to Z, you have to know where Z is, first (personal communication).

Respect the Family

Every family has resources, stresses, strengths, and limitations (Minuchin & Fishman, 1981). The counselor works with the resources which the family has and *does not blame the family* for lacking some attribute which families are "supposed" to possess. On the contrary, On the contrary, it is up to the counselor to design strategies which meet the family's needs. Asking a family to accomplish something beyond its resources is, in fact, disrespectful, and a recipe for failure.

Multiordinality

A counselor cannot and should not rely on any one method or approach and expect a family to adapt to that approach. Instead, it is up to the counselor to adapt techniques or approaches to the family. Thus, if a family enters counseling wanting to talk about feelings, the counselor should fit this need into his or her strategies for dealing with the dysfunction within the system. If a family utilizes humor to cope with pain, the counselor should incorporate humor into interactions with the family. Strategic and structural counseling are not "one size fits all" models.

Be Aware of Your Position

Various subsystems will compete for an alliance with the counselor in order to improve their position within the family. While you are responsible for initiating change within the family, you are not part of the family. Whitaker used to frame this for families in a baseball analogy. *The counselor is the coach* and the family members are the players. Like a coach, the counselor can make suggestions that might help the family "play" better, but it's the family that has to actually hit the ball and run the bases (Whitaker & Bumberry, 1989).

Some families are adept at "inducting" the counselor into the family's dysfunctional pattern, in other words, making the coach play the game for them. I can feel this happening when I catch myself "spacing out"--that is, I catch myself in a trance-like state, discovering that I haven't really heard what has been going on in the session. In such cases, it is perfectly permissible for the counselor to excuse him- or herself from the session for a few minutes, and to use this time to plan a strategy for counteracting such a pattern. In this case, I am not being an effective coach, so I need to amend my "game" strategy.

Basic Microskills of Structural and Strategic Therapy

Like all counseling approaches, there are certain microskills that need to be mastered to be an effective structural/strategic family counselor. I, unfortunately, haven't mastered these, yet. But I am a decent journeyman practitioner, so I would like to provide some insight into what I have learned over the years, in terms of common skills, listed in Figure 4-1.

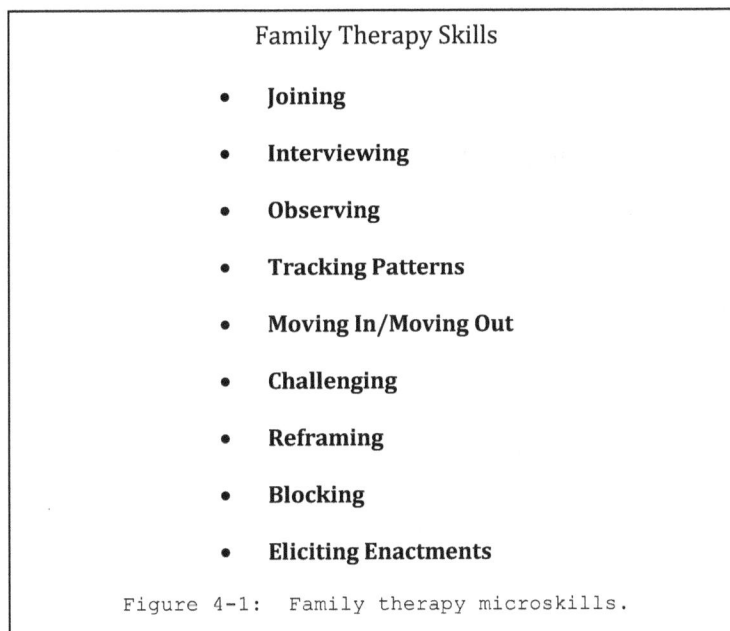

Family Therapy Skills

- **Joining**
- **Interviewing**
- **Observing**
- **Tracking Patterns**
- **Moving In/Moving Out**
- **Challenging**
- **Reframing**
- **Blocking**
- **Eliciting Enactments**

Figure 4-1: Family therapy microskills.

Joining

Joining is the counselor's means of connecting with the family in such a way that the counselor actually becomes another member of the family system. Joining is an important tool which enables the counselor to understand the family's frame of reference and stresses. It is both similar to and different from Roger's condition of empathy (Rogers, 1975). With empathy, the counselor establishes a relationship with the client that allows the counselor to understand the client's experience "as if" the counselor was the client. It is a deeper way of connecting with clients. Joining focuses more on the family as a whole and not on individual relationships among family members. It is, in fact, important that the counselor avoid over-empathizing with individuals in the family because this can cause a family member to think that he/she has an alliance with the counselor and alienate other family members. So, joining is a balancing act: connect with the family and convey understanding of what the family is going through, but maintain distance from individual members in order to reduce the potential for alliances.

For example, when seeing families with adolescent children, I often will share some of the funnier things my own children did as adolescents. This allows me to join with the parents regarding some of the teenage behaviors and issues that they are struggling with and join with the teens in the family regarding understanding their need to be independent.

Interviewing

Interviewing might seem a ridiculous item to include as a microskill since, isn't all counseling interviewing? Yes, but…. First of all, unlike individual counseling, in which the course of the session is guided by the client, in family therapy, the counselor is in charge. The counselor has a goal to achieve (change dysfunctional patterns, reorganize family structure, improve family communication) and develops an agenda or game plan based on that goal.

Interviewing, then, is more complicated because the counselor needs to collect information from a number of individuals in order to synthesize these individual perspectives into a holistic understanding of the family and use the information to implement interventions. Some rules of thumb for interviewing:

- Begin with the parent or spouse who has the most powerful position.

- Move to the other parent (if there is one).

- Then move to the oldest child, and question children in chronological order.

- Make sure everyone has an opportunity to offer their perspective.

- Ask open-ended questions, such as: What do you think? How does this happen? Who does what?

Observing

While conducting the interview, it is critical for the counselor to observe the non-verbal and ancillary behaviors of all family members. Does mom role her eyes when dad is talking? Are other children in the family misbehaving while the identified client sits quietly? Do the parents notice the misbehavior of the non-identified children in the family? Do they recognize the client's good behavior? Is a wife trying to convince you that she is right, and her husband is wrong?

Think about when you were starting out as a counselor and how difficult it was both listening effectively and being aware of an individual client's non-verbal behavior. Now, consider what it is like listening to several people at once and noticing their non-verbal behaviors. What I often find with my students is that when they first start seeing families, they tend to over-focus on the interaction with one parent and completely lose track of what the other parent and kids are doing during this time. Of course, with live supervision, it's easier to redirect the counselor with a call from the supervisor. But if you are working alone, it's easy to lose track.

One thing I do in my practice is to always have a notepad on my lap. This reminds me to scan the room and jot down any important observations periodically during a session. With younger children who are playing while I am speaking with a parent, I try to comment on what they are doing from time-to-time, so that they know that I am paying attention. I also am careful to bring members who are not participating into the conversation by asking for their input on what is being discussed. This helps me stay focused on what is happening with all of the family members in the room.

Tracking Patterns

In addition to watching the non-verbal behavior of individuals in the family, the counselor has to track patterns of interactions. These interactions are the key to understanding the dynamics and structure of the family. Some of these patterns will occur spontaneously: parents setting limits for children, spouses disagreeing or correcting each other, one family member speaking for another, and even who family members sit next to when they enter the room. Others are the result of enactments, which are described below as a specific microskill. It is incumbent upon the counselor to note the patterns as a means of conceptualizing the family's dynamics and deciding where to intervene.

Moving In and Moving Out

Because the counselor becomes part of the family, by virtue of entering the room and joining, the counselor needs to be aware of the amount of psychological distance that needs to be maintained. There are times that the counselor needs to be more engaged with the family or specific family members, and there are other times that the counselor needs to move out and be separate and detached. Minuchin is a master of this, developing emotional closeness and using it to move the family members to interact, then pulling back and allowing them to interact without involving him in the interaction. He does this by simply looking down, looking away, playing with his tie, or engaging the children while the parents interact. This creates a boundary that prevents family members from using him as an ally or getting him to do something that they need to do. They cannot make eye contact or look to him for help.

Conversely, if he needs to move in to motivate or strengthen a particular family member, he might sit next to them or directly coach them on how they should do something. He may get the parents and children playing together with him on the floor, and then move out and encourage the parents to continue the interaction on their own. By doing this, he creates a positive family interaction for the parents who might have a negative view of the identified child, and models appropriate ways for parents and child to engage each other. This provides an alternative to their previous way of engaging through negative interactions.

For beginning family counselors, moving in and out is typically a difficult shift from the constant focus and engagement required in individual counseling. I recommend to my students that they bring a pad or clipboard into sessions, not necessarily because they are going to use it, but because it provides something to focus on when they need to move out. But again, other ways of doing this are by simply focusing on an object in the room, speaking with or playing with children while parents are working on a task, or engaging parents while children work on a task.

Challenging

Minuchin has always seen himself as someone who challenged the status quo in the family (Founders Series, 1991). Families enter counseling because the status quo isn't working for them anymore. They are trying to deal with a stressor by doing more of the same that used to work in the past but no longer works. Attenuating feedback loops are maintaining the unconstructive response, so what Minuchin sees the family therapist's task as, essentially, creating an amplifying loop that will stimulate change. The counselor does this by challenging the family.

What should you be challenging with families you see? It depends on what is getting the family stuck. Sometimes, the family's world view interferes with flexibility that is needed to respond to stress. That is, the parents or other family members have created realities that prevent them from seeing alternative ways of dealing with the issue. They have tunnel vision. By gradually building an argument with information provided by the family, and through the use of reframing, the counselor attempts to expand and then shift the family's reality to one that's more adaptive. We will discuss reframing in detail below.

Other areas of family functioning may also be the focus of challenging. Problems in family structure, such as a child drifting into an inappropriate subsystem or attaining an inappropriate position in the family hierarchy, require the counselor to push the family to NOT accept this as a useful way of operating. Alliances that isolate and alienate an individual in the family from the rest of the family need to be broken. Specific interventions for these situations are discussed in Chapter 6. At any rate, be prepared to challenge, it's your job.

Reframing

Reframing is used in two main ways. One standard purpose of the reframe is to reformulate the family's statement of the problem in such a way as to give it a more positive connotation, thereby making it more solvable. The second is to shift the family's world views, either about individuals in the family, the family's view of itself in relation to the world, or the world at large.

The first type of reframing is essentially what the "spinmeisters" of politics are hired to do. Political operatives try to put the "best face" on negative or damaging situations that impact their candidates. For instance, in a close election in which one candidate wins by only one or two percentage points, the winner may state that she has received a clear mandate from the people, while the loser asserts that he has delivered a message to the winner that the people are "equally split" on the winner's platform. If you follow politics, you will see any number of reframes being used to cast candidates in the best light.

Family therapists are working toward a similar goal with their reframes by spinning the identified client's behavior into something positive that helps the family. This serves to remove the focus off of the identified client and recast the problem as a problem of the family. It also removes the client from the scapegoat position, recasting him in a positive light. For instance, the misbehavior of a child whose parents are in conflict might be reframed as the child's way of getting his parents to work together. The use of alcohol by a teen who has an alcoholic parent could be reframed as the teen's attempt to get the parent help.

The second type of reframing occurs throughout each family session as a way to challenge the family's unproductive world views. Here, the counselor gradually introduces labels that become increasingly challenging. Minuchin stresses the importance of challenging in a measured, step-wise fashion, starting with a reframe that, while distasteful to the family, will not be completely revolting (Unfolding the Laundry, 1984). By doing this, it is more likely that the family will accept the reframe without arguing with the counselor. As the level of challenge increases, the family begins to become uncomfortable, and then even to examine the discordant perspective being presented to them. Members may begin questioning the validity of the counselor's reframe. Or different members will begin disagreeing with each other, some supporting the reframe and others rejecting it. The counselor at this point can move out and let the family work through the discussion that the reframe stimulated.

Take the case of a mother who presents as depressed. During the family session, it comes out that neither her husband nor children help with household chores and have come to expect her to "wait" on them. The counselor may first reframe her role as the husband's maid, then move to a less desirable label like servant, and finally increase the undesirability of the mother's role to one of indentured servant. The purpose of this reframing would be to challenge the wife to NOT accept her role and to rebel and assert herself in the family hierarchy. If the wife can be motivated to do this, she will become less depressed because she will no longer be in an oppressed position in the family. In addition, presenting this new perspective to the husband may open up his eyes to a pattern with which he is uncomfortable. This may lead him to change his behavior in relation to his wife, and to join her in making reasonable demands on the children to contribute to the household.

Blocking

Blocking is a strategy that is used for establishing boundaries during a family session. It is a way to stop a member from one subsystem from forcing his or her way into another subsystem inappropriately. Some instances of this type of subsystem intrusion include:

- A parent speaking for a child who is trying to answer a question the counselor asked.
- A child insisting on sitting with his/her parents when the counselor only wants to address the parents.
- A child advising parents on how to discipline another child in the family.
- One spouse interrupting the other spouse who is answering a question.

Blocking may simply be straightforward limit setting, such as telling a child to not interrupt his parents, or to mind his own business. But it may also be more diplomatic, requiring a respectful explanation. Blocking can also involve a physical reorganization of the family, having members change the location of their seats or sending family members to a different area of the room to do something together.

Eliciting Enactments

Enactments are an important tool in family counseling sessions. Therefore, eliciting enactments is an important microskill that a new family counselor needs to develop. Enactments allow the counselor to actually observe HOW the family functions. Eliciting an enactment requires the counselor to be directive and encouraging. The counselor has to set the stage for the clients and, if necessary, coach them. Here are a few examples of enactments.

- [To two parents dealing with conflict about discipline.] I'd like the two of you to discuss the rules you have for the kids.

- [To a parent who is complaining about her daughter not listening to her.] Have Johnny come over and sit next to you. Explain the new rule for bedtime to him. [As the mother explains]. You need to be clearer.

- [To parents who have a child who is using tantrumming to exercise control over them.] I want you to show me what happens when Jenny throws a tantrum. Dad, have Jenny get down on the floor and throw a tantrum. [To Jenny] Jenny throw a tantrum just like you do at home. [To dad] Show me what you do when Jenny throws a tantrum.

As you, as the counselor, observe the family, you should note how the family members accomplish the task. Does one parent look to the other for help when a child doesn't respond to a request immediately? Does the child respond only when his mother repeats herself several times and then yells? Does one spouse repeatedly correct what the other is doing? Enactments are critical for revealing the real dynamics of the family, no matter what family members tell you.

Now that we have covered some of the basic skills, let's move on and look at how to structure and conduct a family therapy session.

The Family Session

Organizing the First Session

Family counseling differs from many of the common individual approaches in that the counselor does not approach a session as a blank slate; that is, without an impression about what is going on with the family. Family sessions are *counselor-driven*. That is, they are carefully preplanned with the counselor working from one or two basic hypotheses about the family which she has developed based on pre-session information. This pre-session information is obtained primarily from the individuals who make the referral, usually the identified client's parents or, in the case of couples, one member of the couple. Sessions then proceed through specific stages, with the counselor working toward specific counseling goals regarding family organization and problem solution.

The Referral Phone Call. Typically, I attempt to gather the following information from an initial phone call or contact with a parent before the first session:

- What is the presenting problem?

- When did the problem become apparent to the parent?

- What does the other parent think about it?

- Who are the other family members?

I avoid going into any amount of detail in this initial phone call, because this usually leads to blaming or concretizing the identified client as *the problem*. It is also in this first contact that the battle for initiative begins (and sometimes, ends).

Before the session, the counselor then sets up a preliminary "map" which serves essentially as his or her hypothesis about the way this particular family works. After establishing my initial hypotheses about the family, I organize the session *on paper* by writing down relevant questions and to whom these questions will be posed. The purpose of this is to obtain information to test hypotheses, and to gradually work toward a reframe or other intervention that will address both the presenting problem *and* underlying family structure and patterns connected with the problem. For example, I might want to ask, "Is there a time when you and your daughter have fun together? Tell me about it," and specifically direct this toward the father because he is the person who is involved in a negative pattern with the daughter. Or I might want to ask all the children in the family, "What are the rules in your house?" The purpose of this question would be to develop an understanding of the level of organization in the family, and to assess whether or not this is a family in which people are expected to "read minds." I keep my list of questions within my view during the family session to refer to from time to time.

A primary understanding when using strategic or structural approaches is that the counselor is responsible for success or failure in the counseling process. That is, if a family does not appear to be making progress, it is the counselor's responsibility to reconsider his or her hypotheses and interventions, and to attempt different strategies that might work. A family is not blamed for being resistant; it is the counselor's fault if he has not used appropriate strategies to circumvent resistance. Pre-session preparation is not a luxury in this approach, it is a *necessity*.

Stages of the Session

One of the basic assumptions of the strategic and structural approaches is that therapy is not method-driven. However, there are some standard protocols that are used in conducting therapy, one of these being the format of counseling sessions. Family sessions move through a series of stages, the stages being essentially the same for each session with the exception of the first meeting with the family (Figure 4.2).

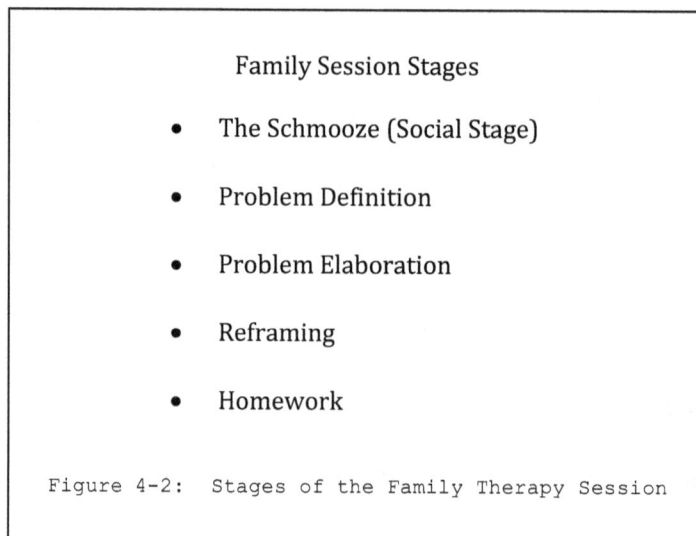

```
┌─────────────────────────────────────────────────┐
│                                                   │
│            Family Session Stages                  │
│                                                   │
│      •   The Schmooze (Social Stage)              │
│                                                   │
│      •   Problem Definition                       │
│                                                   │
│      •   Problem Elaboration                      │
│                                                   │
│      •   Reframing                                │
│                                                   │
│      •   Homework                                 │
│                                                   │
│   Figure 4-2:  Stages of the Family Therapy Session │
│                                                   │
└─────────────────────────────────────────────────┘
```

The Schmooze.   The first session includes two preliminary stages which are not usually present in later sessions. These are the social stage or "schmooze, and the problem definition stage. During the social stage, the counselor "schmoozes," exchanging social amenities, thanking the parents and children for attending the session, and simultaneously, obtaining information regarding the parents' work schedules, babysitters, etc. It is during this stage that the counselor also begins the process of "joining" (Minuchin & Fishman, 1981).

The Battle for Initiative is an idea which comes directly out of Whitaker's family work (Whitaker & Bumberry, 1988). Whitaker sees this as the earliest phase of counseling in which the therapist establishes his belief with the family that working within a family framework is the only way he can be effective in helping the identified client. The counselor then seizes the initiative by being firm and insistent about the family accepting this basic assumption. For example, if a parent says, "I want you to talk with my child about her constant bickering with her father," the counselor replies, "I believe I can be most helpful by meeting with you and your husband with your daughter." If the mother replies, "I am sure that my husband won't come in. Anyway, it's her fault. She just won't listen." The counselor then insists, "It seems clear to me, as I am sure it does to you, that although your daughter is misbehaving, both you and your husband can offer a perspective of what is going on. That is why I prefer to work with your entire family." If the mother continues to keep the problem child focused, the counselor may have to simply state, "I am sorry, but I don't think I can help the situation by just seeing your daughter. If you change your mind and decide to come in with your husband, please give me a call." This may seem harsh, but it is important for me to establish the family focus of the intervention and not allow a parent to maintain the child in the identified client position. As Whitaker used to say, "I don't believe in individuals. I believe in families" (Different Kind of Caring).

While my battles for initiative do not necessarily resemble the hypothetical example provided above, I am gently or strategically insistent when discussing a referral with a parent or teacher. One strategy I use with parents who are utterly resistant about being seen as a family, is to agree to see the child one or two times individually, followed by a family meeting. I use the individual sessions with the child more-or-less to let them know that he or she has been referred, and to do some simple fact gathering, such as completing a genogram. I then schedule and organize the family session as I would any other first session, as detailed below.

The second approach that I use is to appeal to parents' sense' of responsibility for and guilt about their child's difficulties. Typically, I use this approach with families that range from mildly cooperative to mildly resistant. In these cases, I make it clear that "two heads are better than one, three heads are better than two, etc.," telling the parents that other members of the family can offer a broader perspective, and generate more possible solutions for a problem than can a solitary child and myself. These types of families are usually more easily persuaded, particularly if they are experiencing a less tolerable level of stress due to the identified client's behavior. I have found that, outside of the highly resistant family, most families will readily come in for a family meeting if I ask.

Problem Definition. The second stage which is unique to the first session is the problem definition stage. During this portion of the session, the counselor moves from one family member to the next asking each one to define the problem. For example, "What do you think is the problem," or, "What brought you here today?" It is important to address this question to the family in hierarchical order, beginning usually with the mother or father (depending on who seems to be the "power person") and moving to the oldest child, second oldest child, and so forth. The problem-definition is also intended to be brief. If one person begins to give a prolonged exposition about the identified client or other topics, the counselor must politely block by interrupting and asking the individual to hold his or her thought for later. This is designed to avoid focusing blame on any one person in the family, and to establish that the counselor is in charge of the session.

Problem Elaboration. The problem elaboration stage is where information is gathered to deepen understanding of the problem. This stage is common to both the initial and subsequent family sessions. Various individuals in the family are asked to go into detail regarding their view of the problem. This is done by directing specific questions to specific individuals, and by

eliciting interactions between family members that will help illuminate hierarchy, triangles, and isomorphic patterns. The information obtained during this stage serves to clarify aspects of family functioning and forms the basis for the next stage--the reframe. Below are some problem-focused questions for families with children with suggestions for the order of family members to which the questions should be directed.

- To parents: When did the problem begin?

- To parents and children: When does it get worse? Better?

- To parents and children: Which parent deals with the problem the most?

- To parents and children: How does the client respond?

- To children and parents: What happens if they don't respond?

General family functioning questions:

- To children and parents: What are the rules in the house?

- To children and parents: What happens if someone breaks a rule?

- To children and parents: What chores does each child have?

- To children and parents: What happens if chores don't get done? What happens when they get done?

- To parents and children: What does the family do for fun together?

- To children and parents: When was the last time the family did something fun together?

- Starting with youngest child who can answer then moving to older children, and finally the parents: Which family member does each family member worry about the most?

Reframing. Reframing is not so much a stage as it is an ongoing intervention intended to reformulate the family's problem statements and perspectives to make the problem more solvable. It is akin to saying that finding a flat tire on your car in the morning isn't a problem, but rather, the car's way of telling you the tire was worn out and might be dangerous. There are as many kinds of reframes as there are problems. The critical point to keep in mind is that the reframe should be helpful, understandable, and should be explained to the family as being consistent with the information they provided.

Remember, by reframing the family's perception of the problem, the counselor seeks to shake-up the family's perspective and remove the finger of blame from the identified client, consequently getting the family unstuck from the stereotyped kinds of behavior which resulted in the dysfunction in the first place. The reframe is shaped by information provided by the family in the interview, and by the counselor's map of the family's world view, hierarchy, triangles, and isomorphic patterns. While the reframe may fall anywhere on the continuum of reasonable and straight-forward to far-out and even silly, it *must* be logically supported by the accumulation of evidence provided by the family and filtered by the counselor.

One family which I met with provided the following scenario. The father complained about his 10-year-old daughter's continual fighting with him. He revealed that his daughter had been sexually abused by an adult outside the family at age seven, and that the father's greatest concern about her was that she would become sexually involved with boys at an early age because of her premature entrance into puberty (which was already evident). In addition, the father admitted that he had been somewhat of a tomcat in his adolescent years, so he knew how teenage boys think. The reframe I chose to use with this family was that the father was misinterpreting the reasons for his daughter's combative behavior. Father had actually taught his daughter to fight so that she could protect herself from boys. Her fighting with him was actually her way of practicing for the future, and he should be proud of teaching her so effectively. After all, the best defense is a good offense.

This reframe served a number of purposes. First, it provided praise to the father, who was feeling quite incompetent as a parent, about a success in parenting. Second, it converted the symptom of "fighting with father" to "practicing" for her future defense. Third, it communicated to the father that his fears were valid. Finally, it provided the basis for having the parents help the daughter differentiate between father as a threatening male, and other boys as threatening males. Approximately two weeks after this session, the father was finally able to sit down and listen to his daughter, giving her permission to express other issues which had been interfering with their relationship. This resulted in an amazing transformation in the family's functioning, which even I would not have predicted.

Enactments. As the counselor gathers information and reframes the family's various statements and world views, it will be necessary for the counselor to see what the various members of the family are describing. This is where enactments come in handy. The counselor needs to direct the combinations of family members regarding the form and content of the interaction, and then move out and observe. This may be as simple as having parents ask one of the children why he misbehaves. It might be having the family play a game together. Or it could be a role play illustrating what happens in a problem situation.

Homework. The final stage of the session is the assignment of homework. Homework is the vehicle that the strategic counselor uses to provide the family with an opportunity to carry over any changes made within the context of the session to everyday life and/or to implement interventions which will facilitate reorganization of the family constellation. Homework is assigned with specific goals in mind--that is, with a careful plan and rationale for each task that is demanded of each family member. After the first session, the counselor may have one or more homework assignments pre-planned for subsequent family sessions, based on the needs of the family. The counselor then carefully proceeds to work toward these pre-planned assignments through the use of reframes and interactions between specific family members within the session. We will review homework in detail in the next chapter.

Organizing Subsequent Sessions

Homework Check. Subsequent sessions should begin with a review of the homework that was assigned to the family in the previous session. This is very important, as it communicates to the family the importance of the homework as an intervention. If the counselor fails to do this, the family may conclude that the homework was just busy work. The only reason for not starting with the homework review is if the family is truly in crisis over a situation that has developed between sessions. But, you have to be careful about paying attention to every crisis. Some families use crises as a way of avoiding the real issues, and others only function when they are in crisis mode. If you become aware that you are dealing with either one of these types of families, then you should insist that the homework be reviewed first and return to the crisis later. Don't swing at every pitch the family throws at you.

The other important reason for reviewing the homework is that it helps determine the direction of the session based on how the family accomplished their homework. Part of your planning for the session should include what types of interventions you will use if the family completed their homework successfully, and what types you will use if they didn't complete it successfully. Some of the standard questions used during this stage are provided below.

- How did your homework assignment go? Did you complete your tasks?

- Mom (or Dad), how did _____(task)_____ go?

(If the family was successful, get details.)

- Who organized the task?

- Who monitored things?

- To children: What do you think about how it went?

- On a 1 to 10 scale, 1 being "terrible" and 10 being "great" how have things been overall during the past week (or two weeks)?

(If the family was unsuccessful, get details.)

- What happened to prevent them from doing the assignment?

- On a 1 to 10 scale, 1 being "terrible" and 10 being "great" how have things been overall during the past week (or two weeks)?

(If the family is going to make a second attempt at the assignment, plan it in detail and address the things that interfered with the assignment the first time: change of time or day, put someone else in charge of organizing, etc.)

Additional Problem Elaboration. With a positive homework outcome, the counselor then moves on to build on the family's success and sets up the next step in the intervention plan. Assuming that the assignment has facilitated some change in the family, the counselor proceeds to address another component of the dynamics, using the same protocol as was used in the first session: reframing, enactments, and homework.

Summary

This chapter provided you with information about the skills that you will need to use and some general guidelines for conducting family sessions. Now it's time to apply some of this before you move on to the next chapter.

Application Activity: Reframing

Read each of the following scenarios and formulate at least one reframe for each one, using the guidelines in the chapter.

1)   The lights go out just before you and your spouse settle into bed to watch TV.

2)   A 13-year-old girl with no previous history of behavior problems runs away from home a week after her parents separate.

3)   A kindergarten student begins using baby talk and crawling around his classroom shortly after his mother has a baby.

4)   A 12-year-old whose already thin mother has lost a lot of weight refuses to eat lunch unless her mother comes to school to eat with her.

Examples in Appendix B

Application Activity: Organizing the Session

Read the following family case and outline your upcoming counseling session with the form below.

Jessica, a female elementary school student is referred to you by a teacher reporting that the girl is "scared to death." In consultation with the school nurse, you find out that the child has been making frequent visits to the nurse every day, reporting that she is nauseous, dizzy, and experiences rapid heartbeat. In addition, she becomes worried about attending school each night, has difficulty sleeping, and fights with her parents each morning over going to school.

Jessica is the youngest of three girls born to Mr. and Mrs. Smith. Mr. Smith is a rehabilitation counselor with the local community mental health clinic, and Mrs. Smith is a special education teacher. The Smiths have lived in the "country" all of Jessica's life and are currently considering a move to a small town community in the area. Mrs. Smith has changed teaching positions three times during the past year because of dissatisfaction with her employers. Mr. Smith recently changed positions within his clinic and is just now feeling "settled."

Jessica's oldest sister, Jayne, is an outgoing, athletic sophomore in high school of above average achievement. She is involved in a number of social organizations and sports in school. Jessica's next oldest sister, Sarah, is an high achieving seventh grade student who is the family "bookworm." Jessica is an average student who experiences some difficulties in learning math.

Socially, Jessica is quiet but well-liked. She has several friends within her class, but only one or two close friends. She tends to be more of a follower than a leader in class. She sometimes has friends stay overnight at her house but refuses to stay at their houses, as she becomes very anxious when she does not know where her parents are.

Jessica's maternal grandfather, to whom she was very attached, died approximately six months ago of cancer. Her maternal grandmother died about a year before Jessica was born. Both her paternal grandparents are alive, but she has little contact with them, as they live out-of-state, and her father is not particularly close to his family of origin. Jessica's mother (age 38) has two older brothers and two older sisters, in that order, eight years separating the oldest and youngest children. Jessica's father (age 40) is the oldest of nine children, having siblings in the following order: two sisters (38, 37), brother (35), sister (34), twin sisters (31), brother (29), sister (24).

Jessica has seen you one time and has described her symptoms as related above. She stated that she becomes particularly worried when her parents go places at night during the winter, because the roads are bad and she is concerned they will have an accident. In addition, she stated that her parents go for a "meeting" together every Thursday night, although she does not know what type of meeting they are attending.

In a single family session with Jessica's mother and father and Jessica, Mrs. Smith described Jessica's symptoms and stated that she and Jessica were very similar, in that they were both "worry warts." Mr. Smith stated that he and his wife were not in agreement about the impending move from the country to a town, and were seeing a counselor every Thursday night to process this issue. Mrs. Smith appeared very uncomfortable about the sharing of this information and became quiet for most of the remainder of the session. Mr. Smith also stated that when Jessica experienced her "anxiety attacks," Mrs. Smith felt ineffective in helping Jessica and it usually ended up being his role to help Jessica calm down.

1) Complete the DAFFI-DUCC based on the information in the case study.

2) Based on your conceptualization in the DAFFI-DUCC, develop a plan for the next family session with Jessica's family. Assume that all family members, including Jayne, will attend.

   a) Goal(s) of the Session:

   b) Schmooze Stage - How might you *join* with the following:

      Mom:

      Dad:

      Jayne:

      Jessica:

   c) Problem Elaboration Stage – Since the problem was defined in the first session, decide on questions that you would direct to each family member to obtain more information.

      Mom:

      Dad:

      Jayne:

      Jessica:

   d) Reframe – Based on the information in the case study, what are some reframes you might use?

   e) Enactments – What types of enactments might be useful? Be specific about which family members would be involved in each enactment.

Examples in Appendix B

Family Surname _____   **Date** _____

Identified Client _____   **Age** _____

Other Family Members/Ages _____

_____

Person Completing Form _____

DAFFI-DUCC
Dynamic Assessment of Family Functioning Inventory Demonstrated Under Clinical Conditions

by

Jay Cerio, Ph.D.

Directions:

- Complete this assessment after the second session with the family. Experienced family clinicians may be able to complete the instrument after one session.
- Follow the directions for each section, which include identifying specific family patterns and rating the pattern on a scale from 0 to 10.
- Compute the average rating for each section and enter that rating on the scoring summary form.
- Plot the average rating on the profile on the last page.

Genogram

Construct a three-generation genogram for the family that illustrates family membership as accurately as possible. You may turn the form sideways if necessary to fit all members.

Symptom Function

List some hypotheses on how the symptom of the identified client helps the family. Consider the metaphor represented by the symptom.

Hypothesis 1

Hypothesis 2

Hypothesis 3

Now estimate the ***Degree of Interference*** that the symptom is causing in the family's functioning.

Extreme					Moderate					Minimal
0	1	2	3	4	5	6	7	8	9	10

SF Estimated Degree of Interference

Family Developmental Stage

List the developmental stage(s) in which the family is functioning. For each stage, describe developmental tasks and issues that are confronting the family and rate the degree of stress that the family is experiencing related to each task or issue.

Developmental Stage 1:
___ Couple Formation ___First Child (Birth-2) ___One or More Young Children (2-9) ___Tweens (10-12) ___ Adolescents ___ Parent Separation from Young Adult Children ___ Middle-Age Parents with Adult Children ___Aging Parents
- **Task/Issue** _____
- **Task/Issue** _____
- **Task/Issue** _____

	Extreme			Moderate			Minimal	
Degree of Stress	0 1 2 3 4 5 6 7 8 9 10

Developmental Stage 2:
___ Couple Formation ___First Child (Birth-2) ___One or More Young Children (2-9) ___Tweens (10-12) ___ Adolescents ___ Parent Separation from Young Adult Children ___ Middle-Age Parents with Adult Children ___Aging Parents
- **Task/Issue** _____
- **Task/Issue** _____
- **Task/Issue** _____

	Extreme			Moderate			Minimal	
Degree of Stress	0 1 2 3 4 5 6 7 8 9 10

Developmental Stage 3:
___ Couple Formation ___First Child (Birth-2) ___One or More Young Children (2-9) ___Tweens (10-12) ___ Adolescents ___ Parent Separation from Young Adult Children ___ Middle-Age Parents with Adult Children ___Aging Parents
- **Task/Issue** _____
- **Task/Issue** _____
- **Task/Issue** _____

	Extreme			Moderate			Minimal	
Degree of Stress	0 1 2 3 4 5 6 7 8 9 10

Developmental Stress (DS) Lowest Rating

Subsystems

List the subsystems in the family that are evident, and who comprises these subsystems. Then list the various subsystems and rate the clarity of boundaries between subsystems.

Degree of Cohesiveness

Hypothesis 1
Disengaged　　　　　Appropriate　　　　Enmeshed
0 1 2 3 4 5 6 7 8 9 10 9 8 7 6 5 4 3 2 1 0

Hypothesis 2
Disengaged　　　　　Appropriate　　　　Enmeshed
0 1 2 3 4 5 6 7 8 9 10 9 8 7 6 5 4 3 2 1 0

Hypothesis 3
Disengaged　　　　　Appropriate　　　　Enmeshed
0 1 2 3 4 5 6 7 8 9 10 9 8 7 6 5 4 3 2 1 0

Subsystems (SS) Lowest Cohesiveness Rating

Hierarchy

Provide your perception of the family members from most (top) to least (bottom) powerful.
Space is provided for two possible hypotheses.

Degree of Interference

Hierarchy #1

Extreme   Moderate   Minimal

0   1   2   3   4   5   6   7   8   9   10

Rationale

_____

_____

_____

_____

_____

_____

_____

Degree of Interference

Hierarchy #2

Extreme   Moderate   Minimal

0   1   2   3   4   5   6   7   8   9   10

Rationale

_____

_____

_____

_____

_____

_____

_____

Degree of Interference

Hierarchy #3 Extreme   Moderate   Minimal

0   1   2   3   4   5   6   7   8   9   10

Rationale

_____

_____

_____

_____

_____

_____

_____

Degree of Interference

Hierarchy #4 Extreme   Moderate   Minimal

0   1   2   3   4   5   6   7   8   9   10

Rationale

_____

_____

_____

_____

_____

_____

_____

Hierarchy (H) Lowest Interference Rating

Triangles

Diagram the triangles in the family by listing one family member at each point of a triangle. Then, determine the valance in each dyad (positive relationship = "+"; conflicted relationship = "-").

| **Triangle** | **Degree of Interference** |

Extreme					Moderate					Minimal
0	1	2	3	4	5	6	7	8	9	10

Extreme					Moderate					Minimal
0	1	2	3	4	5	6	7	8	9	10

Extreme					Moderate					Minimal
0	1	2	3	4	5	6	7	8	9	10

Extreme					Moderate					Minimal
0	1	2	3	4	5	6	7	8	9	10

Extreme					Moderate					Minimal
0	1	2	3	4	5	6	7	8	9	10

Extreme					Moderate					Minimal
0	1	2	3	4	5	6	7	8	9	10

Triangle (T) Lowest Interference Rating

World Views

List the world views, that is, the beliefs of family members, related to other family members and the family in relation to the world outside of the family. Then rate the degree to which each view interferes with family functioning.

Family Member	**World View**	**Degree of Interference**

Extreme	Moderate	Minimal
0 1 2	3 4 5 6 7	8 9 10

Extreme   Moderate   Minimal
0   1   2   3   4   5   6   7   8   9   10

Extreme   Moderate   Minimal
0   1   2   3   4   5   6   7   8   9   10

Extreme   Moderate   Minimal
0   1   2   3   4   5   6   7   8   9   10

Extreme   Moderate   Minimal
0   1   2   3   4   5   6   7   8   9   10

Extreme   Moderate   Minimal
0   1   2   3   4   5   6   7   8   9   10

Extreme   Moderate   Minimal
0   1   2   3   4   5   6   7   8   9   10

Extreme   Moderate   Minimal
0   1   2   3   4   5   6   7   8   9   10

Extreme   Moderate   Minimal
0   1   2   3   4   5   6   7   8   9   10

Extreme   Moderate   Minimal
0   1   2   3   4   5   6   7   8   9   10

Extreme   Moderate   Minimal
0   1   2   3   4   5   6   7   8   9   10

Extreme   Moderate   Minimal
0   1   2   3   4   5   6   7   8   9   10

World Views of the Entire Family

World View

Degree of Interference

Extreme   Moderate   Minimal
0   1   2   3   4   5   6   7   8   9   10

Extreme   Moderate   Minimal
0   1   2   3   4   5   6   7   8   9   10

Extreme   Moderate   Minimal
0   1   2   3   4   5   6   7   8   9   10

Extreme   Moderate   Minimal
0   1   2   3   4   5   6   7   8   9   10

Extreme   Moderate   Minimal
0   1   2   3   4   5   6   7   8   9   10

Extreme   Moderate   Minimal
0   1   2   3   4   5   6   7   8   9   10

Extreme   Moderate   Minimal
0   1   2   3   4   5   6   7   8   9   10

Extreme   Moderate   Minimal
0   1   2   3   4   5   6   7   8   9   10

World Views (WV) Lowest

Chapter 5

Interventions

Chapter Overview

In this chapter, you will:

- Learn the protocol for assigning homework within the structural/strategic framework.

- Review standard interventions for common family problems.

- Apply standard interventions to case examples.

Homework

"Homework" is an important aspect of the intervention process in the strategic approach. Homework may take different forms, but usually consists of tasks which the family agrees to implement outside the counseling setting. It provides a means for transferring the changes in the family system which are the focus of the counseling session to the family's everyday life. Homework also serves as an ongoing intervention, the implementation of which leads to shifts in triangles, interruption of patterns, and changes in hierarchy. Finally, homework provides feedback to the counselor about the accuracy of her or his hypotheses, the effectiveness of interventions, and the family's willingness to change.

The simplest type of homework is direct assignments, in which the family agrees to engage in specific behaviors or interactions. This may be as simple as setting up lists of chores or rules and consequences, and assigning parents to specific disciplinary, support, and caregiving roles. More complicated forms of homework involve the prescription of ordeals and the use of metaphors and paradoxes. These involve a more advanced level of skill and experience.

An important understanding for the beginning strategic practitioner is that homework is not assigned flippantly. It must be well-thought out so that it addresses the shifts in the family system which are desired. For example, using the simple task of setting up a list of rules, such a list would be formulated by the family right in the family session. If there was a situation of one parent being placed in a position of competence while the other was in an incompetent position, the incompetent parent might be assigned the enforcement role of simpler rules where he would experience some success, while the overly competent parent would be assigned the more difficult disciplinary situations in which she would experience some failure. Although the overt goal of this particular kind of assignment may be to bring more order to a chaotic family, the covert goal is to bring the parent subsystem into balance--to reorder the hierarchy and interrupt a pattern which leads to one parent feeling incompetent, and the other, possibly overburdened. The guidelines for assigning homework are discussed below.

Homework Protocol

- Address the entire family.

- Ask one member to write down the tasks.

- Explain the rationale for the assignment.

- Give each family member a task.

- Speak with a lilting singsong intonation and nod.

- When the assigning is completed, ask each member to review his or her task.

- Always begin subsequent sessions with a feedback about the homework.

Figure 5-1: Guidelines for Assigning Homework

Address the entire family. It's very important to get the entire family together and have their attention when you deliver the homework assignment. You want to communicate that you are "mobilizing the troops," calling everyone together in a cooperative effort to help the family. If children are playing in another part of the room, ask the parents to call them over. Seat the family in appropriate subsystems, with the parents sitting next to each other and the children sitting together. You want to deliver the message that this is important stuff!

Ask one member, usually the identified client, to write down the tasks. If the identified client is old enough and capable, ask him or her to record the homework assignment. This gives the client a positive role and will provide some insight into how he or she operates, as well as providing some comic relief. I have seen the latter in the way a child records the assignment, embellishing it with his own take on what he or his parents should do, rather than the actual tasks. When I have the client read back the assignment, it gives me an opportunity to correct his revisions.

Explain the rationale for the assignment in the context of the information provided during the session. The directives that are included in the assignment must make sense to the family and will be viewed as more acceptable if explained within the family's world view. This means that the counselor has to use the family's language and information from the session when explaining each task. For instance, if I am trying to get an over-involved, enmeshed parent to decrease involvement with discipline and an under-involved parent to take more responsibility for discipline, I DON'T explain this as my rationale. That would set up resistance because it threatens the parents' status quo. Instead, I might approach it from the perspective that the overly involved parent has been working "too hard" and needs a "vacation" from being the disciplinarian, and the under-involved parent needs "more time" with the kids. What I am doing is reframing the parents' roles to avoid blaming one parent or the other for the problem.

Give each family member a task*.* Everyone in the family must feel invested in working on the solution to the problem. Excluding any one member may cause that individual to sabotage the tasks of the other members. If I have no specific task for a particular member, I at minimum assign them a monitoring role. If members aren't present, I send a message to them about how important it will be for them to take on certain tasks. ***It's all about getting everyone on board.***

Nod and modulate your intonation. This may sound silly, but it comes from Haley's work with Milton Erickson. Erickson employed this approach as part of the induction process with clients. What you are trying to do by using this technique is to induct the family into complying with the assignment. Gunnison (2004) calls this hypno-suggestive language patterns and uses this technique with his hypnocounseling approach with a similar goal in mind. Interestingly enough, I have found that family members will gradually pick up on my rhythm and begin agreeing with the explanation being provided.

Be specific. Make sure the "who, what, when, and where" of each assignment is clearly established. The more specific the components are, the more likely the family is to follow through. So, if the family is supposed to have a "fun night," you need to have them determine which night of the week they will use, when they will get together, and what they will do. If the family fails to follow through on their assignment, this provides the counselor with data on the function of the problem, and whether or not direct interventions will work. The counselor can then decide if a new approach needs to be used to circumvent resistance.

When the assigning is completed, ask each member to repeat back his or her task. This provides an opportunity to clarify any confusion and stress the importance of each member fulfilling his/her assignment.

Always begin subsequent sessions with feedback from the family about their homework. As I discussed above, it is very important to review homework assignments. This communicates that the assignment is an integral and critical component of the therapeutic process, as it should be. Occasionally, crises will arise that will have to be addressed before the assignment review. But it is important for the counselor to differentiate between real crises and a family that operates on the "crisis du jour." With the latter, you will need to set limits and address the homework first.

Homework: How You Might Present It

Counselor:	[To parents.] Have the children come over and a sit over here [counselor gestures to two chairs next to the parents].
Father:	Come over here Josh and Jeremy. [Kids ignore him.]
	Stop playing and come over and sit. [Kids ignore.]
	[Father looks to counselor for help.]
Counselor:	Do what you need to do to get the boys over here.
Father:	[Gets up and takes the toys out of the kids' hands.] Get over there and sit.
Counselor:	I have a few things that I want you to do before I see you next time. It's your homework. [Kids groan.]
	Josh, how's your writing?
Josh:	Okay. I can write in cursive.
Counselor:	Good, I'd like to ask you to do me a favor. If I give you my pad, will you write down what everyone needs to do for homework?
Josh:	Mom and Dad, too?
Counselor:	Yes, mom and dad will have homework, too.
Josh:	Oh boy! Sure, I'll write it down [takes pad and pen from counselor].
Counselor:	Okay. Mom, you have been having a pretty hard time trying to get Josh to behave. I think you need a break.
Mom:	You can say that again.
Counselor:	I think you've been letting dad off the hook with the discipline, so I'm going to ask him to do a little experiment for me. [To dad] Would you be willing to try something for me?
Dad:	It depends what it is.
Counselor:	Nothing weird, of course. But it may require that you spend less time on your projects in the garage and more time in the house.
Dad:	Maybe. Let me hear it.
Counselor:	I would like you to take over the discipline with the boys for the next two weeks. You are going to be the one who has to enforce the rules that you and mom just set up.
Dad:	That seems easy enough.
Counselor:	But you will need to be present in the house to do this. Unless of course you want to take the boys out in the garage with you.
Dad:	I suppose I can try it.

Common Intervention Strategies   While strategic and structural strategies do not

adhere to standard interventions, there are some common strategies that are useful for specific

types of problems. Structural therapists tend to implement strategies in the session, usually

through directives and actions, then encourage the family to process and or continue using a task

after they leave the session. Strategic therapists also use in-session interventions, but specifically

extend interventions to homework assignments that continue the therapeutic process outside of

the session. I generally use the latter approach, as it keeps the family focused on the goal of

finding a solution that works.

Purpose of Intervention	Intervention
Subsystem and Hierarchy Problems	Rearrange seating of family members in session. Re-direct a family member who involves himself/herself in interactions of other members inappropriately. Assign a task to family members in the same subsystem to get them to collaborate in a positive way. Create a pretend that has family members act out appropriate subsystem/hierarchy interactions. Have family play a game in which parents are in-charge and kids have to listen to parents to win.
Increasing Benevolence	Establish "family time" for regular positive interaction. Catch a kid being good. Have family members "surprise" each other with positive behavior. Have family play traditional games together to have constructive time together. Special time spent with the identified client on a regular basis.
Organizing the Family	Helping parents develop appropriate rules and consequences. Assigning developmentally appropriate and reasonable chores. Encouraging consistency and firmness.

Figure 5-2: Common Intervention Strategies

Purpose of Intervention	Intervention
Improving Communication	Standard communication exercises. Creating private time for the couple or a parent and child. Teaching/modeling effective negotiating.
Decreasing Oppositional Behaviors	Monitoring/tracking oppositional behaviors. Prescribing the symptom. Creating an ordeal. Creating pretends about the problem behavior.

Figure 5-2 (con't.)

Subsystem and Hierarchy Problems

Problems with parent-child subsystems and hierarchies are often manifested in disciplinary situations. For instance, a parentified child who has risen above a parent in the hierarchy, or who has entered the parent subsystem, may resent being disciplined by that parent and refuse to conform to limits. The child perceives herself to be an equal or better of the parent, so why listen? This may be due to a conflict in the spousal subsystem which has spilled over into the parent subsystem. One parent may look to the child for support and inappropriately use the child as a confidante, thereby forming an alliance with that child and isolating the other parent. This may also occur when a child becomes a caretaker for a parent, as is typical in alcoholic families.

Hierarchy problems within subsystems can also occur. A younger child may assume a position above older siblings if that child becomes a parent's confidante, as in the above illustration. Children with chronic illnesses who require substantial care by parents often rise to the top of the sibling hierarchy just because of their caretaking needs. A spouse who insists on controlling all money matters of the couple pushes the other spouse down into an inferior position in the couple subsystem. In single-parent families, children who are depended on to help with caretaking of other children in the family attain the highest position in the sibling hierarchy, which has the potential of engendering resentment and conflict among siblings. Let's look at some of the possible interventions for these issues.

Rearranging seating. Goal: To physically relocate members of the different subsystems with other members of the appropriate subsystem as a way of starting to reorganize the family. This is akin to rearranging the deck chairs on the Titanic, but, this rearrangement has a positive impact. With parental children who insist on sitting with the parent(s) while siblings play during the session, I direct the parent to *make* the child join the other children in their play, or, in the case of a single child, insist that the child play by himself away from where the parents are sitting. In the case of parents who are "not on the same page," that is, not supportive of each other, I ask the parents to sit together if they are not already seated in that way.

Rearranging Seating: How You Might Present It

Intact Families with Parentified Child

Counselor:	(To both parents) I want you to have Colin go over where his brothers are playing.
Father:	Colin, go play with your brothers.
Colin:	I don't want to.
Counselor:	Do what you need to do to get him do this. If you need to lead him by the hand, go ahead.

Single Parent with Parentified Child

Counselor:	(to mother) Mom, we need to talk about some parent business, so I'd like you to have Amanda go over and play with her sister while we talk.

Parents who Disagree about Discipline

Counselor:	(to father) Dad, I want you to come over here and sit with Mom.
Father:	Why?
Counselor:	It's important for you and Mom to be on the same page. You each need to support the other and that's easier if you are sitting together when you present your plan to Amanda.

Blocking. <u>Goal</u>: To prevent family members from becoming inappropriately involved in the business of subsystems to which they DON'T belong, or in issues between individuals that don't involve them. This can be done directly by telling the individual to wait or to stop interfering, or indirectly through another family member. The former tends to work better with individuals who are concrete and simply not aware of what they are doing, while the latter is often used with individuals who may become resistant if directly confronted about their behavior.

Blocking: How You Might Present It

Direct Block (Counselor Statements)

- ✓ I'm speaking with your mom right now. You will get your turn in a few minutes.
- ✓ Hold that thought for a minute until I finish up with your daughter.

Indirect Block (Counselor Statements)

- ✓ (To father) Does your wife always work this hard for you?
- ✓ (To parent) Let's do a little experiment. Mom, I want you to sit over there and observe Tanner and me while we chat.
- ✓ (To child) I'm confused. Are you the parent?
- ✓ I bet you can't go longer than 2 minutes without saying something. I'm going to time you.

Giving members of the same subsystem a collaborative assignment. <u>Goals</u>: 1) To pull members of a subsystem together so that they feel connected in a common purpose; and 2) To correct the hierarchy within a subsystem. Any number of tasks or activities can serve these goals, as long as they involve the participation of all members of the subsystem being targeted. A few examples of tasks are provided below.

Parent Subsystem

- Work together on establishing two rules and consequences for breaking the rules.

- (Where one parent is in a higher position) Have the "weaker" parent take over discipline duties for a week, and have both parents discuss how things are going every night after the children have gone to bed.

- Work together on establishing chore list and enforcing it.

Couple Subsystem

- Go on a date together (important to be specific that they should be dating *each other*).

- Plan a getaway.

- Go parking.

- Cook dinner together.

Sibling/Child Subsystem

- Plan a surprise for the parents (breakfast in bed, etc.)

- Cook dinner together.

- Commit some minor mischievous behavior together.

- (Where a younger child is in a higher position than an older sibling) Have the older sibling teach the younger child something the older child is skilled at that the younger child has not learned yet.

- Plan ways that siblings will behave that parents won't expect.

Collaborative Assignment: How You Might Present It

Siblings Planning to Misbehave

Counselor: (To kids) I want to ask you boys to try something that may sound a little weird, but I think it will be fun. You know how your parents are always expecting you to misbehave in some awful way. During the next week I want you to misbehave, but I want you to work together to find something that you can do that won't please your parents, but won't get you in big trouble either. You have to do this together to win at this assignment, so you have to do some planning. And you shouldn't tell your parents what the misbehavior is until we meet next week. You'll understand why in a minute.

                    (To parents) Your job is to try to figure out what the minor misbehavior is that the two boys are planning. The two of you have to keep track of what you notice about the boys' behavior each day and compare notes after the boys go to bed. But, you are not to tell the boys if you think you've figured out what they are doing. You also have to wait until we meet next week to tell the boys what you've noticed.

                    Any questions about the assignment from anyone?

Pretends of appropriate subsystem/hierarchy interactions. <u>Goal</u>: To use an indirect method of communicating appropriate boundaries and hierarchy. Pretends are a particularly useful strategy for providing direction for a family without telling the family members that they need to change and how to do it. Pretends introduce ideas in a fun, non-threatening manner. The basic pretend is a story or role play that the family has to act out together. The counselor creates the story and "coaches" the family on how to play it out, then directs the family to play this "game" during the intervening period before the next session. Developing a pretend requires creativity, flexibility and a sense of humor on the counselor's part. Getting the family to follow through requires assertiveness and a sense of purpose regarding the importance of the pretend to facilitating change in the family. Some common types of pretends:

- Develop a story that mirrors the family's problem and provides some constructive possibilities for solutions.

- Have the story mirror the family's problem but be open-ended with the family being asked to brainstorm multiple solutions.

- Have the family act out the family interactions, but switch roles, with the children playing the parents and the parents playing the children. Encourage them to embellish and be creative in their roles.

- Develop the pretend around a common children's story or fairy tale that mirrors the family situation.

Once the pretend has been developed, have the family act it out the first time in the session and direct them through it. Then, assign the re-enactment of the pretend as homework, stipulating the days, times and number of times that the family will "pretend."

Pretend: How You Might Present It

Counselor 's Explanation

I've been thinking about what you've been telling me, and I think it would be good to try something a little different. I'd appreciate it if you will go along with me for a few minutes. You all have not been happy campers for a while, so I want to have you do something that should be fun for everyone. I am going to tell a story, and I want you to act the story out as we go along. But the different thing about this story is that I want you (indicate the parents) to be the kids, and I want you (indicating the children) to be the parents.

(To kids) How do stories usually start? Once upon a time? Okay. Once upon a time, there was a mommy and a daddy. Okay kids, step; forward. This is mom (indicate daughter) and this is dad (indicate son). And there were two kids, a brother (indicate dad) and a sister (indicate mom). Mom and dad were very, very frustrated because the kids never listened to them.

(To real kids) Tell "your kids" to do something, like chores, or turn the TV off, etc.

(Give real kids time to act this out.)

(To real parents) Now you two need to misbehave like kids.

(Give parents time to act this out and coach them if necessary) Come on, you can do better than that.

Now kids, you need to try again. You can try anything you want, except physical punishment, to get them to do what you are telling them.

(Allow parents and kids to develop the story on their own and act it out for a few minutes.)

(To real kids) Mom and dad, if you were kids, what would get you to do what you want your kids to do? Would a reward? Time with mom and dad? Is there a punishment that would definitely work if you were the kid?

(To everyone) Now pretend that mom and dad (indicate real kids) are going to try what they suggested and the kids (indicate real parents) are going to listen. Play that and show how things might end.

(Allow time for the family to develop this final scenario. Again, coach if necessary.)

The end! What did you think about your story? (Go around to each family member and process the pretend. If they want to modify or make changes at this point, incorporate these into the story.)

Now we are going to play our story one more time with your changes. (Narrate as the family acts out the story again).

(After the family finishes, assign the pretend as homework.) Now, the big surprise. This seemed like a very good story that helped you come up with good ideas for getting along. So, during the next week, I want you act out this story together at least 2 times. Each time, after you are finished, I want you all to get together and write down any new ideas for getting along that you come up with in the story.

What 2 days can you definitely get together to do this? (Have family identify the days.)

What time would be best for you to do this? Remember, you need time to act out the story and time to write down any new ideas. (Have family identify the time.)

Finally, who is going to write down the new ideas? (Try to encourage at least one of the kids to do this.)

(Review the assignment with everyone and end the session.)

You can see how this particular pretend introduces pre-planned confusion (the children pretending to be parents who are pretending to be children) as a way of shaking up the family's normal, ineffective way of responding to the problem. This is a way to get the family out of the rut that it's been in, and to force them to "think outside of the box." You can also see how this type of intervention requires creativity and humor on the part of the counselor. You need to be able to help the family develop the story, tease the parents and children as they play, and then pull it all together to be used as a tool in the counseling process.

Games. <u>Goal</u>: To correct hierarchy problems by communicating metaphorically through a common childhood activity. There are a few common games that can be used as metaphors and methods for correcting the parent-child hierarchy. These are particularly useful in situations where a child or children have assumed a position above a parent, making it difficult for the parent to be effective as an authority figure in the family. Some of the games I have used in the past are discussed below.

Mother May I. This is the traditional game in which the person who is "It" is "mother," and gives each player a directive, such as "You may take…one giant step; one baby step; two hops; an umbrella twirl, etc." Each player must then respond, "Mother may I?" If mother says, "Yes you may," the player may then execute the directive. If mother says, "No you may not," the player must stay where she is. If a player fails to ask, "Mother may I," or does not follow the directive, he must return back to "start." In my therapeutic version of this game, the parent is ***always*** "It" and the children are always the players. This provides a structured situation in which the parent is in charge and the children must listen in order to "win." It also serves as a metaphor for the correct hierarchical organization, with the parent on top in the authority position and the children below, having to acknowledge the parent's authority.

I typically have the family play the game in session, then use the game as part of the homework assignment. It has been my experience that the family may expand the parameters of the game and play it during an everyday family activity, such as dinner or when cleaning the house. I have taken these ideas from families and used them as homework assignments with other families. So, when the family is eating dinner, if a child says, "I want more milk," the parent responds, "What do you say?" The child must respond, "Mother or father may I," and wait for the parent to say, "Yes you may," before proceeding. Parents can add a behavioral component by having a special reward for the child who does this most consistently during dinner.

Red Light-Green Light. This is another traditional childhood game that I have found useful with parent-child hierarchy problems. The game format is similar to Mother May I. The players line up at "start" approximately 20 to 30 feet from the person who is "It." "It" turns her back and shouts, "Green light." When this happens, the players begin walking forward. They are not allowed to run. At any time, "It" turns around and shouts, "Red light." Any players who continue moving at all (including stumbling forward from momentum) or who are running, must go back to start. "It" can also say, "Yellow light," which means that the players must slow down but not stop. Whoever touches "It" first, wins.

I use this game in a similar way as "Mother May I." The parent is *always* "It" and the children are always the players. The children must then listen to the parent's directions in order to win the game. The purpose, as with Mother May I, is to provide a fun, metaphorical experience that communicates that the parent is in charge.

Games of Tag. Any of the various games of tag can be used in the above ways. These include Frozen Tag, Marco Polo, Relievio 1-2-3, and Farmer McGregor, to name a few. Most games of tag include a safe spot where players can go and not be tagged and allow for players who have not been touched by "It" to "untag" and free those who have been tagged. I use tag as an intervention by again, having the parent be "It," but also by giving the parent all the rule change authority. So, only the parent can declare "electricity" (players touching a player who is touching the safe spot cannot be tagged), slow motion (all players must move in slow motion), or "everyone free" (everyone is untagged). In order to win the game, the children have to listen to the parent's directions.

Increasing Benevolence in the Family

Families that are under stress often get so caught up in their problems that they forget the good times, such things as:

- They once had fun together.

- The identified client isn't or wasn't always a problem.

- They once liked each other.

- Having fun together is a lot better than being in conflict.

Strategies for increasing benevolence are designed to remind members of the family that they have the potential for having fun together and to refocus them from a negative to a positive frame of mind.

Family fun time. <u>Goal</u>: To create a structured, positive activity that involves the entire family. Essentially, what the family is asked to do is establish a regular time each week that everyone can be at home, do something that is fun but not demanding, and enjoy their time together. Most families that I have worked with translate this to "family fun night" and choose a weeknight to do something together. The activities are based on the family's needs. Families that find it almost impossible for members to tolerate each other might be asked to watch a mutually agreed upon video together. Families that need interaction are usually directed to choose an activity that requires members to do something with each other, such as playing games. Families with younger children might settle on joint play times during which parents and children engage in developmentally appropriate play (finger painting, building with blocks, playing house, etc.). Often, when given the opportunity, families, particularly children, will think of very creative ideas to incorporate into their fun time, and will include multiple activities (playing a game, making cookies, watching a movie). The important thing for the counselor to keep in mind is that the following things be addressed.

1) A specific day and time need to be selected.

2) There can be no competing activities (one child having a soccer game, or a parent possibly working late).

3) Everyone needs to be included in the decision. Don't allow parents to speak for children, or to not participate in the planning process.

4) Everyone needs to be satisfied with the plan.

5) Everyone needs to commit to follow through.

6) NO CONTIGENCIES. Family time is not contingent on good behavior. It happens even if the family has had a bad day. In fact, it is even more important that it happen if its been a bad day.

Interestingly enough, the idea of "Family Fun Night" has been hijacked by such toy makers as Milton-Bradley as a way to sell more games. But in spite of this, it is a healthy activity for families.

Catch a child being good. Goal: To force parents to focus on the identified client's desirable behaviors. This is an old strategy that has been used off-and-on for years in school settings. It is the simple use of positive reinforcement to increase the desired behaviors of child, instead of punishing him or her for negative behavior. Parents are asked to watch for the client's positive behaviors and then tell the child that they noticed the positive behavior. Usually there is a simple token reinforcer, such as a cutout that says, "I was caught being good," or a sticker. This can be paired with a concrete reinforcer, such as being able to earn a privilege, a toy, or the like, for accumulating a specific number of tokens. But, more often than not, just recognizing the child's good behavior is reinforcement enough. The child's perception that the positive things he's doing are being noticed goes miles in mending relationships.

Surprises. Goal: To improve relationships through non-contingent recognition. I often use the strategy of surprising someone in the family when I am working with couples and with stressed out parents who feel unappreciated. The surprise can be a gift, an act of kindness, or a special time for the recipient. But the important aspect of the surprise is that it is completely unexpected, and the recipient isn't required to do anything to receive it.

With couples, surprises can be useful when a couple gets "stuck in a rut:" One spouse feels under-appreciated, the spark has gone out of the relationship, or spouses have lost a sense of being a couple because of parental responsibilities. I usually do not use this strategy with couples where the issues are critical to the couple's survival, such as major power struggles, infidelity or abuse. With the stuck-in-a-rut couple, a surprise can serve to interrupt the unfulfilling patterns into which the couple has fallen. Think about how nice it is to get a card from someone who just wants you to know how much you mean to them. That's what a surprise can do for a couple.

Couple surprises I have used over the years:

- Flowers, candy or similar traditional gifts.

- A date to a favorite activity of the recipient, such as a play, concert, or sporting event.

- A "kidnapping" where the presenter takes the recipient to a "secret" destination.

- A "mini-vacation" of a night or two at a nearby destination.

- "Intimacy time" when the kids are at school.

With families, the surprise is usually something that the children do for the parents. Again, the issue is typically a parent feeling isolated (especially a single parent) and that no one appreciates how much she is doing for the family. Some child surprises for parents that I've used include:

- Breakfast in bed.

- Cleaning the house without being asked.

- Making dinner and cleaning up.

- Surprising a parent with a favorite dessert.

- Making cards for the parent that tell them how much they are appreciated.

- Giving the parent a "day off" (usually with the help of the other parent or other adult family member).

The Surprise: How You Might Present It

1) When meeting with the couple or with the entire family, ask the recipient of the surprise to list things that she would like to do for herself or have done for her that make her feel special.

   "Mom, you've really had your hands full these past couple of months. What are things you used to like to do to relax? What kinds of things did you like to get as gifts on a special occasion? What are some things that you wish people would do for you now to reduce your stress?"

2) Assign general homework to the couple or family. Then indicate to the couple or family that you want to spend a few minutes with the *presenter* of the surprise. Assure them that this is not about anything unusual, that, in fact, it is about something positive that everyone else (or the recipient spouse) will find out about in the near future. This message will serve to set up some suspense on the recipient's part.

   "Everyone seems clear on what they are supposed to do this next week. So, I'd like to take a few minutes to talk to the kids alone about something. This isn't anything bad. I just have a couple of little things I want them to work on privately, and, in fact, if they do these, mom and dad will probably feel better."

3) Discuss with the presenter the need to surprise the recipient. With a couple, you can go over ways that the recipient feels neglected, discouraged, or underappreciated. With children, you can discuss how stressed the parent is and how nice it would be for her if the kids let her know that they notice how much she is doing for them.

   "You know that she has been working very hard to make sure everything is going okay for you guys, right? And right now, she's tired and doesn't feel like anyone appreciates the things that she has been doing. So, I have a proposition for you. What would you think about surprising mom by doing something special for her?" (Get kids' reaction). "It doesn't have to be anything complicated, just something to let her know that you notice all that she is doing for you, like on Mother's Day."

4) Then go over the things that would make the recipient feel special, that he had previously listed. Have the presenter think about which of these things is something that she can do.

   "What are some things that your mom just talked about that would make her feel special?" (Give kids time to list things and prompt them if necessary.) "Would you like to do one of these for her, or do you have some ideas of your own?"

5) Plan the surprise. Go through the specifics: what the surprise will be, when to present it, how much it will cost (if there's a cost), where to present it, etc. With children, make sure that they are developmentally able to present the surprise, and be specific and concrete in the planning. If they need to enlist the help of the other parent, help them do this.

   "So, you want to give mom breakfast in bed. Okay, then you need to decide what you want to make her. Alyssa, you're old enough to use the stove, have you ever cooked anything?" (If child replies affirmatively) "Good, then you can be the cook. What do you think your mother would like? Do you need to buy…pancake mix, eggs, etc?" "You need to talk this over with your father so he knows what you are doing. Be sure to tell him that it's a secret!"

6) Go over the plan and bid the presenter good luck.

Special time. <u>Goal</u>: To help members of the family reconnect in a positive way. Special time is a strategy that is useful for parents and children or spouses to have undivided attention from each other. In the case of parent-child problems, this is a way for the parent to give positive attention to the identified client that is not related to behavior. As with other strategies in this section, special time allows the parent to see the identified client in a positive context, hopefully interrupting the pattern of seeing him/her as the problem or "bad" child. Special time does not have to be anything complicated. In fact, the simpler, the better. Simple activities are more likely to be repeated on a regular basis. Some examples of special time activities:

- Reading a chapter book every night at bedtime.

- Telling an ongoing story to the child.

- Playing a card or board game.

- Baking or cooking together.

- Playing outdoors – catch, basketball, Frisbee, fishing, etc.

- Playing indoors, such as in filial therapy.

- Having girls' or boys' day or night.

- Going to a movie together.

The important thing about special time is that it be uninterrupted by other children, adults, or activities. If there are other children in the family, arrangements need to be made for them to be watched by someone else (the other parent), doing something else, or in bed, if they are younger than the identified child. The parent needs to give the child undivided attention during special time.

Special time for couples operates under the same rules. Since this is a strategy I use with couples with children, this means that they may have to use extended family or friends for child care, if they are unable or unwilling to use a babysitter. As parents, the couples usually have been so caught up in the responsibilities of child rearing that they have lost their sense of couplehood. Some couples even think that they don't have a right to have couple time. Special time, then, is a way of giving them permission and forcing them to schedule regular couple time. As with parent-child special time, the simpler, the better. Some examples of couple special time:

- A regular date night every week or two.

- Exercising together.

- "Quiet time" to talk after the kids are in bed, without distractions such as TV or the internet.

- Playing a favorite adult game regularly when children are occupied, such as chess, cards, backgammon, or Monopoly.

- Going parking…really!

Organizing the Family

The most common problem area with which I have dealt is family organization. This area involves the "nuts and bolts" of parenting, such as discipline, fostering cooperation with children, garnering respect, meeting children's physical and emotional needs, and organizing the household. These seem like obvious things that any parent should know, but, in reality, it's an area with which too many parents struggle. The strategies are relatively concrete and straightforward, as long as the parents are motivated to change. All too often, by the time that parents bring their families to counseling, they are frustrated to the point of wanting to give up, feel completely incompetent as parents, and are looking to the counselor to take over and fix things. So, while the actual strategies are simple, the implementation requires the counselor to be very careful to NOT take over for the parents. The overall goal of family organization interventions is to help the parents both become and *feel* more competent.

Developing rules and consequences. One of the primary questions I ask the family in the first session is, "What are the rules at home?" The responses from parents and children can be quite discrepant, especially in families that are chaotic. It is not unusual for parents to assume that there are rules, but never really establish the rules with the children. Or, in an attempt to gain control over the chaos, parents establish so many rules, the rules are essentially unenforceable. The counselor's task, then, is to help the parents establish a few necessary rules and to help them be successful in enforcing them.

Consequences that are used in chaotic families are also problematic, and not necessarily due to parents relying on corporeal punishment. It is more the case that the consequences tend to lie at too extremes: arbitrary and overly reactive or non-existent and without action. At both extremes, consequences are inconsistent. Physical punishment is often the end product of these approaches being ineffective, leading to the parental feelings of frustration and incompetence. Children, being astute observers of behavior, gradually learn what to expect and how to get around their parents' attempts to set limits. They become "parent deaf," knowing that they don't really have to listen to a parent until after the third or fourth attempt to set limits, when the parent finally yells. Or they know how to outwait their parents, particularly in situations where grounding is used as a consequence. Parents will ground their children for extended periods of time, such as a week or month, but lack the capacity to enforce such a sanction. Kids learn this and know that after a day or two of grounding, their parents will lose the will or interest to continue, allowing the children to return to the same misbehavior that led to the punishment.

Thus, you, as counselor, have your work cut out for you in these situations. The consequences should fit the infraction. Help the parents establish reasonable consequences that are enforceable and that leave them with further alternatives if the initial consequences don't work. For instance, if using grounding, ground children for a half day or day at a time. This leaves the option of adding a day if necessary. If using suspension of privileges, such as using the computer, again, do this in small chunks.

Developing Rules and Consequences: How You Might Present It

1) Limit the number of rules that parents have to enforce. Have the parents focus on no more than one or two important rules.

   "I'd like you two to take a few minutes to talk together about what rules you would like to have in the house." (This is an enactment, so the counselor needs to move out, observe and direct the parents to talk to each other. With a single parent, this will be a straightforward counselor-client interaction.)

   (If parents start coming up with a laundry list of rules for every little behavior) "I know these things are important to you, but I want you to pick out the two things that are most important to start with."

2) Help them be concrete and specific. Get them to define what they mean.

   (If parents state that one important rule is, "Everyone will respect each other.")

   "What do you mean by respect? Sometimes we think kids know what we mean, but they really don't. This is important so the kids understand the rules clearly."

   (If parents can't define what they mean, prompt them.) "Do you mean, "listen to each other?" "Refrain from cruelty or teasing?"

3) Encourage the use of positive reinforcement for desired behaviors. Sticker charts, additional privileges and the like are much more powerful supports for good behavior than punishment is a deterrent for bad behavior.

   "I know what you DON'T want the kids to do. But what do you want them to do? What are some good behaviors that you want to see?" (Use the "Dead Man" rule: Don't define a behavior as something a dead man can do. e.g., Dead men don't tease people. Dead men don't hit.)

   "What can you do to reward the kids for good behavior?"

   (If parents say that rewards are bribery, and they aren't going to bribe kids to do what they are supposed to do.) "You're right, it is bribery. But there's good bribery and bad bribery. Your employer uses good bribery—they pay you for coming to work, and, son-of-a-gun, you keep showing up, even if you hate your job—and it works. This is the same thing that you would be doing with the kids.

4) Keep the rules and consequences within the parents' capacity to implement them.

(If the parents come up with an unreasonable punishment, challenge them.) "If you ground them for a week, are you going to be able to be present all the time to enforce it? Do you really want to spend a week as their jailor? This is more of a punishment for you than the kids. So, what's a more reasonable time period to ground them that you can enforce without causing you even more stress?"

5) Be the cheerleader. Support the parents' successful attempts to follow through. Help the parents revise parts of their plan that don't work for them.

"Okay, so the plan worked a couple of times but not all of the time. That's a great start! Just remember, when you are trying to change behavior, the old behavior gets worse before it gets better. It's like going on a diet. When you know you are going on a diet, you try to eat as much of the foods you like and are going to cut out, before you start the diet. Same thing applies here. You are trying to break some bad habits, and that takes time. So, you have to stay with it. So far, so good."

Establishing chores. <u>Goal</u>: To facilitate the development of responsibility and a sense of cooperation with the children in the family. It is important to instill in children the idea that they are valuable contributors to the family's functioning. The process of establishing chores is similar to that of developing rules.

1) Don't go overboard. Start with one or two chores.

2) Chores need to be developmentally appropriate. Have little chores for little people and bigger chores for bigger kids.

3) Don't pay children for chores. Chores are a necessary contribution to the family. Kids do them to help out. Allowances should not be tied to chores.

4) Establish reasonable consequences for failing to complete chores.

5) Again, be the cheerleader for the parents. Support their successes.

Improving Communication

Distorted and disrupted communication are characteristics of families and couples under stress. Sometimes the disruption is simple, such as failing to listen, interrupting, or trying to dominate. Other times the distortion is subtle, such as incongruence between the verbal and non-verbal message. In this section, I will limit the discussion to the simpler forms of communication interventions.

Communication exercises. <u>Goal</u>: To change unconstructive communication habits that are causing problems among family members. These are the same types of basic exercises that you used as beginning counselors: listening actively, summarizing the other person's message, noticing non-verbal cues, and using "I" messages. These types of exercises are commonly used with couples that are experiencing communication problems and with parents and teenage children. Some of the typical strategies are listed below.

- Active Listening. Have the two family members sit facing each other. One person will speak for two minutes and the other listens without interrupting. Then, the listener summarizes what the communicator said. After, the communicator provides feedback about the accuracy of the listener's summary. Then, the two change roles and repeat the procedure.

- I Messages. Two family members sit facing each other. One has to tell the other something that bothers her using I messages, without accusing or blaming. Then they change roles and repeat the procedure.

- Identifying Non-Verbal Cues. In session, the counselor points out non-verbal behavior of each family member as they talk. Then, the counselor has the family members talk to each other, and as they do, stops them and asks them to identify non-verbal behaviors that they observe.

Private time. <u>Goal</u>: To establish boundaries with children and other family members which allow them to have appropriate privacy to communicate with each other. Some strategies for accomplishing this goal:

- Have the couple establish a time each day during which they will sit down with each other and discuss issues or topics of their choosing, without interruptions from children, work, etc.

- Establish periods of time for specific types of communication, such as a 15 minute period for the "Complaint Department," when each child can come to a parent individually to complain about something they feel is unfair. Other types of specified communication: "Award Department" for providing positive feedback without any complaints; "Family Storytelling Time" for sitting with a child and relating stories about the parent's childhood or extended family legends; and "Cuddle Time" for two individuals to simply hold each other and be affectionate without any verbal communication.

Modeling effective negotiating. Goal: To teach parents and children the art of compromise. This is a common developmental problem for families with adolescent children. As children become older, they question the absolute rules that parents established when they were younger and expect the parents to go along with every request made by the children. Simultaneously, parents get stuck trying to deal with the teens in the same way that they did when they were younger and expect their authority to go unquestioned. In this strategy, the counselor uses a conflict between family members to model negotiation and compromise. The counselor works through the conflict with each family member, while having the other family members observe. In doing this, the counselor models how to listen to each side of a request; how to modify expectations that everything that is requested will be granted; how to be calmly assertive and not aggressive; and, finally, how to settle on a compromise that will probably not be entirely pleasing to either party. The next time a conflict arises, the counselor then coaches the individuals in conflict as they negotiate their way through the situation.

Dealing with Oppositional Behaviors and Positions

From time to time, you will encounter families that are dealing with an oppositional child or a family in which the parents are oppositional, basically daring the counselor to help them effectively. While the traditional psychotherapy view of this type of behavior is that the family is *resistant*, in strategic therapy, there is no such thing as resistance, only the failure of the therapist to develop and utilize an effective strategy to help the family change. Just as there is no "I" in team, there is NO "resistance" in "strategic." Typically, with these types of families, the counselor needs to employ a special group of interventions, once it is clear that direct interventions are not useful. These comprise what is usually referred to as indirect interventions or paradoxical intent.

A word of caution before I discuss these interventions. The rule of thumb when using paradox is that ***the worse outcome of the intervention should be that nothing changes.*** Let me repeat, ***at worst, the strategy that is prescribed should do nothing, and, most importantly, it should not make things worse!*** Therefore, when using paradoxical intent, *the law of unintended consequences* is definitely in play. You need to think very carefully about what you want to accomplish and what the unforeseen outcomes may be. And, you ***never, never, never*** use paradox directly when someone in the family is a danger to themselves or others. In other words, ***NEVER PRESCRIBE SUICIDAL, HOMICIDAL OR AGGRESSIVE BEHAVIOR.*** In addition, in most situations, it is important to try direct strategies with a family first as a way of assessing their commitment to change, before employing an indirect intervention. With those caveats in mind, I will continue my discussion on some common paradoxical strategies.

Prescribing the symptom. <u>Goal</u>: To reduce or eliminate the power that the problem behavior exerts in the family. Prescribing the symptom is what in popular culture is thought of as "reverse psychology." In some situations, a child or adult in the family derives secondary gain from a symptom by controlling others in the family. One common situation I have run into in this area is tantrumming by older children (above the age of 7). Usually, when a parent brings a child in with this problem, I obtain a thorough history regarding what the parents have done to try to eliminate the problem. If it is clear that the child is getting reinforced by the parents' direct attempts to manage the tantrums, and that strategies like planned ignoring have not been successful, then I use the following protocol.

- I meet with the parent or parents and child together.

- I have the parents describe the child's tantrumming behaviors very specifically.

- I instruct the parents to have the child throw a tantrum in the therapy room, eliminating any behaviors that may hurt the child or someone else while he/she is tantrumming.

- If the child is unable to do so spontaneously, then I ask the parents to tell the child to engage in specific tantrumming behaviors as they have described them to me.

- After giving the child a reasonable amount of time to tantrum, I then instruct the parents to tell the child to tantrum every time they see the first cues of defiance from him or her. I am also very open about the fact that, if the child throws a tantrum in response to the parents' directive, then the child is actually doing what the parents want him to do and is not being defiant.

I have used this intervention many times over the years with the following results. Most kids look at me like I am completely out of my mind. The prescription of the behavior totally contaminates their perspective and confuses them. Parents also think I am a little peculiar, but, using appropriate reframes, such as, "this is his way of holding on to his pre-school years," helps to convince them that they have nothing to lose in trying this approach. Only one child has actually thrown a tantrum in my office when instructed to do so, but it fizzled out. He couldn't keep it going on demand.

This is what I call a "no lose" intervention. If the child throws a tantrum, the parents win because the child is following their rules. If the child refuses to throw a tantrum, the parents win because the child has given up the behavior. Underlying the change is that the child no longer experiences the secondary gain from the disruptive behavior (doesn't get attention, doesn't control the parents' reactions) and the symptom loses its usefulness.

I have also used this approach with parents who enter treatment hell bent on proving that their problem is so bad that it can't be solved. These are the parents who have the standard response that, "Nothing works," or, "I tried that already and it didn't work." They will also leave a session with a homework assignment to implement a direct intervention and either not follow through or use the intervention in such a way that it will not be useful. In these situations, I prescribe the parents' helplessness by reframing their proven ineffectiveness as their way of being good parents. Some examples:

- It's clear to me that Justin must keep misbehaving, because it helps you feel like he needs you. So, it is very important that you do nothing to change things.

- It's apparent that you want Justin to misbehave so that you have something to keep you occupied as a parent. So, Justin, it is important for you to keep misbehaving so that your parents have something to do.

The purpose of these statements is for the parents to continue to prove me wrong by rejecting my statement as complete idiocy or by going home and trying something on their own to resolve the problem. Either way, it forces them to give up their position of helplessness, which is the beginning of change in the family.

Ordeals. Goal: To make a symptom so cumbersome or the consequences so distasteful, that the client or family reduces or gives up the symptom. In the vernacular, the ordeal makes it such a pain-in-the-ass to engage in the symptom that the client stops. Developing an ordeal requires that the counselor obtain specific information from the client about the symptom: how the client engages in the symptom, antecedents, emotional reactions, reinforcers, and consequences. The counselor then needs to form some hypotheses regarding the function of the symptom for the client and needs to find out about alternate symptoms or activities that the client would find aversive or repugnant. With this information in hand, the counselor then sets up the situation so that the symptom is made more complicated, the amount of time for the symptom is increased or decreased to an unrealistic length, or that the client engages in an alternate aversive activity if he/she exhibits the symptom.

Ordeals can be simple or complicated. Some ordeals that I have used are described below.

The "Complaint Department" is an ordeal I use in families where the kids or one of the parents complains incessantly about others in the family.

- I ask the family to establish a specific time of the day for complaints, similar to a complaint department in a business.

- The complainer is not allowed to complain any other time of the day except during the complaint time and must save all complaints for that time.

- The established time incorporates a time period that is unrealistically long for complaining, such as 30 minutes.

- If the complainer begins complaining outside of the complaint time, he/she is reminded once that complaints have to be reserved for the complaint time. I usually build in a reward that the person receives if they listen and stop complaining. If they continue, there is a consequence that usually involves "paying" in money or time for something they like doing.

- When the complaint time arrives, the Complaint Department opens. The "listener," usually a parent, sits at a table across from the complainer, tells the complainer that he/she has 30 minutes to complain, and starts the timer. The listener cannot defend against any complaints. If the complainer runs out of things to complain about (which almost always happens within five minutes), the listener must then encourage the complainer to complain more and, if necessary, suggest new complaints.

- The complainer must remain at the table for the entire time period, even if she/he runs out of complaints. At the end of the time period, the complainer receives a reward for complaining at the appointed time.

This strategy usually makes complainers aware of how little they have to complain about and restricts their complaining so that they stop rehashing one complaint over and over. The complainer also eventually gets bored with complaining because they cannot fill the 30-minute time period, while at the same time receiving positive reinforcement for the desired behavior (not complaining).

I have used a similar strategy with anxious children whose anxiety is controlling the parents because the children are constantly seeking out the parents for comfort. Worry Time follows the same protocol, but substitutes worrying for complaining. I sometimes also incorporate concrete activities, like the parent instructing the child to write down worries on slips of papers and then throwing them away or putting the slips in a "worry box" that is kept in a safe place where the worries can't escape. Again, the purpose is to limit the habitual worrying and make the worry time so intrusive that the child loses interest in the symptom.

I used a more complicated ordeal with a female college student who was suffering from bulimia and waiting to enter a residential treatment program. The client's purging, which in her case was vomiting every time she ate, had reached a frequency of four or more times per day, and was causing dental and esophageal problems as a result. The goal of the ordeal in this case was to reduce the frequency of purging until the client could enter the residential facility. In speaking with the client, I found out that she was Jewish, and I used this information to develop an aversive ordeal. I asked the client to identify an anti-Semitic group that she absolutely abhorred for their anti-Jewish attitudes and propaganda. When she had done so, I told her that she would have to begin placing five dollars in a jar each time she purged. Each time she returned for a session, she had to bring the jar with her and give me the cash and a deposit slip for her checking account. She then had to write a check to the anti-Semitic group equal to the amount in the jar, address an envelope to the group, and place the check in the envelope. I deposited the money to her account, donated the postal stamp, and mailed the check. This was set up to be a time consuming and painful procedure for the client so that each step of the process would keep her focused on the fact that she was sending money to people who hated her and her culture. The client agreed to follow the procedure because she really wanted to stop purging but felt unable to do so.

The first week of the ordeal was costly, and the client ended up sending $40 to the hate group, which, while representing eight episodes of purging, was an improvement from previous weeks. The client showed marked improvement the second week, paying only $15 to the hate group. After that, she was able to control her purging to between one and three times per week until she entered the residential program.

The important thing to keep in mind with ordeals is that they need to be tailored to each family's specific circumstances and you have to both convince the family about the importance of following through and know with relative certainty that they will follow through.

Monitoring oppositional behavior. Goal: To use a child's oppositional style against the child as the vehicle for change. Monitoring behavior is another "no lose" strategy that is very simple. With the oppositional child in the room I ask the parents to track the child's behavior for the week to two weeks between sessions. They are to identify when, how many times, and the situations in which the behavior occurs. When they return for their next session, they are to bring their findings to me to discuss. The typical reaction of truly oppositional children is that they will not give their parents the satisfaction of being able to demonstrate to me how "bad" the children are. So, they stop engaging in the behavior. If the children aren't really oppositional, they usually will improve their behavior so that their parents will bring a good report back to me. If neither of the above happens and the children continue to misbehave, the parents will return with useful behavioral information that will allow us to develop new interventions. Any way you look at it, the monitoring yields something positive.

Technology and the Family

Since the turn of the century, the rapid development of electronic devices—smart phones, tablets, iPads, readers-- has had a pervasive impact on families, particularly the ways in which families interact and communicate…or not. In my practice, I have seen more and more families whose members are so absorbed in using their smart phone or tablet, and accessing social media, that they essentially cut themselves off from the rest of the family. This not only happens with teenagers, who tend to derive the essence of life from their devices, but also parents, and spouses. Although less technologically savvy than their children, they also get drawn into the ongoing communication mazes of Facebook, Twitter, and the like. The social media interaction becomes reality to them, while their face-to-face contacts with family members pales in comparison to the excitement of "the net."

I want you to understand that I am not a Luddite who wants to destroy the terrible and fearsome machines. I like the conveniences of technology as much as anyone else. But I am disturbed by the trend that I have observed: we are allowing technology to control us, rather than controlling it so that its use does not impair our human interactions. It is this interference with normal social conventions that has become yet another roadblock to functional family interactions. It is no coincidence that many of the developers of popular technology have disclosed that they have instituted "technology-free" days for their own families during which everyone in the family turns off their devices and actually interacts with each other (Fleming, 2015). It is also no accident that one of the most popular private schools in Silicon Valley The Waldorf School of the Peninsula, where many of our technology leaders send their children to school, uses no computers for instruction, as a means to foster creativity (Richtel, 2011). Hmmm. Do you think they know something that they aren't telling us?

The practical challenge for the family counselor, is to help parents practice and teach moderation in the use of technology. Let me say that again. MODERATION. And again, moderation, moderation, moderation. For parents, this means modeling reasonable use of the smart phone or iPad and enforcing limits on children's use of devices and social media. This seems particularly difficult for current parents of teens, as they themselves grew up with technology as an integral component of their lives. But there is no commandment that says,

"Thou shalt not turn off thy iPad," or, "Thou shalt not take away thy child's cell phone." Some parents actually believe that they are depriving their children of being "plugged in," and thereby limiting their opportunities in life, if they don't allow them to be constantly using an electronic device. Well, my response to them is, it's time to take charge of technology and to be a parent!

Family Interventions with Technology

I lump interventions that are required to reduce the negative impact of technology into the area of "improving communication and relationships." These interventions are designed simply to create boundaries for electronic devices and the internet, so individuals in the family can have direct interactions.

Technology or "screen free" zones. These are times and places when everyone, and I mean EVERYONE—parents, children, spouses—power down their devices. Really. Meal times are a good place to start. The rule is, everyone turns off their phone or other device and places it in the basket in the middle of the table, until parents determine that the meal is over. It will take time, but eventually, the members of the family will actually start looking at each other and speaking. You'll think it's a miracle.

Technology holidays. This is what some of the biggies in Silicon Valley do. They make weekends technology-free. No cell phones, computers, tablets, or other devices. This is a bigger stretch, so you might want to start off with a couple hours after dinner, or a half day on a weekend first, and give the kids ample time to prepare for the first experiment with this. If a half day or a day work for reducing the distraction of technology, that might be all you need to do: one day per week as a technology holiday. When kids and parents realize that the world doesn't end when they were offline, AND that their relationships improve, they will begin buying in.

Family fun night. I also have families combine the above two ideas with family fun night.

One of the rules for fun night is that all technology gets turned off and put away during the two or three hours that the family is engaged in the activities they planned. When fun night is done, people can turn on their devices again.

Technology and Privacy

Parents constantly struggle with privacy as it relates to electronic devices, particularly cell phones. While I believe that teens have to have a zone of privacy, the abuse of technology in ways that can lead to emotional and physical damage of a child dictates that there needs to be limits to this type of privacy. Call me conservative, but I'd rather have a child who is mad at me because I checked her texts, than one who exchanging texts with a stranger she doesn't know, becomes a victim or perpetrator of cyberbullying, or gets in trouble for sexting. To wit, here is what I now recommend to parents.

Dealing with sexting. The phenomenon of sexting has moved from the area of strange adult paraphilia to everyday teen behavior. Don't misunderstand me. It is not something I condone or turn a blind eye to. It is problematic and, depending on the age of the participants, illegal. But it has become a regular part of adolescent sexual exploration and experimentation. And that is one of the main problems with it. Sexting is accepted by teens as just another type of intimate behavior. They don't see anything wrong with it, and, especially with younger teens, they don't project the potential consequences of sending electronic images of themselves in compromising positions.

What most teens and parents don't realize is that, the way that federal and state law anti-child pornography laws are written, if a teen is in possession of just one picture of themselves on their cell phone, they are breaking the law and can be arrested. There have been a number of situations like this around the country that have presented all kinds of problems for law enforcement officials, school administrators, and parents, when trying to apply the laws as they were intended.

The other thing that teens don't necessarily realize is that once an electronic image or salacious text is sent out into cyberspace, it never goes away, no matter what the app or website tells them. It is somewhere on the internet. Years ago, just at the beginning of the use of cell phones as cameras, I saw a seventh-grade female who was refusing to go to school. As the story unfolded, what had happened is that this young lady had taken a nude picture of herself with her cellphone and sent it to her best friend forever. As is typical in middle school, "forever" didn't last long and the friends had an argument that led to the BFF texting my client's nude picture to a large percentage of the seventh and eighth graders in the school. Thus, my humiliated client refused to go to school because she simply could not face the other students, justifiably so. The resolution was not a great one. My client ended up having to transfer to a different school where she could start with a clean slate. But that meant that she had to leave the school that she had attended all of her life at that point.

There is no easy way for parents to broach the topic of sexting with their kids besides tackling it head on. Parents need to have "the talk" with their children, which should include making them aware of the legal and social implications of sexting. Parents also need to remind children on a regular basis about these implications. In addition to this, monitoring children's electronic devices is reasonable, as will be discussed in the next section.

Up front disclosure of monitoring. Inform your child that you will be checking their texts, emails, and search histories whether they are getting a device for the first time, or you have decided to institute monitoring with a device they already have. Don't expect them to like that you are doing this. As I tell parents that I see, there's nothing in the "children's manual" that says that kids are supposed to like or agree with parent decisions. But if you are up front and clear about this, it will avoid the need to "snoop" if you think that your child is getting into something inappropriate or downright dangerous online.

Electronic monitoring. There are ways for parents to electronically monitor devices, either directly through the device, or as part of the wireless plan. I have parents check with their internet carrier to find out how to do this, and then proceed to set this up. Again, up front disclosure is important. The child should know that the parents are taking these steps.

With either of these types of monitoring, it is important to have a reasonable consequence for a child accessing an inappropriate website or communicating in an unacceptable manner. The typical consequence is loss of the device, or all devices for a period of time. Again, the child is not supposed to like this, but follow through is important. If parents stick to their guns and are consistent, their children will, at minimum, be careful about what they are doing online, a main goal of parental monitoring.

Summary

This chapter provided guidelines for assigning homework and a list of common interventions that are used to intervene with specific types of family dynamics. Figure 5-3 provides a summary as a quick reference.

Strategy	*Subsystem/Boundary Problems*	*Hierarchy Problems*	*Increasing Benevolence*	*Family Organization*	*Improving Communication*	*Decreasing Defiance*
Rearrange seating of family members in session.	X	X				
Block a family member who involves himself/herself in interactions of other members inappropriately.	X	X			X	
Assign a task to family members in the same subsystem to get them to collaborate in a positive way.	X					
Create a pretend that has family members act out appropriate subsystem/hierarchy interactions.	X					
Have family play a game in which parents are in-charge and kids have to listen to parents to win.	X	X	X			X
Establish "family time" for regular positive interaction			X		X	X
Catch a kid being good.			X			X
Have family members "surprise" each other with positive behavior.			X			X
Have family play traditional games together to have constructive time together			X		X	
Have parents read to identified client every night.			X			
Help parents develop appropriate rules and consequences.	X	X		X		
Assign developmentally appropriate and reasonable chores	X	X		X		
Encourage consistency and firmness.				X		
Standard communication exercises					X	
Create private time for the couple or a parent and child.	X		X		X	
Teach/model effective negotiating.	X				X	
Monitor/track oppositional behaviors.						X
Prescribe the symptom.						X
Create an ordeal.						X

Figure 5-3 Summary of Intervention Strategies

Chapter 6

Using Systems Approaches
in Schools

Chapter Overview

In this chapter, you will:

- Examine various types of triangles that develop in school settings.

- Learn basic strategies for neutralizing such triangles.

- Review common home-school interactions within a structural-strategic framework.

Introduction

As the use of systems approaches has proliferated among the various helping professions, the applications of systemic thinking has broadened to include not only nuclear and extended family members, but also agencies and social institutions which impact the family (Nichols & Schwartz, 1991). The school, as one of the primary social institutions with which almost all families have contact, has become an area of recent interest for proponents of systemic approaches to problem-solving (Fine & Carlson, 1992; Power & Bartholomew, 1987).

Family approaches have been adopted more slowly by school practitioners (psychologists, counselors, social workers) than by their counterparts in mental health settings, despite the fact that family counseling courses are included within the framework of school training programs. A number of factors probably contribute to the reluctance of school practitioners to work with families. First, school psychologists, counselors, and social workers are public servants, making it difficult to "take the initiative" (Whitaker, 1988) with parents, in getting them to accept a family focus for a child's difficulties. Second, the school setting itself complicates systems-oriented counseling, as it presents the counselor with several more systemic components--teachers, administrators, social service agencies--which enlarge the nuclear family system. Third, these other components of the larger family-school system unwittingly sabotage family counseling by viewing the child as the focal point of social, emotional, and academic difficulties. In other words, the emphasis of these "others" is "fix the child," without paying attention to how the child's difficulties are embedded in the larger systemic context.

The School-Age Family

The school-based family counselor is in a slightly different and in some ways, more difficult, position than his or her colleagues in mental health settings. Parents come into the schools with preconceived assumptions about what a "guidance counselor" is supposed to do, family counseling not usually being considered to be a guidance counselor skill. Typically, the problem is seen as child-focused, a view which is reinforced by teachers and administrators. And it is more often the case than not, that parents either want the counselor to see the child individually or prefer speaking with the counselor without the child present. All provide barriers to even initiating family counseling in school settings. There are some primary tasks that I have found to be almost universal with the families I have counseled. While I operate primarily from a strategic/structural framework, my approach is gradually becoming more eclectic. Thus, the discussion in this section does not represent a purely strategic/structural approach.

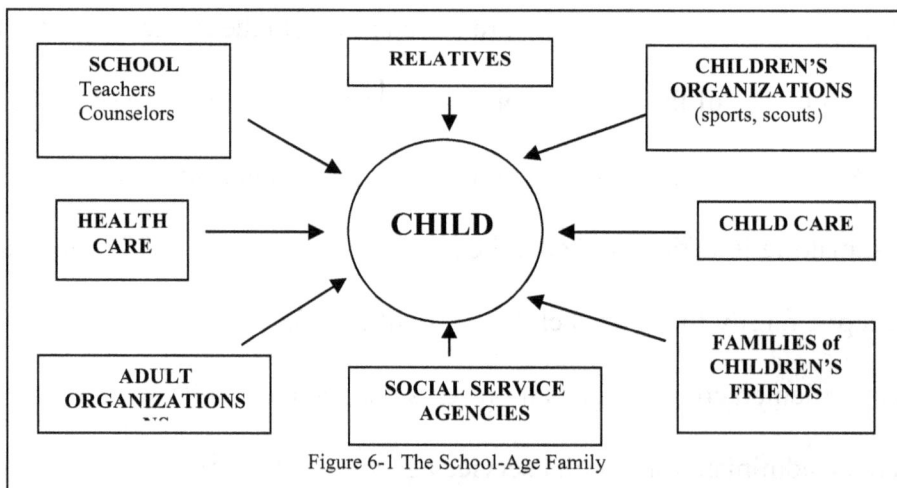

Figure 6-1 The School-Age Family

Home-School Interactions

Power and Bartholomew (1986) described a number of interactions between parents and school personnel within a family systems framework. They identified four common interactions that interfere with helping a child who is experiencing school problems: avoidant, competitive, merged, and one-way. They based their ideas on two systems phenomena: complementarity, described in chapters 1 and 2, and symmetrical transactions. Symmetrical transactions occur when more of a behavior from one party results in more of the same behavior from a second party. For instance, arms races tend to be symmetrical. One country obtains a certain number or kind of weapons, and this leads to the country's enemy doing the same, which leads to the first country obtaining more weapons, and so on.

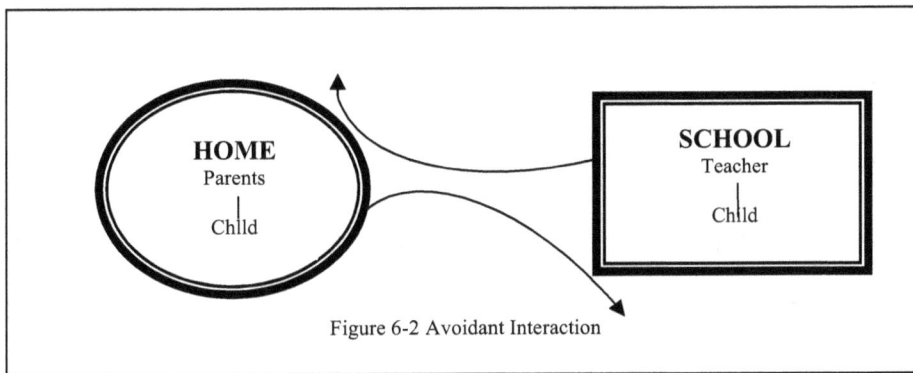

Figure 6-2 Avoidant Interaction

Avoidant Interactions. In these types of symmetrical interactions, the boundaries between the school and home subsystems are too rigid and the subsystems, therefore, are disengaged. Thus, when someone from the home subsystem tries to communicate with someone from the school subsystem, and vice versa, the receiver of the communication avoids the contact. Subsequently, when the first receiver tries to make contact with the initial communicator, that person avoids contact. Each party then continues their avoidant behavior whenever the other party attempts to make contact.

An example of this was my interaction during my time as a school counselor, with a parent who I found particularly demanding and unpleasant to deal with, who I shall call Mrs. Jones. I hated talking with her because I knew it meant spending an extended time on the phone listening to a complaint about a relatively insignificant issue, then having to spend time following up on her complaint. If Mrs. Jones called when I was not available, I would tell myself that I would call her back as soon as I had a few uninterrupted minutes. The day would go on and I would get busy, so I would tell myself that I would call her as soon as the students left school. The students would eventually be dismissed, and I would get tied up talking with teachers about students with whom they were concerned. So, I would tell myself that I would call Mrs. Jones first thing in the morning. Morning arrived, and I would get busy dealing with students. Finally, around noon the next day, I returned the call, and Mrs. Jones was not available, so, I left a message on her answer machine.

Meanwhile, Mrs. Jones was rightfully upset about my not returning her call in a timely manner. When she heard my voice on the answer machine, she decided not to pick up the phone. On my end, I began feeling guilty that I hadn't returned her call immediately, so I called back several times trying to contact her. Each time, Mrs. Jones wouldn't answer the phone. Consequently, the problem she called about never was addressed.

Competitive Interactions. Competitive interactions are also symmetrical in nature, but this time the pattern has to do with the boundaries between home and school being poorly defined and, therefore, causing enmeshment between the parents and school personnel. In this case the enmeshment has to do with members of one subsystem forcing their way into the other subsystem. When this occurs, the members of the subsystem on the receiving end reciprocate and attempt to force their way into the first subsystem.

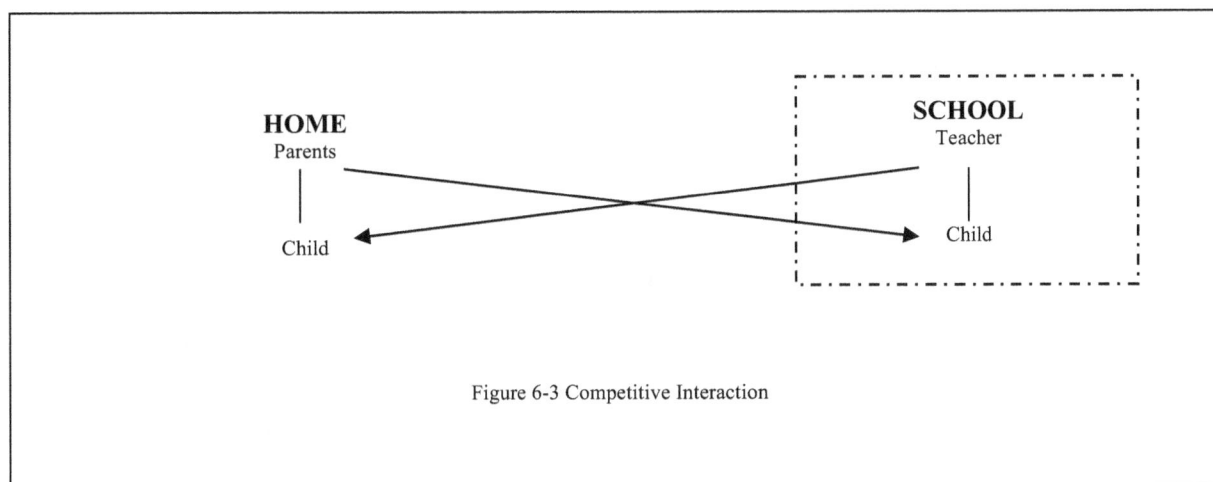

Figure 6-3 Competitive Interaction

Here's how this might look in a common school situation. A father whose son is failing math calls his son's teacher upset about how the teacher is teaching math. The teacher explains that she is following the state guidelines and that this is how the students have to learn math in order to meet state standards. The father, an accountant, tells the teacher that this is ridiculous, that it is clear now why his son is failing, and that he is going to teach his son math the "right" way. The father begins helping his son with his homework but refuses to use the approaches being taught in school. The teacher, rather than trying to argue with the father, simply lowers the student's homework grades because he is not using the correct procedures, even though he is able to find correct answers to problems. Consequently, the son keeps getting poor grades and the father becomes more adamant about not trying to use the methods being taught at school.

The problem here is that the father is trying to *make* the teacher do things his way, and the teacher is insisting on doing things *her* way, each insisting on being the "expert" on the problem. The more one of them pushes his/her position, the more the other resists and becomes entrenched in his/her position, and the more frustrated both of them become. Thus, the situation escalates, becoming a competition between the adults, but nothing constructive is done to resolve the son's problem with math. The only communication that occurs is adversarial, and there is no compromise or collaboration.

Merged Interactions. Merged interactions are complementary transactions that occur when the boundaries between home and school are again poorly defined, but in this situation, a member of the other subsystem is invited into the initiating subsystem. As the invited members help the members of the initiating subsystem, a complementary process occurs in which the members of the initiating subsystem who needed help lose power and the members of the other subsystem who were invited to help gain power. The end result is that the members of the initiating subsystem (the helpees) and those of the invited subsystem (the helpers) become enmeshed, with the helpees becoming dependent on the helpers, and, therefore, less able to handle their problems on their own.

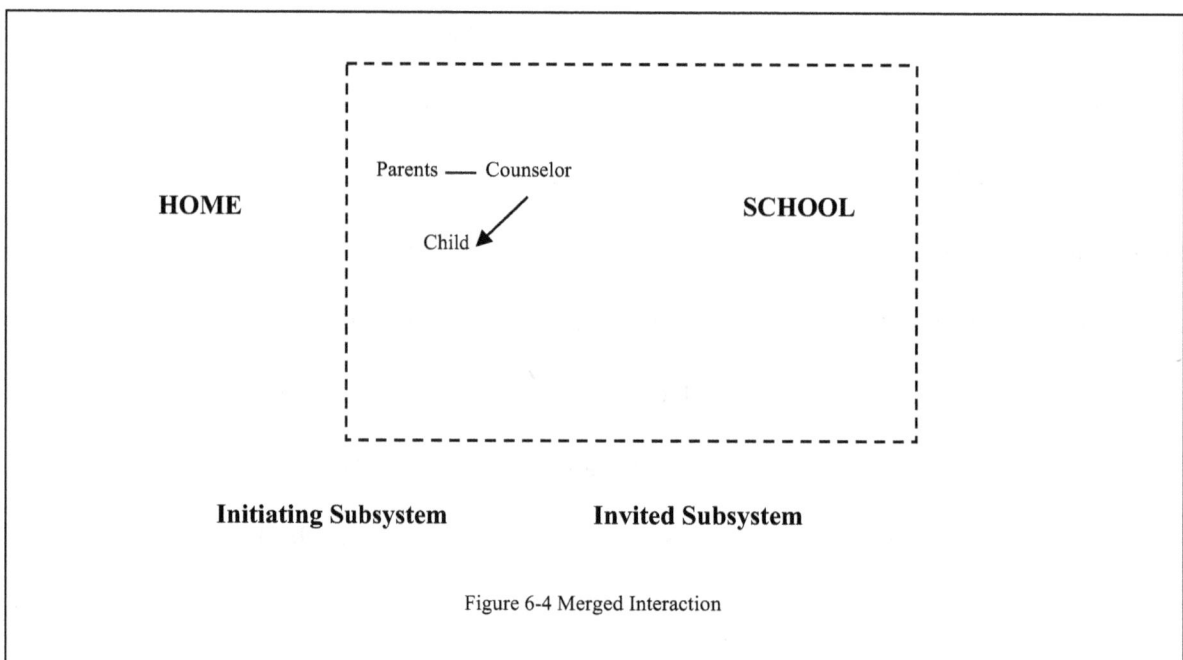

Figure 6-4 Merged Interaction

The most common type of merged interaction is when parents feel incompetent to deal with a problem of their child's, or when they are simply exhausted from dealing with a chronic problem. For instance, a single parent who is having difficulty with limit setting at home may

contact the school counselor for advice. The school counselor, with the best intentions, then sees

the children in the family and "fixes" things for the parent, and the children settle down at home.

The parent, then continues to look to the school counselor for help in resolving a multitude of

problems with her children, becoming dependent on the counselor. The problem here is that the

parent continues to feel incompetent in dealing with the problems at home, and the more the

counselor helps, the less competent the parent feels. Secondly, the parent and the counselor have

become allies against the children, which will interfere with the counselor's work with the

children in school.

   One-Way Interactions. One-way interactions begin in a positive way, with one

subsystem trying to appropriately contact the other subsystem. The problem is that the

boundaries of the initiating subsystem are appropriate, but those of the receiving subsystem are

rigid and impermeable. Therefore, the receiving subsystem does not reciprocate the attempts of

the initiating subsystem. The disengagement of the receiving subsystem leads members of the

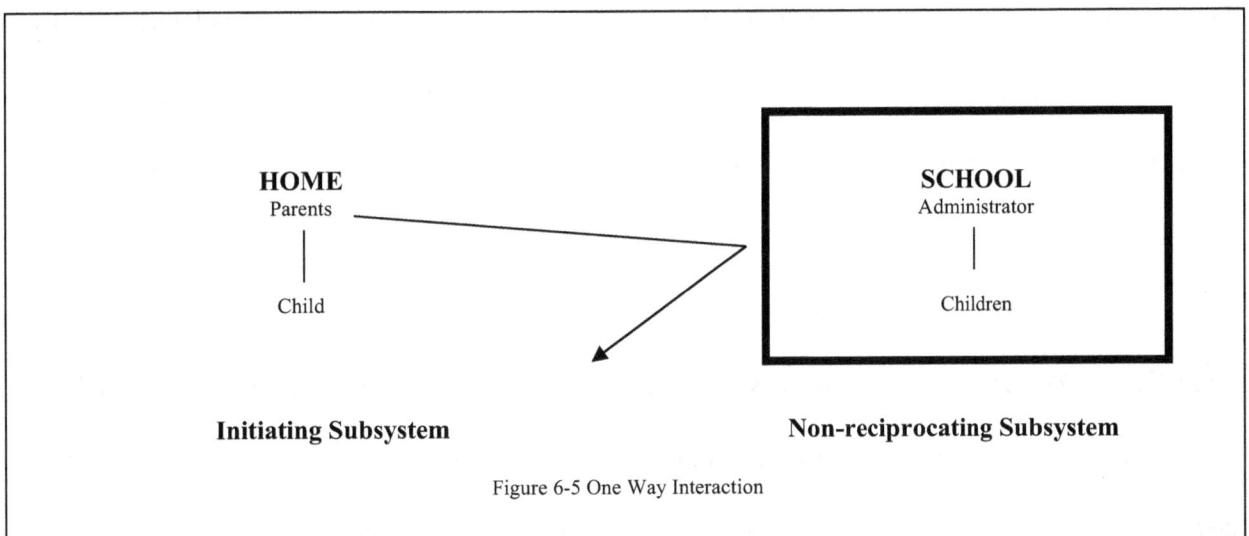

Figure 6-5 One Way Interaction

initiating subsystem to continue their efforts to engage the receiving subsystem. If the receiving subsystem simply avoids responding and the initiating subsystem gives up in frustration, this pattern becomes an avoidant interaction. If the receiving subsystem responds with the message, "Mind your own business," and the members of the initiating subsystem become angry and more intent on becoming involved with the receiving subsystem, this pattern will become a competitive one. As the adults continue to play out their dysfunctional patterns, the child's problem goes unresolved once again.

I observed this type of pattern occurring in a school district with which I had regular contact. Parents would offer their help to their children's teacher in efforts to be supportive of the school. The school administrators, however, were threatened by this, seeing this as a way for parents to interfere with their planning and implementation of the curriculum. So, the administrators decreed that only certain parents were allowed to help teachers, and then, the parents were limited to copying and delivering materials between classrooms. The parents eventually became frustrated and felt that the administration was patronizing to them, so they eventually stopped trying to help and, in fact, became quite adversarial with the administration. The situation became so bad that parent groups were formed to monitor the school and work to defeat the school budget. Thus, reasonable attempts to collaborate with the school by parents were rejected by the administrators, with the effect of creating an ongoing competitive interaction with the parents that interfered with the children's education.

Cooperative Interactions. The one constructive type of home-school interaction identified by Powers and Bartholomew is one in which the boundaries of both home and school subsystems are appropriate: flexible enough to allow interactions between the subsystems, but clear enough to prevent members of one subsystem to inappropriately enter the other subsystem. This type of structure allows parents and school personnel to collaborate on problems, each party listening to and valuing the contributions of the other and compromising to resolve the problems of the child. For example, a teacher and parents would conference about a problem that the child is having. Parents would offer their input regarding how they have dealt with a similar problem at home. The teacher might offer suggestions regarding what has worked for her with other

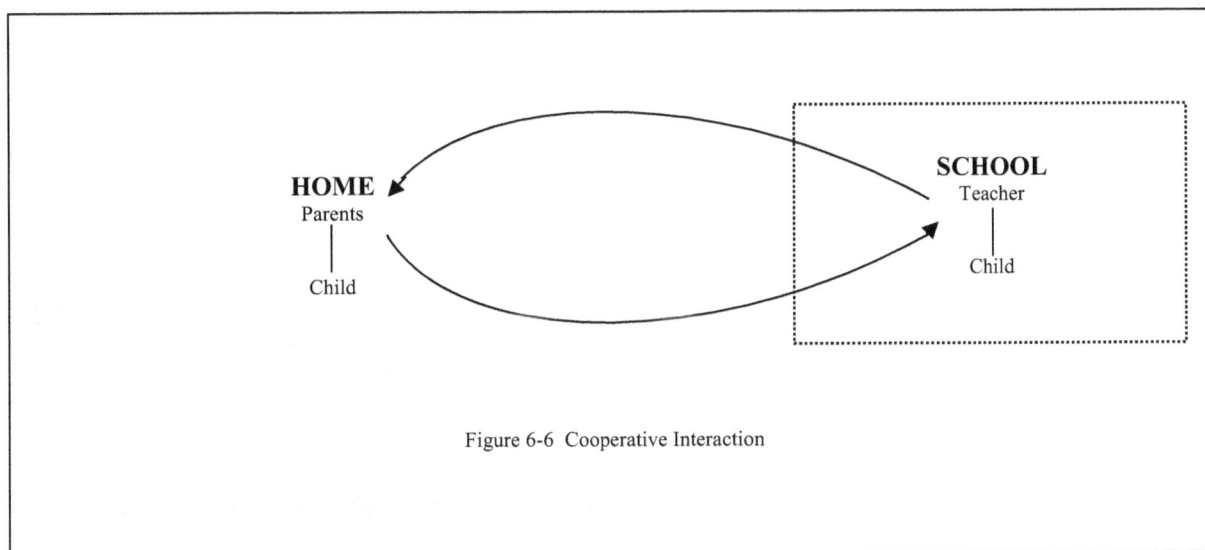

Figure 6-6 Cooperative Interaction

children in the past. Together they develop a plan on how to address the problem, which includes strategies that the teacher will use in school, strategies that the parents will try at home, and how the teacher and parents will keep each other informed about how things are going (such as passing a daily notebook back and forth).

Family-School Triangles

Schools are complex systems that are perfect breeding grounds for conflicts, competitions and alliances. There are two basic types of triangles that develop in schools: ones that involve the family and ones among school personnel. An important task of the school-based family counselor is to de-triangle themselves from alliances within the family and the school.

This is usually easier if the counselor is seeing the identified client with his or her family from the beginning of counseling than it is if the counselor has been seeing the identified client individually beforehand. It is important for the family to perceive you as a somewhat neutral member of the system who is trying to understand what the family's life together is like. By successfully removing yourself from an existing triangle and avoiding being drawn into a new triangle, the counselor can more effectively exert his or her power as a change agent and implement intervention strategies that will help reorganize the family.

Triangles within the Family. How does the counselor do this? It is my experience that when counselor and client have been involved in an individual counseling relationship, the parents approach the first family meeting fearing that they will be judged or blamed by the counselor for the child's difficulties. It is important in this case to "join" with the family (Minuchin, 1981) in a non-threatening way, letting them know that you understand the difficulties, stresses, and anxieties that parenthood brings into people's lives. Another pitfall of seeing the family of a child who has seen the counselor for individual counseling is that the child has developed an image of the counselor as an ideal adult who understands him or her better than his or her parents do. One way of dealing with this is to point out your shortcomings in other adult-child relationships; for example, telling a story about a time you really "blew it" with a child. You may also have to discuss things which the child has told his or her parents at home about individual counseling sessions and use the family meeting as an opportunity to correct any miscommunications on the child's part.

Another way that the counselor can extract him- or herself from or avoid triangles is by insisting that both mother and father attend the family meeting (except in single parent homes). This helps reduce the possibility that the "left out" parent will feel blamed and sabotage the work done in a session. In custody cases, where it usually is unwise to do this, it is important to clearly differentiate between legal issues and family issues. In these situations, I find I have to be relatively firm and assertive, particularly when a parent insists on trying to have me as a school representative interpret a custody agreement. In addition, I make it clear that any discussions around custody may come under the scrutiny of the court and be open to the absent parent.

Sometimes de-triangulating requires the counselor to deliberately anger the family member with whom an alliance has been mistakenly formed. This can be accomplished by supporting a family member who the ally sees as an adversary, or by challenging the ally on points where he or she sees him- or herself in the right.

Triangles between the Family and School. Triangles also develop between members of the family and school personnel. Sometimes, this serves to reduce stress between family members. For instance, it is not uncommon for divorced parents who are involved in a custody dispute to "create a crisis" with the school by drawing in a teacher or counselor into the disagreement. This is simply accomplished when the parent who does not have physical custody of the child comes to school and demands to see the child. If the there is no custody decree, or the parents have failed to provide a copy of the decree to the school, the school administrator or counselor will have to deny this request. The non-custodial parent then becomes angry with the school personnel, re-directing the focus of the conflict from the spouse to the school. The custodial parent becomes angry because the school is dealing with the non-custodial parent, and both parents are essentially united by their anger with the school.

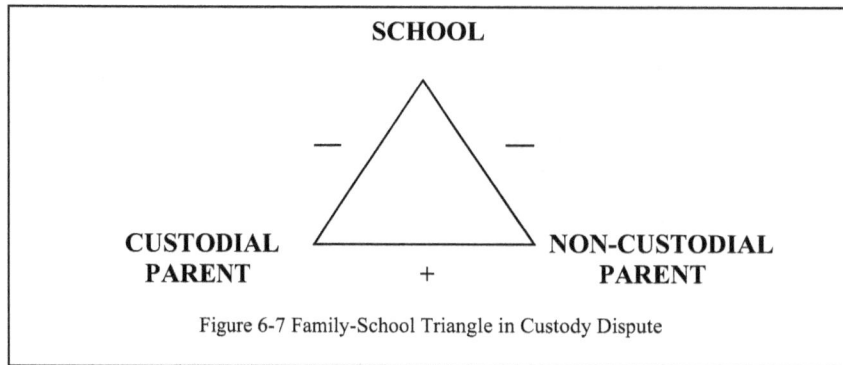

Figure 6-7 Family-School Triangle in Custody Dispute

Another type of triangle that commonly occurs between the family and school is when a parent asks a member of the school staff, such as the counselor, to "keep tabs" on his/her child. This is similar to the merged relationship described above. The school counselor, then, becomes allied with the parent against the child, which will make it difficult for the counselor to advocate for the child.

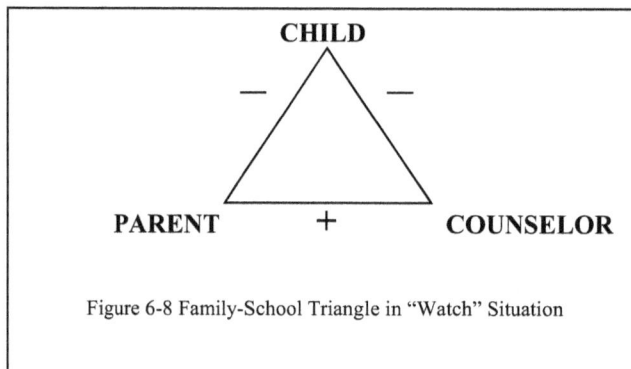

Figure 6-8 Family-School Triangle in "Watch" Situation

Triangles within the School. There are other types of triangles which are unique to school settings, such as parents-student-teacher, student-teacher-counselor, and parent-teacher-counselor. These triangles may be the most difficult to navigate because they involve school personnel who want their expertise with a child recognized, and, many times, want their views to be the only views that are considered legitimate. For instance, a teacher consults with the school psychologist regarding a child's behavior in her class. The psychologist recommends some behavioral strategies for the teacher to try. The teacher isn't sure she likes what she heard from

the psychologist, so she seeks out the school counselor and asks her opinion. The counselor

offers to see the child because she thinks that there is an emotional issue underlying the behavior

that needs to be addressed. The teacher likes this approach better because it means that the

counselor will be dealing with the problem. A few days later, the psychologist stops in to see

how the behavior intervention is going, and the teacher tells him that the counselor had different

recommendations and is seeing the child. The psychologist feels insulted and becomes angry

with the counselor, marching down to the counselor's office to give her a piece of his mind. You

could replace the main players with administrator, social worker, bus driver, safety officer, and

the outcome would be the same. Two people end up in an alliance, the third feels disrespected,

and the problem with the child does not get effectively addressed.

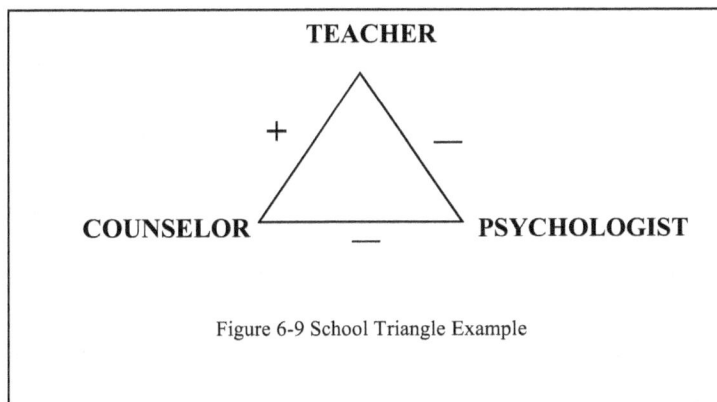

Figure 6-9 School Triangle Example

Dealing with Triangles

The important point of the previous discussion is that if you, as the counselor, get drawn

into a triangle, you will lose credibility with other members and/or subsystems of the larger

family-school system. This, in turn, diminishes the possibility that you can effectively facilitate

the family's change. So, you need to neutralize these triangles by minimizing the potential for you being pulled into one. A few ideas are provided below.

In the first example, the custody dispute, the school is being asked to mediate a legal issue that is the parents' problem. So, the important task for school personnel is to make sure that it stays the parents' problem. The main way to do this is to ask both parents for copies of the custody order before the school will allow any contact with the children in school. If a parent is insistent and accuses the school of siding with the other parent, the school representative has to be equally insistent in stating that BOTH parents need to contact their attorneys, and that the school must follow the court decision, but can only do so if copies of the court order are on file at the school.

Triangles within the school can be even more problematic because they include people who are the counselor's co-workers and peers, and who, themselves, like to be perceived as "experts" with children. The primary means I use for dealing with such triangles is to enlist the teacher's or administrator's cooperation by asking his or her advice on how I should deal with a specific situation when I meet with the family. Whether I use the suggestion or not, I am careful to send a message back to the teacher or administrator thanking him or her for his or her advice and stating how helpful it was in the counseling session. This strategy serves a minimal purpose of acknowledging the colleague's expert status and reduces the possibility of sabotage by that individual because of a hurt ego. Yes, it is manipulative, but in a positive way, with the goal of helping the child.

The Family Intervention Action Team (FIAT)

Most people think of a FIAT as an inexpensive but dependable Italian car. But my FIAT is the Family Intervention Action Team, an approach to the types of family-focused counseling problems which can be very frustrating to the psychologist, counselor, or social worker who is counseling a child individually. This is an idea I proposed a few years back which I think could be very useful in dealing with family-school issues.

The problem with approaching such presenting problems with individual counseling is that this focuses attention on the child, whose problem typically is only a symptom of difficulties in the larger family system. This removes the focus from other members of the family and other professionals in the school who may be contributing to the problem situation.

The purpose of the FIAT is to decrease and/or eliminate the possibility of this type of "triangulation"; that is, the type of situation described above in which the helper exacerbates the problem by buying into the family's need to identify the child as the person in need of help. The FIAT is intended as a systemic approach to counseling intervention in which the child is viewed as becoming symptomatic in order to help the family, albeit in an inappropriate manner. For example, a child whose father is away from home frequently and whose mother is becoming depressed by this situation may begin acting out and disobeying his mother. This allows his mother to demand that father spend more time at home in order to help her discipline the child without forcing her to confront her anger and depression over her husband's neglect of their relationship. A counselor working individually with a child would probably focus on the child's misbehavior and utilize such interventions as a behavior modification program or establishment of logical consequences. However, a counselor or team working systemically would not only address the presenting problem of the child's misbehavior, but also intervene with the parents to get them more involved with each other.

So, why do we need to be doing this in the schools? As anyone who is working as a helping professional in schools knows, a significant number of children who are referred for counseling come from families which are experiencing some level of dysfunction. This ranges from mild developmental problems, such as difficulties adjusting to a previously cooperative child becoming a rebellious adolescent, to severe dysfunctions involving child abuse or parental separations. What often happens is that, in the heat of the situation, the child becomes symptomatic--in school and/or at home--and the parents or teacher or school nurse, seeking to relieve some of the pressure they are feeling, turn to the school psychologist, counselor, or social worker to "fix" the child. The school psychologist, counselor, or social worker, recognizing the complexity of the situation, becomes frustrated about being asked to "fix" the child, and begins feeling helpless about the situation and/or resentful toward those who are expecting a quick fix.

How do we avoid this trap? The purpose of the FIAT is intended to bring everyone who has contact with the child "on board;" that is, working with the child from the same set of basic assumptions. These assumptions include: 1) Problems presented by children are part of complicated set of interactions within the family which go beyond simple cause-effect relationships; 2) The school and school personnel represent subsystem components of the larger family-school system; and 3) In order to impact a child's problem, one must intervene with any elements of the system which contribute to the problem. The professionals who will be members of the FIAT will include psychologists, counselors, teachers, social workers, nurses, and administrators--that is, as many members of the school subsystem as possible. The focus will be *action*, not recommending. Who will be taking what action will be a function of the group's conceptualization of a particular problem and formulations of interventions. For instance, in the case example discussed above, the FIAT might designate the teacher as the person to help the family with the presenting problem (misbehavior) and the psychologist as the person to work with the parents regarding their roles with the child and, implicitly, with each other (under involved father, over-involved mother), and the counselor as the person to make a home visit to work with the family within their natural environment. All these professionals will be assigned their roles and tasks and will implement them in conjunction, not competition, with each other.

Working toward this end will not be an easy task. It will require that the helping professionals in the schools relinquish some of their "turf" and recognize both their unique and shared areas of expertise regarding children. In-service training will be necessary in order to educate all those involved in systems models and interventions. Finally, time will be needed, particularly during the start-up period of the team--organizational time, team meeting time, team consultation time, and family meeting time. Communication and cooperation will be key elements of making this approach effective.

This may sound like a "pie-in-the-sky" idea, but, in reality, I have worked with schools that have developed family-based programs similar to this which have been effective in helping kids. The FIAT would simply be a more formal approach to programming.

Chapter 7

Systems Troubleshooting

Chapter Overview

In this chapter you will review structural-strategic approaches for dealing with:

- Suicide crises with children.

- Families that are going through divorces.

- School phobia.

Risk-taking and Self-Harm

Situations in which a family member is engaging in risky behavior in which he or she is potentially endangering him/herself, or in which the family member is openly suicidal of course require immediate attention. Within the context of a family approach, these situations require mobilization of the family to help the member who is at risk. The counselor's goal is to get responsible family members to do something to ensure the client's safety.

Keep in mind that the mandate of the system is to maintain homeostasis, so it is not unusual for family members, particularly parents, to deny the seriousness of the situation. I see this in statements from parents such as:

- "If someone talks about suicide, they won't really do it."

- She's just being a drama queen."

- He's just being a boy.

This is, in effect, an attenuating feedback loop that maintains the family's homeostasis in a situation in which an amplifying feedback loop is required that will help the family move to a different level of homeostasis. The family's acceptance of the behavior as normal has to be exploded in order to spur them to act.

I follow some basic guidelines for addressing these situations with parents.

- Assess the level of benevolence in the family.

- Don't play into ***denial*** (and I don't mean the river).

- Raise the parents' level of anxiety. A certain amount of anxiety drives action.

- Put the parents in charge.

- Make a plan.

Assessing Benevolence. First, it is important to assess the parents'/family's attitude about the client. Do they seem to be emotionally attached to the client? Are they showing genuine concern about his wellbeing? Is their anger simply frustration over not being able to help up to this point? Or, are they cold and indifferent? Has their anger toward the client led them to reject and abandon him? Do they want to get rid of the client because he has become such a burden or interference to them? It is important to clarify the parents' position in relation to the client, as this will determine how you will proceed in getting them to act. You do this through observing what the parents say about the client and how they act toward the client.

Unfortunately, I have dealt with many families in which the parents are emotionally disengaged from the client and just want to get rid of him. Their statements about the client are extremely negative and punitive, and they typically are pushing for the client to be placed outside of the household. In these situations, I cannot trust the family to insure the client's physical safety because it is possible that the parents might be relieved if the client was "out of the picture" and off their hands. When I deal with these types of families, I think it is in the client's best interest to be placed outside of the home and I move the parents in that direction (which is usually fairly easy, since this is what they want). I DO NOT use strategies that require the parents to be responsible for the client's safety, beyond transporting him to an appropriate agency or facility where the placement can take place.

However, when dealing with families where the emotional attachments are secure or even enmeshed, and where the family's interactions with the client demonstrate their concern, albeit frustration, I am more likely to use strategies that appeal to the parents' sense of responsibility and worry for the client's wellbeing. I will also put the parents in charge of the client's safety and treatment planning in situations in which the client's life isn't in imminent danger. The strategies discussed below would be used with this caring type of family and NOT with the disengaged and emotionally detached family.

Dealing with Denial and Raising Anxiety. In situations that are not acute—that is, not an immediate threat to the client's life—I have used strategies designed to push parents to recognize the absurdity of their denial and to raise their anxiety enough so that they don't accept the situation as normal. These situations include things like alcohol and drug use, risky sexual behavior, unsafe driving, and other thrill-seeking behavior. In other words, the child is making inappropriate choices but not in immediate danger. If the parents' inertia is due primarily to passivity, that is they are not completely avoiding the situation, but are more like deer caught in a car's headlights, I usually refer to the possibility of the child's death if the behavior continues.

- If she keeps doing this, she will die.
- It's clear that his drinking will eventually kill him if nothing is done.
- Kids who do this sometimes accidentally kill themselves without intending to.

The purpose of this is to push the parents to get beyond a helpless position and do whatever they need to do to inhibit the child's behavior.

With more serious situations of denial, such as, parents acting like the behavior isn't even occurring, I sometimes take more drastic action. The most powerful strategies involve having parents prepare for the client's unavoidable demise. In these cases, I want to "hit the parents over their heads" with the possibility of a tragic outcome for the behavior. I want them to be frightened enough to not be able to rationalize the behavior away and, consequently, to take action. So, the strategies are more extreme.

- ***Christmas or birthday gifts.*** In this strategy, I tell the parent that it's clear to me from the child's behavior that he will not be alive for their next birthday or Christmas, whichever is coming up sooner. So, it is important for the parent to give the child their gift now, while he is still alive and able to appreciate it. The parents are to buy a gift and wrap it for the holiday and bring it to the next session to give to the client. The hope is that the parents will do at least one of the following:

1) Recognize that what they are doing is absurd and get angry with the counselor about the directive. When they return for the next session ready to unload on the counselor, the counselor can use their anger to get them to act.

2) Follow through and return with the presents. If the parents do this, the counselor then needs to set up the session so that the giving of the gift is very dramatic. Explain to the client why the parents are giving him a gift now instead of waiting for the holiday. Emphasize the parents' love and concern about the client and their confusion about how to help him. Then, direct the client to give the parents his undivided attention as they present the gift. After the gift is open, ask the client what he would like the parents to do with the gift when he's gone. Ask the parents if they want to put the gift in a special place where they can see it, so that they can remember the client. At this point, everyone should be upset enough so that they either recognize the absurdity of

just allowing the client's behavior to continue, or so the counselor can confront them with the absurdity and push them to act.

- ***Goodbye letter.*** This is a strategy designed to push the parent/family to act and to make the client realize that, no matter how bad things are now, the parent/family still loves and wants to help the client. I direct the parent (or other family members, if old enough) to write a letter to the client expressing their feelings and hopes for the client. As above, they cannot share this with the client until they return for the next session. In the next session, I first have the parent read the letter to me without the client present and help them revise it, if necessary, so that it has the necessary impact. Then, I invite the client in and orchestrate the session so that the parent stands facing the client, gets the client's undivided attention, and reads the letter to the client. The client is directed to sit, listen, and say nothing until the parent is done. This procedure needs to be dramatic and as emotionally laden as possible because it is supposed to upset the family and client enough to force them to act. So, it is important to NOT try to reduce the level of emotion or comfort people. In fact, as the counselor, your goal is to make everyone uncomfortable with their complacency. Thus, you may have to try to instigate more emotion if everyone is being under-reactive. Once the procedure is done, the counselor then asks the family if they want to prevent the impending tragedy and helps them plan how to do it.

Putting Parents in Charge. Once the counselor has the parents' attention and has generated some energy, it's time to get them to take action. The message to communicate to them is that the client can only change and get better if the parents do something to help her get better. The parents are in charge. As the counselor, I support the parents in asserting that they will not allow the behavior to continue, and that, if the client insists on continuing the behavior, they will do what they need to do to stop it. This leads to the next step.

Making a Plan. Now, it is time for the counselor to help the parents formulate a plan. The goal of the plan is to disrupt the client's potentially self-destructive behavior, ensure the client's safety, and get the client the appropriate type of intervention that will stabilize him.

- *Crisis Planning.* For crises such as suicidal ideation (without a plan or means), threats of hurting someone else, and issues of running away, the counselor has to help the parents plan for the crisis. This typically includes a "watch," which requires the parents to keep the client under their supervision, 24-7, line-of-sight; that is, the client cannot be left alone, even when sleeping. If the parents don't feel that they can maintain this level of supervision, then they may have to consider seeking help from an agency (mental health, probation, hospital) that can provide this level of oversight. Even if the parents can monitor the client to this extent, they need to have backup plans. For instance, they should clearly identify the mental health emergency services, law enforcement, or family court agencies that they will contact and have the phone numbers readily available. The counselor should also lay out the specific criteria that they will use to determine when it is time to seek additional help, and make the client aware of the plan.

- *Non-crisis Situations.* In situations that aren't emergencies, the counselor needs to aid the parents in deciding what reasonable steps they need to take to get help for the client. For instance, in the case of a client with a severe eating disorder, identifying treatment programs, scheduling an evaluation, and committing to follow through, even if the client claims things are better (remember, don't allow denial). The counselor then provides support and encouragement for the parents as they take action.

Divorce and Custody

In the previous chapter, I discussed custody issues in relation to the family-school system. Divorce and custody is one of the common issues with which family therapists are confronted.   Typically, the parents seek help from the counselor because of issues they are having with their child regarding the divorce or visitation. The important thing for the counselor to keep in mind is that conflict between the parents makes it more difficult for children to adjust to the divorce. The more conflict, the harder the adjustment. Usually this is related to the fact that the more adversarial the parents are, the more likely that they will draw the children into their conflict.

Although divorce is, unfortunately, all too common, it presents a unique situation to the family because it pushes it into a different developmental sub-process than the typical stages of development discussed in Chapter 2 (Figure 7-1).

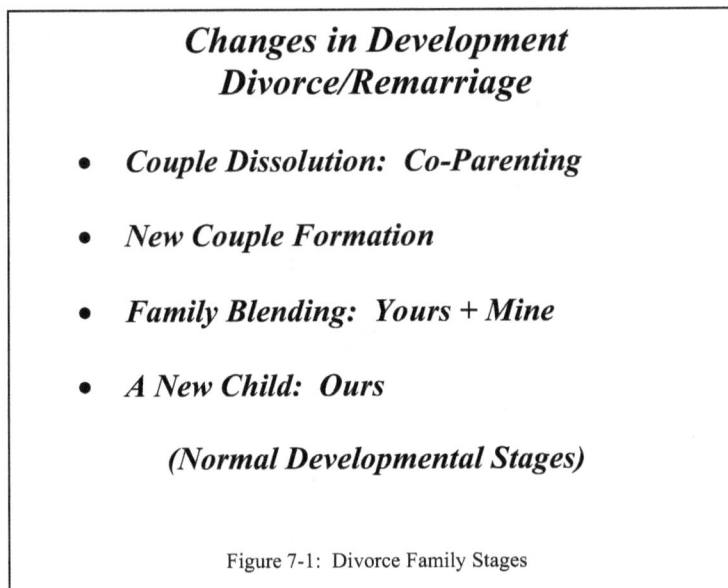

Changes in Development
Divorce/Remarriage

- *Couple Dissolution: Co-Parenting*

- *New Couple Formation*

- *Family Blending: Yours + Mine*

- *A New Child: Ours*

   (Normal Developmental Stages)

Figure 7-1: Divorce Family Stages

Couple Dissolution. When the decision to divorce becomes final, whether it is made by one spouse or is by mutual agreement, the family's normal developmental stages are disrupted by the couple dissolution sub-stage. The difficulty of this stage is that the couple subsystem is dissolving, while the family and the parent subsystem must remain intact for the children. Simultaneously, the individuals who are the couple must distance themselves from each other, while still remaining emotionally together and available as parents. They must do this to co-parent effectively, while at the same time not giving the children mixed messages about the fact that the marriage, not the family, is over. This obviously is a difficult task in any divorce situation, even an amicable one; and it is nearly impossible in situations in which the couple is in conflict. And this has to be accomplished during a time when the couple is working out the nitty gritty details of the divorce: finances, property, custody, support, and the like.

New Couple Formation. If one or both parents become involved in new relationships, the divorced family enters the stage of new couple formation, in which the adults are navigating the typical couple formation tasks, while at the same time dealing with the tasks of co-parenting, as well as the normal developmental stages of families with children. Children's loyalty is a big issue during this stage, especially if the divorce was initiated by the parent who is starting the new relationship, and the other parent is not in a relationship. The new couple is then faced with additional issues, such as children who do not want to see the relationship continue, or who may want to punish their parent who is in the relationship.

Family Blending. If the new couple succeeds in staying together in spite of the additional stress, then there are a number of tasks that need to be resolved related to forming a new nuclear family unit. Will the family live at one of the new spouse's current residences or move to an entirely new, neutral home? If one or both spouses have children from previous marriages, who will live with them? Will children reside with the new couple for any length of time, as in joint placement situations? Will the children come for visits with the step-parent present? Will they visit at the spouse's residence, or will the biological parent maintain a separate residence for visits? Will step-parents be involved in disciplining their stepchildren, or will only the biological parent be allowed to do this? Whose rules will be used? How will bedrooms be divided up among step-siblings? Will the step-parent be involved in co-parenting with the biological parents?

A New Child. Whether all of the above issues get resolved or not, if the new couple is of child bearing age, there is always the possibility that they will have children together. If this occurs and one or both parents have children from previous marriages, the status of the children may be an issue. Will the joint child of the couple (ours) be treated differently than each spouse's children? Sibling rivalry becomes an issue if stepchildren perceive the couple's biological child as being favored, even if this isn't the case. And, as is indicated in Figure 7-1, underlying all the unique issues raised by divorce and family blending, are the usual tasks and issues of family development.

Strategies for Helping the Family

I use the following protocol with parents who are going through a divorce.

- *Establish Realistic Expectations.* It has been my experience with parents who are seeking a divorce that they verbalize their desire that their children not be impacted by their decision. My response is that divorce always has an impact on children. The research is pretty clear on this point. Even children whose parents divorce amicably and have positive relationships following the divorce are affected by the breakup of the family. BUT, conflict, again, is the key: divorces that are less conflicted have less of a negative effect on children. So, I emphasize the need for the parents to establish clear boundaries around the adults' business and children's business, and to make a conscious effort to minimize conflict.

- ***Clarify the Subsystems***. One thing I have found useful with divorcing parents is to provide a realistic perspective of the subsystems involved in relation to the children. In other words, I explain that the divorce is between the couple, not the parents. For the children, their parents will always be their parents, so it's normal for them to want to see their parents together. The couple's business should be kept between the couple and not involve the children. The parents' business is the children, so it is critical that both parents remain involved with the children and figure out how to co-parent effectively. It is equally important that the parents not fight over the children or use the children as weapons in the couple's disputes. I continually differentiate couple from parents whenever discussing issues with either spouse.

- ***De-triangle the Children.*** Similarly, I try to block attempts by parents to pull children into a conflict triangle. This is a pretty straightforward task for me. I continually tell parents that their issues are not their children's issues. If I hear the parent describe a situation in which the children have been pulled into a triangle, I point this out and tell the parent that this is inappropriate and needs to stop. I then have the parent self-monitor their behavior in this respect.

- ***Obtain the Adults' Agreement to Respect the Children's Neutrality.*** Finally, I ask the spouses to agree to keep their kids neutral. Specifically, this means that if one of the children tries to involve themselves in the couple's business, the child is told that it's not his business. I also have the parents give the children permission to tell the parents not to involve the children in their business, if one or the other parent slips and complains about the other parent. The parents then have to agree to abide by this rule.

- ***Be Aware of the Children's World Views Regarding Loyalty.*** Children usually feel that they must remain loyal to their parents, particularly a parent who appears to be in a losing position in a divorce. Even in amicable divorces, it is not unusual for a child to think that she cannot like or accept a parent's new spouse if the parent becomes involved in a new relationship. So, even though it may be difficult, it is important for the divorced parents to encourage the children to be open to each other's new relationships (providing, of course, that these relationships are not harmful to the child in any way).

- ***Children Need Time.*** Divorce is a process that requires time for everyone to adjust to new circumstances. One thing I stress with parents is that they need to assume that every change related to the divorce will disrupt the children's sense of stability. Change disrupts every new level of homeostasis that develops. Therefore, parents need to be patient and allow the children to get used to new situations related to the divorce, such as a parent moving in to his own living quarters, a new relationship, or the children of a future step-parent. It is unrealistic for parents to expect their children to just accept such changes and get back to what used to be "normal" for them.

School Phobia

School phobia is a particularly difficult problem that confronts school helping professionals with some regularity, affecting from one to eight percent of school children (Clarizio & McCoy, 1976; Kahn & Narsten, 1962). Despite the relatively high prevalence of this problem, the literature on this disorder is limited (Morris & Kratochwill, 1991). The school phobic child often exhibits emotional distress frequently and excessively, is fearful, and verbalizes multiple physical complaints (Berg, Nichols, & Pritchard, 1969). Parents of these children feel frustrated, worried, and guilty about their children's emotional well-being, the possibility of impaired school achievement due to absences, and about doing the right thing to help their children (Clarizio & McCoy, 1976).

While there is general agreement about the symptoms of school phobia, there are differing views regarding causes and treatments of this problem. These range from psychodynamic perspectives which relate the phobic behavior to the mother-child relationship (Kelly, 1973) to behavioral models that view the child's behavior as produced by an aversive school setting combined with the positive reinforcement of parental attention that the child receives when the child stays at home (Scott, Cully, & Weissberg, 1996; Tahmisian & McReynolds, 1971). What the models have in common is that they relate the phobic behavior to interactions among the child, parents, and school. Because of this, it seems reasonable that a more systemic approach to dealing with the school phobic child might be effective.

A useful differentiation when approaching school phobia within a family systems framework is to separate children whose predominant symptom is anxiety from those whose primary symptom is opposition and attempts to control the responses of adults. This differentia-tion is important for determining the focal point of intervention. The intervention approach described in this article will focus on the first group described above, those exhibiting classic symptoms of school phobia. This approach has also been found to be useful with children in the second group, who exhibit signs of school refusal. However, the actual strategies used are slightly different. Strategic and structural therapy concepts that are important to consider when intervening with school phobic children are discussed in the next section.

Application of Structural-Strategic Concepts to School Phobia

Symptom Function. The first is the idea that the identified client--in this case, the child-- is merely the symptom-bearer for the family system. Thus, the initial hypothesis with the school phobic family is that the child's anxiety is related to at least one of the parents being highly anxious. The child's symptoms provide a focus for the parent, distracting the parent from his/her problem, and increasing the parent's feelings of being needed by the child.

Subsystems. Problems occur when boundaries are overly rigid (disengaged) or poorly defined (enmeshed) (Minuchin & Fishman, 1981). With school phobic families, it is not unusual for one parent, typically, the anxious one, to become overly involved with managing the child's problem, leading to enmeshment with the child, while the other parent is under-involved or disengaged from the child.

Hierarchy. The "normal" hierarchy is one in which the parents are on top in lateral positions followed by the children in chronological birth order. In the school phobic family, this hierarchical arrangement becomes disrupted by the anxiety symptoms of the identified client. The parents' acquiescence to the demands of the phobic child (e.g., allowing the child to miss school) eventually place the child above the parents in the family's hierarchy, making it difficult for the parents to parent.

Triangles. The process of triangulation serves as a means of reducing stress within the family system by involving a third family member in a problematic interaction between two other members of the family system. With school phobia cases, this often occurs within the family-school system when parents, frustrated by the demands of a symptomatic child, seek the assistance of school personnel. The situation becomes problematic when parents disagree with each other regarding management of the problem and seek support for their positions from school personnel, or when school personnel offer to manage the problem for the parents, thus reducing the parents' competence for dealing effectively with the problem in the future (Power & Bartholomew, 1987). An important task for the professional working with the school phobic family is to prevent such triangles from developing.

World View. This understanding of how the family views the problem will influence the form and direction of the intervention. The task of the practitioner working within a systems perspective is to understand the family's frame of reference and, as much as possible, work within it, taking the path of least resistance.

Family Systems Protocol for School Phobia

A standard procedure for intervening with school phobic families is outlined below. This protocol is based on clinical experience with a number of school phobic children for whom other interventions, such as behavior management and individual counseling failed. At least two of these children had been absent from school for an uninterrupted period of more than one month, two others reported symptoms of panic attacks, and all had physical complaints, including nausea and headaches. A feature of this approach that differentiates it from other approaches is that the focus is not on symptom remission. The assumption of this approach is that if the family system is functioning adequately, the identified client's symptoms will abate. Thus, unlike other interventions described in the literature (Scott, Cully, & Weissberg, 1996), this approach focuses on the family-school system rather than the child as the basic unit of intervention. The steps to this approach are outlined below.

Meet with as many members of the nuclear family as possible. At minimum, the school counselor should meet with the parents and identified client. However, it is helpful to include siblings, as this will provide a more complete picture of family interactions around the problem and increase the number of people who will generate solutions.

Have each member of the family define the problem. This is the typical problem definition phase of strategic family therapy. After obtaining this information, ask each individual in the family, including the identified client, to provide more detailed information, such as time of onset, precipitating events, who helps the client, who is responsible for getting the client to school, who is more understanding about the problem, and what, if anything, has worked in the past. The information obtained in this phase of the family meeting will help the school counseling professional develop initial hypotheses regarding the family's world view, subsystem interactions, triangles, and hierarchy.

Reframe the problem. Based on the information obtained in the interview, redefine the problem away from any psychopathological connotations to more manageable terms. For example, "That doesn't sound so much like a phobia to me as it does a child who is allowed to worry too much." This reframe transforms the illness to something that parents can relate to--worrying--and also communicates that the parents have some control over the symptom because they <u>allow</u> the child to engage in the worrying behavior.

Determine which parent is over-involved and which parent is under-involved with managing the child's phobic behavior. The general hypothesis that grows out of this is that the over-involved parent is the more anxious parent. This also provides information for organizing the intervention.

Have the parents articulate the basic goal of the intervention. The basic goal from the counselor's perspective is to get the child back in school as soon as possible. The counselor needs to challenge the parents to commit to this goal by emphasizing the importance of not allowing the child to miss school, followed by the pre-suppositional question (Gunnison, 1990),

"What do you want to happen?" This is also the point at which it is established that while symptom remission is a reasonable long-term goal, it is not an attainable short-term goal. In fact, if the parents make the expectation that their child be in school absolutely clear to the child, the child will develop appropriate coping mechanisms. This particular component of the intervention is similar to other flooding techniques used with school phobic children (Scott, Culley, & Weissberg, 1996).

Shift parental interaction patterns related to the identified client. Assign primary management of the problem to the under-involved parent, and involve the over-involved parent in different ways. The under-involved parent, then, becomes the person who deals with the child's complaints, gets the child to school, and contacts school personnel. The over-involved parent, rather than working with the child's problem directly, provides advice and support to the under-involved parent and spends quality time with the child that may or may not be associated with the phobic behavior. Goals of this intervention include equalizing parental responsibility for helping the child, interrupting the relationship between the more anxious over-involved parent and the symptomatic child, increasing contact between the under-involved parent and the child, and reducing the potential of sabotage by the over-involved parent who might feel that his or her position of "expert" regarding the child is being threatened.

Challenge the parents to commit to a united front. The parents must be in agreement regarding the course they will take to resolve the problem. If there is any disagreement, a triangle might develop with the identified client in which one parent becomes the child's defender and the other, the child's tormentor. The school counselor must listen for even the slightest hint of disagreements between the parents and challenge them on these points. The importance of the parents convincing the child that they mean what they say must also be stressed. In this way, the parents are placed in the executive position of the family, a hierarchically appropriate position within the strategic and structural models (Madanes, 1981; Minuchin & Fishman, 1981).

Incorporate interventions that address both the symptom and the cause of the school phobia. While symptom relief is not a primary goal, including interventions that may directly impact symptoms is perfectly reasonable. However, such interventions should also target the underlying cause of the phobia. Since a general hypothesis in this approach is that the child becomes symptomatic for the overly anxious parent, it is important to include that parent in the intervention. For instance, provide a relaxation training tape that the overly anxious parent will use to provide "instruction" for the identified client as a means for controlling the anxiety symptoms. On the outside, this intervention appears to be targeting the child's symptoms. However, the underlying goal of this intervention is for the parent to learn how to control his or her anxiety, which in turn will reduce the child's need to become symptomatic for the parent.

Involve other members of the family-school system. The school phobic child's problem not only impacts parents, but also siblings and school personnel. When appropriate and possible, include these subsystems in the interventions. An example of this is scheduling "special time" to read books or play games with non-symptomatic siblings to compensate for the inequitable attention being given to the symptomatic child. It is especially important to include teachers, school nurses, the school psychologist, and administrators, because of the potential for therapeutic sabotage if these professionals feel that their expertise and/or competence is being challenged. Thus, school personnel who are affected by the school phobic child's problem should at least be consulted, and the message should be communicated to them that their input was helpful, even if the information was not actually used. The goal of this strategy is to diminish the possibility that negative triangles will develop in which the school subsystems compete with each other for the parents' alliance. A case in which this approach was applied is described in the next section.

Case Study

Case Information

Steven S., an 11-year-old fifth grader, was referred by his school counselor because of the high level of anxiety he was experiencing. He complained about headaches and stomachaches before boarding the bus in the morning, and typically fought with his mother about attending school. He made frequent visits to the school nurse and demanded that his mother eat lunch with him because of his fear of vomiting during lunch. Steven related this particular fear to the fact that math class, his reported source of anxiety, immediately followed the lunch period. The symptoms had been present for approximately three months at the point that Steven was referred to a family counselor by the school counselor for treatment of school phobia.

Session 1

The family counselor entered the first session having hypothesized that Steven's anxiety was probably a symptom of his mother's anxiety, as she was the parent who attended the session with Steven. Information that supported this theory included Mrs. S.'s worrying about Steven since he was an infant because of his sickliness and the revelation that she had been diagnosed with multiple sclerosis, although she had been asymptomatic for a long period of time. It also became apparent that there was some friction between the family and the school--that Mrs. S. felt that the teachers in the school were biased against Steven because of his history of anxious behavior. At this point the reframe was used that Steven's symptoms didn't sound like school phobia, but instead simply like worrying too much. The counselor labeled Steven a worry wart, after which Mrs. S. stated that Steven was a lot like she. A second interview was scheduled with the entire nuclear family.

Commentary. In this first session, the working hypothesis was that Mrs. S. was enmeshed with Steven because of her primary role in managing his phobic behavior and her statement that Steven was like her. Noting this, the counselor requested that the entire family meet in order to include Mr. S. as a counterbalance for Mrs. S's over-involvement. The counselor also moved quickly to reframe the problem as "worrying" in order to remove the clinical label of "school phobia" that had been placed on Steven by the school counselor. This was done in a way that did not negate the school counselor's observations of Steven's behavior, but simply to emphasize the symptom of worrying.

Session 2

Information gathered in the second interview confirmed the world view of the family as being "us [the family] against them [the school]." Both Mr. and Mrs. S. were convinced that most of the teachers did not understand Steven's difficulties and that the principal sided with the teachers. While Steven was adamant regarding the "meanness" of his math teacher, Steven's older brother stated that the math teacher was strict but not particularly mean, and that the teacher was most strict with students who disrupted class. It was pointed out to Steven that he had little to worry about since he was a relatively quiet and well-behaved student. At the end of the session, Mr. S. formulated a plan to discuss the problem with the principal and to meet with Steven's math teacher. Mrs. S. was skeptical regarding the value of this plan, as she had met with Steven's teachers several times without any notable change in their behavior toward Steven.

Commentary. In the second session the counselor obtained information that suggested that the boundaries between the school and family subsystems were somewhat rigid (the "us vs. them" world view). It was also evident that Mr. S. had been quite under-involved in the situation and that Mrs. S. saw her position as the "competent" parent threatened when Mr. S. proposed that

he talk to Steven's teachers. The challenging of the parents by the counselor served more as an

indirect message that Steven had taken advantage of his parents' lack of agreement regarding the

problem. Input provided by Steven's brother helped to confirm this, as his experience with the

teacher in question had not been particularly bad. The encouragement of Mr. S. to pursue his

plan was simply a beginning point for increasing his involvement with the problem.

Session 3

The third session began with Mr. S. reporting that Steven had decided that his math

teacher wasn't as bad as he previously had reported. Because of this, Mr. S. had elected to not

follow through with his plan. Mrs. S. was somewhat amused, stating that Mr. S. tended to "make

a lot of noise" without any intention of following through on his decision to confront the

teachers. Since the parents did not seem to be in agreement about how to proceed, the question,

"What do you want Steven to do?" was posed. Mrs. S. was very clear about wanting Steven to

go to school without a fight and to eat lunch without her. Mr. S. stated he wanted Steven to feel

better but did not want to increase his anxiety by forcing him to do things against his will. These

statements confirmed that the parents disagreed over the handling of the problem. However,

Mrs. S. prevailed, and the parents tried to formulate a schedule for Steven to begin eating lunch

without his mother.

Their disagreement escalated at this point, Mrs. S. insisting that Steven begin eating

lunch by himself the following day, while Mr. S. made excuses about why they should give

Steven more time and not push him too quickly. Steven became more agitated during this

exchange, refusing to go along with any of his parents' plans. Finally, Mrs. S. stated her

frustration with the entire situation, particularly with the fact that she had been managing the problem almost entirely on her own. At this point, the counselor stated that as long as the parent's could not convince Steven that they agreed on how to solve the problem (united front) Steven would continue to be symptomatic (challenge). The counselor continued to challenge the discrepancies in the parents' expectations until they agreed on a decision to have Steven begin eating alone the next day. They then were instructed by the counselor to make their intentions clear to Steven.

Steven, who had been complaining during this process, unsuccessfully tried to manipulate his parents into backing down from their decision. When this appeared unlikely, he ran out of the room yelling that he was going to kill himself. Mr. S. was asked to retrieve Steven and did so, carrying him back into the room and sitting in front of the door to prevent another escape. While Mr. S. was shaken by this incident, Mrs. S. appeared unruffled, stating that this was a common tactic used by Steven to get his way. Despite this, a suicide plan was formulated that included locking Steven's BB gun and bow-and-arrow away, watching Steven constantly for the immediate period after the session, and making it clear to Steven that he would be hospitalized if his parents felt that he was actively suicidal.

Again, Mr. S. was wishy washy about this plan, worrying that Steven would feel punished. This was another sign of the parents' disagreement over how to deal with Steven, and again the counselor challenged them by stating that Steven would use his knowledge of their disagreement to remain symptomatic and keep his mother coming to school every day to take care of him during lunch. Mrs. S. became angry in response to this challenge and made it perfectly clear to Mr. S. and Steven that she would no longer go to lunch with Steven.

This matter settled, a new plan was put into place for managing Steven's phobic behavior. Mr. S. was put in charge of getting Steven to school and going to school should Steven become ill or have other phobic symptoms. It was made clear to Steven that this would mean that Mr. S.

would have to leave work and would lose pay for the time he missed. Since Mr. S., like Steven,

was a worry wart, Mr. S. was directed to spend 10 minutes each night with Steven, encouraging

him to worry about as many things as possible. Both parents were to forbid Steven from

worrying at all other times. Mrs. S. was to spend 30 minutes everynight with each of her sons

(individually) doing something fun (playing games, doing puzzles, reading together). Mr. and

Mrs. S. were also directed to spend at least 10 minutes each night after the children had gone to

bed discussing how the day went with Steven and making any changes they felt were necessary

in their plans for the next day.

As the session ended, the counselor stressed that Steven probably would remain

symptomatic for some time and that this in itself was not important. The parents' goal was to get

Steven functioning on his own in school, and once this was accomplished, he would figure out

how to cope with his worrying. It was also emphasized that this could only happen if the parents

convinced Steven that they would stick to their plan. An appointment was scheduled for three

weeks later, with the agreement that the family would be seen sooner only if Steven was in crisis.

Commentary. The pivotal third session more fully illuminated the family dynamics

connected with Steven's phobic behavior. First, Steven's manipulations suggested that his

behavior allowed him to exert some control over his parents, raising him above them in the

hierarchy, and allowed him to maintain the enmeshed relationship with his mother. Second, Mr.

S's reaction to Steven indicated that he was actually the more anxious parent and that his

noninvolvement with the problem may have been a way he avoided his own anxiety. Third, Mrs.

S. signaled that she was ready to be relieved of the primary responsibility for managing the

problem.

This data was used in the series of strategies employed by the counselor. Mr. S. was the parent who was asked to retrieve Steven when he left the room, moving primary management to the father. Mr. S.'s involvement was increased further by putting him in charge of the most difficult management tasks--getting Steven to school and dealing with Steven's behavior in school. Mrs. S. was not allowed to remove herself completely from the situation. Instead, her involvement was changed to more pleasant tasks that were not connected to direct management of the problem, and that allowed her to begin enjoying her interactions with Steven once again. Finally, the boundaries between the parent and child subsystems were more clearly defined through the counselor's challenges to the parents to form a united front in dealing with Steven. This served as a message to Steven that he no longer could manipulate his mother into supporting his symptoms. Thus, at the end of the intervention, the parents and Steven had been moved back to their respective appropriate positions in the family hierarchy; Steven had been removed from the parent subsystem and placed back into the child subsystem; and the triangle involving Steven, mom, and dad had been shifted by placing mom and dad in an alliance to help Steven.

Session 4

In the fourth and final appointment, Steven reported that he was no longer as worried as before, that he had stopped feeling nauseous at lunchtime, and that he had discovered that his math teacher wasn't as mean as he had previously thought. The parents reported that Steven had begun eating lunch without his mother the day after the third session and had done so ever since. The fighting and complaining about attending school in the morning also had ceased shortly after the third session. Mr. S. reported that Steven had been unable to worry on purpose after the third or fourth repetition of this exercise, leading to the parents deciding to forego additional sessions unless Steven began worrying too much again. Mrs. S. particularly enjoyed her quality time with the boys in the evening, and also appreciated not being the "bad guy" with Steven.

The final component of the intervention was to encourage the parents to acknowledge each other's competence in dealing with the situation effectively, and to have them reward each other. Each parent was encouraged in a humorous way to name several desirable rewards. They eventually agreed that a "date" would be most desirable to both of them, and Mr. S. proceeded to formally ask Mrs. S. out. The parents planned their date, including babysitting arrangements, in the session. The session concluded with the parents' competence being supported by the counselor and with an agreement that future sessions would be scheduled only if needed.

Follow-up

In a follow-up phone contact two months after the final session (just before the end of the school year), Mrs. S. reported no re-occurrence of the phobic behavior. A second follow-up in the fall of the following school year also showed no re-emergence of the phobic behavior. Finally, information provided by Mrs. S. two years after the completion of therapy indicated that there had been no re-emergence of the presenting problem and no symptom substitution, a therapeutic outcome that is considered clinically significant (Jacobson, 1995).

Implications for School Counseling Professionals

The family systems model for dealing with school phobia offers an alternative way of thinking about this problem and new options for interventions. Systems conceptualizations help illuminate the complicated inter-relationships among factors that impact problems encountered within the school setting. Thus, the application of such models is useful for understanding factors that need to be addressed in order to impact a child's presenting problem, and factors that may prevent change from occurring. In addition, this approach aids in decreasing the possibility of institutional triangulation which is common when dealing with such family-focused problems as school phobia and school refusal.

While family systems approaches would seem to be one of the interventions of choice with a disorder like school phobia, a number of factors contribute to the reluctance of school practitioners to work with families. First, school counselors, psychologists and social workers are public servants, making it difficult to "take the initiative" (Whitaker & Bumberry, 1988) with parents, in getting them to accept a family focus for a child's difficulties. Second, the school setting itself complicates systems-oriented counseling, as it presents the counselor with several more systemic components--teachers, administrators, social service agencies--that enlarge the nuclear family system. Third, these other components of the larger family-school system unwittingly sabotage family counseling by viewing the child as the focal point of social, emotional, and academic difficulties. In other words, the emphasis of these "others" is "fix the child," without paying attention to how the child's difficulties are embedded in the larger systemic context. Thus, the school counseling professional who chooses to work within a systems framework needs to be critically aware of the many elements of the family-school system that impact the child's problem. Finally, most school counseling professionals do not receive adequate enough practical training in family counseling as part of their graduate programs to allow them to be proficient in the use of these approaches.

Summary

The family systems approach to school phobia described in this chapter provides a reasonable alternative for understanding and intervening with a relatively common school problem within an ecological perspective. This solution-focused short-term intervention facilitates the use of family resources and the development of parental competencies for effectively dealing with this problem. In short, this approach expands the repertoire of interventions of counseling providers beyond the typical individual counseling and behavioral methods used.

Chapter 8

Introduction to Couples Counseling

Chapter Overview

In this chapter you will:

- Contrast couples counseling with family counseling.

- Understand issues and dynamics that are prevalent in couple conflicts.

- Develop a framework for counseling couples.

A Different Animal

The couple presents a unique challenge to counselors, because when two individuals come together, the system they create as a couple is a whole new organism. One of the big mistakes made by counselors that are inexperienced with couples work, is that they approach counseling as if they are interacting with two individuals. While each partner may have individual issues that impact the couple, the couple responds to counseling in different ways than does each spouse as an individual. This is related to the unique dynamics between the couple that do not exist with each partner as an individual. Some common dynamics of couples are discussed below.

The Role of Power

The dynamics of power within the couple are a primary element of the couple interactions and, when there are problems, of the struggle between the partners. On the functional end of the continuum, where there are not major issues, power is played out in the way the partners adopt their ways of operating as a couple. Who does the laundry? Who pays the bills? Who cooks? Who mows the lawn? At the extreme dysfunctional end of the continuum are grotesque manifestations of domineering behavior and spousal abuse. One spouse completely controls money in the family and uses this as a means of getting the other spouse to conform to his wishes. One spouse belittles and bullies the other spouse, breaking down their emotional defenses and undermining their self-esteem. One spouse physically dominates and abuses the other spouse. In between, there are many nuances on how power is distributed between the partners in reasonable or unreasonable ways.

One of the main battlegrounds of power is finances. How the couple unintentionally or intentionally manages the finances of the couple affects the power distribution. In fact, the number one reason that marriages end is due to conflicts over finances (Dew, Britt, & Huston, 2012). Money is power. If one spouse feels that he or she is not getting their fair share of the money in the household, that's a problem. If one spouse thinks that the other is misspending money, that's a problem. If a spouse feels that they have to sneak to spend money, that's a problem. I have seen these situations play out over and over in my practice. And it's the spouse that feels that they have little or no control of the money that feels powerless, abused, downtrodden, and dissatisfied.

The other common area where power dynamics are played out is when the couple has children. Here a power struggle can be more subtle, because it is not always the spouse that seems to be in control that has the power with the children. One parent may seem to be the one who is effective with discipline because when children misbehave, he responds in a verbally or physically aggressive manner that frightens them into submission. But the other spouse may have more power by being the nurturing, supportive parent who quietly undermines the other spouse. For example, dad may keep the kids in line when he's home by yelling and threatening, but when he's not home, mom gives the children permission to disobey dad's directives. Soon, they learn to go to mom when they want anything and simply avoid dad. Mom ends up being the more influential of the two parents, thus gaining power in their spousal relationship without dad even being aware of what has occurred.

Understanding the power dynamics when a couple begins counseling is critical to understanding the severity of the problem and the potential for appropriate resolution. And by appropriate resolution, I do not mean that the spouses maintain the couple. In some situations, the best resolution is for the couple to end their relationship. I do not necessarily advocate for this, but in extreme situations, where one spouse is incorrigibly a bully there may be no better alternative.

The Role of Development

As was discussed in Chapter 2, understanding the developmental issues impacting a family is necessary in order to understand if some of the issues are due to difficulties with transitioning to a new stage, or if they are manifestations of more significant issues. With the couple, the first stage of family development, Couple Formation, is a critical one. Let's review the tasks of that stage.

Redefining boundaries. This needs to occur with both friends and family. Minuchin (1991) pointed out that when a couple comes together, "it changes everything." The individuals that comprise the couple must change their primary loyalties from their families of origin to the couple. That is not to say that they give up their loyalty to their families, just that their loyalty to each other must be more important. This means that they establish boundaries with their families that make it clear that their priority is the couple. I have seen couples where one of the primary complaints is that one spouse did not defend the other against a criticism from the spouse's parents. If you want to see an angry wife, just watch when her mother-in-law criticizes her

---

Tasks of Couple Formation

- **Redefining Boundaries**
    - ○ **Which spouse's family are you closer to?**
    - ○ **Time with the family and friends vs time as a couple.**

- **Establishing roles in the home mechanics.**
    - ○ **Who does what?**

- **Intimacy and Sexuality**
    - ○ **Physical affection**
    - ○ **Preferred practices, frequency, satisfaction.**

- **Finances**
    - ○ **Joint vs individual accounts.**
    - ○ **Who pays what?**
    - ○ **Who gets spending money?**

- **Conflict Resolution**
    - ○ **Fight or flight?**

Figure 8-1: Couple Formation Tasks

---

cooking, and the wife's spouse goes along with the mother, or even agrees with her. The task of the spouse is to defend their wife, no matter what they really think of her cooking. Allowing the mother to criticize the wife without defending her, allows the mother to intrude into the couple subsystem. The spouse failed to define the boundary by not defending the wife, and this is also a failure in loyalty to her.

Similarly, boundaries need to be defined with friends and siblings. Where it might have been okay for one partner to go out five nights a week with friends or siblings before the couple was together, that's not going to work after the couple is together, if they want their relationship to be successful.   In addition, the couple needs its space and "alone" time. It's not acceptable for friends or family to drop by the couple's residence unannounced whenever they feel the urge.

Again, the couple needs to define for itself and for others what is acceptable related to relationships outside the couple.

Establishing roles in home mechanics. This relates to some of the power dynamics discussed previously. Couples gradually define their roles in the everyday home activities. This includes which partner does specific chores, whether or not they take turns doing various chores, and who is better or more skilled at getting certain things done. This is one of the areas in which the complementarity of the couple comes into play: One partner does more of one thing and the other does less, until this becomes established as the couple's state of homeostasis. It is as simple as one spouse doing more of the cooking, while the other does more of the lawn mowing. The important thing to keep in mind is that this works if both partners are satisfied with their roles. But if one feels that he/she is being taken advantage of or underappreciated, there will be conflict.

Intimacy and sexuality. Of course, at the beginning of a relationship, this isn't something that couples necessarily think about, especially if there is a strong physical/sexual attraction between the partners. But after the honeymoon period is over, how affection and intimacy is expressed becomes more important. If one partner is a "huggy bunny" and the other is an "only necessary contact" person, this can cause conflict. The more affectionate partner may feel that his/her needs are not being met, or the less affectionate partner might feel intruded upon by the other's demands for physical contact. If one spouse dislikes PDA's (public displays of affection), while the other wants to hold hands, hug and kiss anyplace, this may cause tension in the relationship.

Sexuality is another area in which the couple needs to find balance that is mutually satisfying. One simple compromise is frequency of sexual relations. If one spouse enjoys frequent sex and the other is satisfied with occasional relations, this can engender feelings of being neglected in the first case, and pressured in the second. Beyond this, there are things like the types of sexual practices each partner likes or dislikes, the level of spontaneity, and even the time of day and day of the week that each spouse prefers.

The important thing to keep in mind is that disagreements in these areas need to be resolved, whether it is done implicitly by partners gradually accommodating each other, or intentionally through discussion and negotiation. But it needs to be worked out in some way if either of the spouses feels dissatisfied or upset in this area.

Finances. The role of money and finances was discussed above in relation to the power dynamic in relationships. In addition to that, there are some concrete decisions that need to be made related to managing money. These include who takes care of the actual activity of paying bills, how accounts are established, and if each spouse has "their own" pool of money for personal expenses. There are many ways that couples work this out in a manner that is satisfactory to each partner. Some keep a central joint account for common living expenses to which each partner contributes a percentage of their income. Some keep separate accounts, and agree on the bills for which each spouse will be responsible. This only becomes a problem if one spouse feels that they are being taken advantage of, or that the other isn't paying their fair share. This is one of the common conflicts I help couples work through in counseling.

Conflict resolution. It is not unusual for individuals to enter a relationship so in love and happy that they think that they will never ever argue or disagree with one another. Then reality hits, and they have their first spat. The important thing isn't whether or not a couple has conflict; almost all will. The important thing is how the couple fights and how they resolve disagreements. Conflict resolution styles may exacerbate and escalate a minor disagreement.

For instance, if one spouse is an "approacher" who needs to deal with the conflict and try to resolve it immediately, and the other is an avoider, who prefers to withdraw and allow things to cool down, this creates a secondary, "meta-conflict" that centers on whose style of conflict resolution is the one that the couple will use. If both partners have a "let it all hang out style," while this might be similar and congruent, it may not be a constructive way to resolve disagreements. Thus, this is a very important area that couples often intentionally need to negotiate to arrive at a mutually agreeable way to handle conflict. If spouses have incongruent ways of dealing with conflict and don't try to find an effective way to do so, this becomes a problem area.

Couple Formation developmental tasks provide the foundation for the stability of the relationship, but there are other developmental stages that present at-risk challenges to the couple. In particular, tasks during the First Child, Families with Adolescents, and Parent Separation from Children stages present critical tasks that can destabilize the couple relationship.

The First Child. One of the critical tasks during this stage is balancing the mother's focus on and attachment to the new baby with the father's/non-pregnant same-sex spouse's need to feel included as a parent, and the couple's need to maintain connection and intimacy. This is analogous to the juggler that has to keep several plates spinning on poles at the same time. If he fails to pay attention to each plate equally, one or more will crash to the ground.

With the birth of the first child, it is normal and necessary for the mother's attention to be focused almost exclusively on the baby. At the same time, the mother needs to allow the father/non-pregnant same-sex spouse, to form an attachment and have a role with the child. In other words, the non-pregnant parent needs to feel needed in some way and not marginalized. Just as important is the need for the spouses to maintain some sense of "couplehood" at a time when the focus of their relationship is shifting to parenthood. And all of this needs to be accomplished with the finite amount of time available being stretched to meet all of these needs. Not an easy task, to say the least.

However, failure to at least partially accomplish these tasks may have consequences ranging in severity from mild to dire. This is the stage in which Bowen (1993) asserted that triangulation can begin to impact the couple relationship. If the non-pregnant spouse feels excluded from the parent relationship with the child, and that their emotional needs as a spouse are not being met, they may seek to get their needs met by someone or something else through an affair, friends, work, or other activities. This serves to push the mother and child closer together and the spouses farther apart, and a self-defeating cycle gets established. This situation may be a short-term transitional problem that will resolve itself as the child gets older and the non-pregnant spouse becomes involved with the child in a different way (playing with them, coaching, helping with schoolwork). However, if the marginalization of the spouse is extreme, coupled with a very, very close mother-child relationship, the couple relationship may be endangered and eventually fail.

Families with Adolescents. This is another particularly stressful period for the couple. Teenage children (and, now, tweens) present particular challenges to parents' abilities to agree on discipline, coordinate with each other, and negotiate. This is further impacted by the natural tendencies of teens to play one parent off of the other, in order to get what the teen wants, and to challenge parents. Disagreements between parents can spill over into the couple relationship, if one parent begins to feel disrespected or undermined by the other parent. This gets translated to the couple as a struggle over power in the relationship, and may lead to conflict in other couple areas, such as finances. In my own practice, this is one of the major reasons that parents end up seeking counseling for their teenage child, but end up in counseling as parents/couples.

Parent Separation from Children. Tasks during this stage pose the most serious threats

to the couple relationship. It is the stage where "the chickens come home to roost" if the couple

has failed to maintain any sense of couplehood during the period in which they have been

primarily focused on being parents. With children growing up and leaving home for college,

work, the military, etc., the parents are now faced with primarily being a couple once again. If

they have lost their sense of couplehood, and now lose their roles as parents, the spouses are left

drifting, trying to figure out how they fit with each other. As discussed in Chapter 1, there are

many potential outcomes during this stage.

- Couple reformation, where the spouses get reacquainted and redefine their relationship at
  this more mature stage of their lives.

- Roommates, where they are friends, live together, and do some things together, but
  primarily live separate lives.

- Peaceful coexistence, which occurs when the spouses don't like each other but live
  together for financial, religious, or other reasons, and lead completely separate lives.

- Couple dissolution, where the relationship is ended by one or both spouses through
  separation or divorce.

This is the other primary reason that I see couples, and it is the stage in which there is a

greater probability that the couple will divorce.

Family of Origin Patterns

As was discussed in Chapter 1, Bowen (1993) believed that the patterns of the family of

origin, to which children are exposed and part of, are repeated with each successive generation of

the family. While the primary focus of his theory is the interaction between fusion and differentiation, the practical expressions of this interplay are seen in many everyday family situations. If these patterns are dysfunctional and not changed intentionally, they will be subsequently passed on to the next generation, and the dysfunctional pattern will continue, if not become worse. This is what Bowen called the multigenerational transmission process (Bowen, 1993).

It is important for the family counselor to help the couple identify the patterns of their families of origin, good, bad or indifferent. There are different methods for doing this, including constructing a genogram of family of origin relationships with the couple, and having the couple "tell the story" of their families of origin. Once the relationships, interaction styles, and patterns of fusion and differentiation are mapped out, the couple has a tool for examining their own relationship and interaction style, and how this impacts their children, if they have them. This is typically an eye-opener, as many children enter adulthood thinking that they aren't going to be like their parents, only to discover that they are replicating the same parental behaviors and even saying the same things that they experienced with their parents. I will discuss this in more detail in the next section.

Counseling Couples

My approach to counseling couples is an integration of structural-strategic and Bowenian ideas. I have developed a practical and relatively simple style for helping couples deal with relationship issues. It doesn't adhere to any one theoretical framework but incorporates elements of several counseling approaches that I have found useful.

Components of Couples Counseling

- Establish the couple as the unit of intervention, NOT the individual.

- Establish your position as neutral consultant in charge of the session.

- Assess the stability of the relationship.

- Assess the severity of conflict.

- Identify strengths and areas of agreement.

- Map the family of origin patterns.

- Frame current issues in the context of ongoing family of origin patterns.

- Use homework to shift dysfunctional patterns and improve quality of the relationship.

- Provide concrete feedback on progress.

- Know when the ship is sinking.

Figure 8-2: Elements of Couples Counseling

The Unit of Intervention and the Counselor's Position

Couples typically enter counseling due to conflicts that cause a high level of distress for one or both spouses. Thus, they are looking for immediate relief of that distress as individuals, and will seek out the counselor for their own emotional relief versus the problem with the couple dynamics. It is important for you, as the counselor, to make it clear that you are working with the spouses only as a couple, and that you will remain neutral in regards to individual issues and conflicts. If one spouse is seeking individual counseling, he/she will have to do this with another counselor. This is the only way that a counselor can be effective with the couple: Both spouses need to view the counselor as not taking sides. This is sometimes frustrating to the individual spouse, especially if one spouse is feeling particularly wronged or victimized. But failure to establish these boundaries will undermine the counselor's effectiveness.

A second boundary that needs to be established is how confidentiality will be observed. The client in couples counseling is *the couple*, not the individuals. Confidentiality, then, exists for the couple in relation to external subsystems. It does not exist within the couple subsystem. This means that, if one spouse discloses something to me individually, I will ask them to discuss this in the couple session, and make it clear that if they don't, I have to. Thus, if one spouse calls me in between sessions to discuss a counseling-related issue, I remind them about this rule, and give them the option of waiting until the next session. If they insist on continuing the conversation, then I have to bring up the phone call and information at the next session.

It is important to keep in mind that you as the counselor cannot be a part of a secret that one spouse is keeping from the other. By keeping a secret, you become an ally of one spouse against the other, and you lose your neutrality and effectiveness as the counselor of the couple. This rule is not going to make people happy, but your job is not to make the spouses happy. It is to help the couple resolve conflicts and function better.

Stability of the Relationship and Level of Conflict

This is very important to establish in the first session. My experience over the years is that only about 50 to 60 percent of couples enter counseling with both spouses intending to stay together. With the other 40 to 50 percent of couples, one or both spouses have already decided that the relationship is over. In order to know what kind of counseling I am doing (marriage vs. divorce counseling) I need to know where the couple stands in this respect. I do this in two ways, with the couple together and with each spouse separately. My questions are very intentional.

Questions for the couple. Early in the first session, after each spouse states their definition of their issues, I ask the following questions.

- Do you love each other? The typical immediate response from most couples is, yes. But after the kneejerk response, it is not unusual for one spouse to qualify their answer with something like, "…but not in the same way as when we were first together."

- Do you like each other? This is a more loaded question, especially with high conflict couples. "Liking" implies acceptance, appreciation, positive regard, and agreement. "Loving" is a statement of emotional connection.

I have met with many spouses who tell me they love each other, but can't stand many things about the other spouse. Or, they tell me that they love each other, but based on my observations of them, it is clear that they don't like each other. It's my job to point this out to them, and not pretend that "love conquers all." It is easier to have a relationship if you like someone and enjoy and value your time with them, versus loving them and experiencing distress whenever you are together.

Questions for the Individual Spouses. Later in the first session or in the second session, I see each spouse separately for 15 to 30 minutes to explore their perceptions of the relationship and the possibility of success. I usually do this with couples that are experiencing significant and chronic conflict, where the relationship appears to be endangered. I also start out these individual sessions informing each spouse that there can be no secrets in the couples counseling. Anything they disclose in this session will be brought up in the follow-up couple session   Important questions for the couple:

- Is your suitcase packed? Do you have one foot out the door, or have you left already and are heading down the road? I ask these questions when it appears that one or both spouses are very dissatisfied or actually making statements about leaving the relationship.

- What will it take for you to unpack the suitcase? What will it take for you to pull your foot in the door? I want to know if the spouse has made a decision to leave, or is open to the possibility that things can improve and the relationship be salvaged. If a spouse indicates no hope or possibility of repair, then I ask the next question.

- Am I doing marital counseling or divorce counseling? I want each spouse to clearly state what their goal is for the counseling. If there is a discrepancy between their statements, that is, one spouse responds, "divorce" and the other, "marital," then it is my responsibility to inform the spouse who has already decided on divorce that he/she needs to be honest with their spouse.

- On a one to 10 scale, one being "unrepairable" and 10 being "wonderful," how bad are things? Are you hopeful that things can get better? Are you willing to work and do things that might be out of your comfort zone? I want to know if each spouse thinks that counseling can help and is committed to working on the relationship. If one or both are hopeless, or have already given up, that provides me with guidance for how I will approach the counseling process. It doesn't mean that I will just give up and tell them that this is a hopeless situation. It simply gives me direction on strategies that I might use to elicit commitment and hope. However, at the extreme, I may recommend that we begin talking about how to end the relationship in the least destructive way possible.

Strengths

Up to this point we've been negative, negative, negative, and I don't want to give the impression that that's how couple counseling goes. It is important to explore what the couple identifies as strengths, both as a couple and as individuals. So, I ask questions that focus on positive aspects of their relationship.

- How did you two meet?

- What did you find attractive about each other?

- What are some helpful things he/she does for you?

- What is a memorable experience you had together?

- What is his/her best trait?

My goal in asking these types of questions is to interrupt the negative pattern or set that the couple has settled into. When a couple has been in conflict or distressed for an extended period of time, it is easy for them to lose sight of the positive aspects of their relationship. For most couples, except for those that are in severe and destructive conflict, those positive aspects are still there. They have just been minimized by the ongoing stress. By eliciting a discussion of the positives, I am simply trying to change the figure-ground experience of the couple and bring the positives to the forefront, as a means of interrupting the negative pattern. This in and of itself, can have a powerful positive impact on a couple.

Mapping Family of Origin Patterns

I use the second counseling session to map the family of origin patterns, using the genogram method developed by McGoldrick (McGoldrick, Gerson, & Shellenberger, 1999). This is a more detailed approach than a simple genogram that displays family members and the biological and family connections. McGoldrick's approach maps the quality of relationships (distant/close) and conflicts. It also displays family communication patterns and conflict styles. Thus, in addition to the usual questions about biological relationships, marriages and divorces, and health information, the counselor asks the following questions.

- What was your relationship like with your mother and father when you were growing up? Who were you closer to? Who were you less close to, or distant from? If they are still alive, what are your relationships like now?

- What were your relationships like with your siblings when you were growing up? Now?

- What did you observe about your parents' way of dealing with disagreements with each other? Did they talk, yell, stop talking, etc.? Did they resolve disagreements, or did they just leave them unresolved? How do they behave now when they disagree?

- How did you and your siblings argue/fight? How did you resolve disagreements? Did you leave them unresolved?

- How would you describe your family's connection? Were you a close family, or did everyone just do their own thing? How would you describe this with your children?

- Did your parents pay attention to how you did in school? What were their expectations? How involved did they get with monitoring your performance and helping you? What do you do now with your children?

- Did your parents attend most of your school events, sporting events, etc.? Did they care how you did on things? Did they force you to get involved in activities? What about you with your children?

Genogram Family Dynamics Symbols

----------------   **Dashes between 2 members indicate distant relationship.**

Double solid line indicates close relationship.
Triple line indicates closer relationship.

Divided line indicates disengagement between 2 members.

Zigzag line indicates conflict between 2 members.

Example

Close relationship.

Distant, disengaged relationship.

Conflicted relationship.

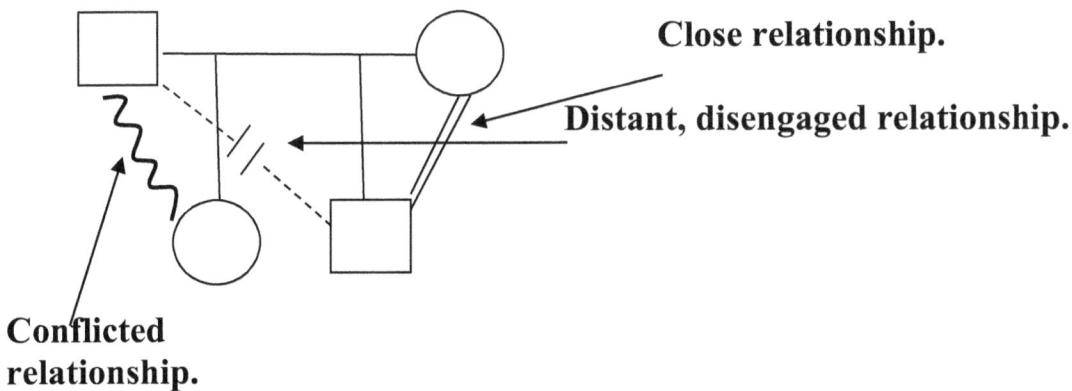

Figure 8-3: Genogram Symbols for Family Dynamics

Framing Issues in the Context of FoO Patterns

The counselor records this information on the genogram, either by just writing descriptions or using symbols that reflect various dynamics (McGoldrick, Gerson, & Shellenberger, 1999). Examples are shown in Figure 8-3.

Once completed, the genogram becomes the reference tool to use when discussing current issues of the couple and how this is related to the past patterns in the family of origin. This is when the counselor adopts the consultant/coach role. The goal is to illuminate the dysfunctional patterns that the couple continues to repeat, and to educate them on the importance of changing these to more functional patterns.

Example

Wife:	Anytime I bring up the fact that he doesn't defend me with his mother, he just gets quiet and goes to another room.
Husband:	I don't know what to say. She gets so loud when she's mad.
Counselor:	Let's look at what you said about what happened when your parents argued, Brendon. From what you said, when your mom started arguing with your dad, he would say nothing and go to the garage and drink.
Husband:	Well I'm not drinking.
Counselor:	No, but you are going to your version of the garage. And when you do this, what happens?
Husband:	Jennifer raises her voice and tries to get me to respond.
Counselor:	Which sounds like what?
Husband:	My mother.
Counselor:	You told me that that didn't work for your parents. They ended up splitting up. How's it working for you two?
Couple:	It's not.
Counselor:	Let's think about how to change this so it works.

Thus, as each ongoing dysfunctional pattern is described, I take the couple through this process of analysis, self-reflection, and problem solving, helping them intentionally formulate ways to shift to more functional patterns.

Sometimes the issue is not dysfunctional patterns, but differences in the family of origin experiences of the spouses. Mapping the family patterns helps the spouses realize that, although their family experiences were different, both families had ways of operating that were functional. For instance, one spouse may have grown up in a family in which the children had input into family decisions, while the other spouse grew up in a family in which parents made all the decisions and simply informed the children. This can contribute to a spousal conflict if the spouse from the parent-directed family makes decisions for the couple without seeking input. The other spouse is then placed in an infantile or submissive position in the relationship, which creates an imbalance in the power distribution. In this case, by illuminating how this pattern reflects the different family experiences, the spouses can decide on how to accommodate each other and develop a more functional way to make decisions that works for both spouses. This rebalances the power distribution and equalizes the spouses' positions in their relationship.

Homework

The use of homework or directives is a standard component of the couple counseling process, as it is when working with the entire family. I have two primary goals for homework assignments.

- To interrupt or shift dysfunctional patterns.
- To re-establish or introduce constructive/benevolent/positive interactions into the couple relationship.

Hence, any homework assignment usually has at least two directives to meet these goals.

The actual process of assigning homework is similar to the one outlined in Chapter 5.

Homework Protocol

- Address both spouses.

- Explain the rationale for the assignment.

- Give each spouse a task.

- Separating the spouses for different components of the assignment is acceptable if necessary to the success of the assignment.

- When the assigning is completed, check with each spouse to review his or her tasks.

- Always begin subsequent sessions with a feedback about the homework.

Figure 8-4: Guidelines for Assigning Homework

As I stated above, I try to incorporate at least one assignment that targets a specific area of conflict or dysfunctional pattern, and a second assignment that focuses on the positive interactions or sense of couple-hood. Since the former depends more on the specific problems and family of origin dynamics, it is difficult to provide standard assignments that can be modified for specific couple situations. However, there are more standard interventions that can be used for couple-hood assignments. As always, the actual assignment depends on the couple's resources, including finances, available time, and support system, if the couple has children. It also depends on how negative and chronic the issues have been for the couple. Some rules of thumb:

- Start small, so the couple has opportunities to be successful.

- For high conflict couples, early assignments should require less emotional involvement and avoid competition or situations involving choices. These can create conflict.

- For couples who have not been intimate or affectionate for an extended period of time, start with simple, low level exchanges of affection.

- As time goes on and the couple is experiencing success and satisfaction, challenge the spouses to have more constructive interactions that require more commitment.

- Build in reward experiences. Make sure that each spouse acknowledges and appreciates the other.

Some examples are provided below.

Couple time. This can be as simple as going for a walk together and as complicated as a weekend away. Couples with limited resources can do things like scheduling "adult" time together at home where they do something fun, like playing a game, going for walks, cooking together, or doing hobbies. If they have children, then these things need to be done when the children are asleep, or being watched by another family member.

A date night or date day is an alternative if the couple has the financial means. This can include things like going out for coffee or dessert, dinner and a movie, or other recreational activities. If the couple is having great difficulty being together, then going out with friends or family members is acceptable at first. But the goal is for the couple to eventually be able to enjoy time together without having to be with other people.

More complicated or expensive activities include a night or weekend trip that allows the couple to be on their own without interruptions of work or family. This requires substantially more financial and support system resources, especially if the couple needs to arrange for child care. It also requires that the spouses are at a point where they desire to spend an extended amount of time with each other.

Surprises. These types of assignments are especially important when spouses feel taken for granted or unappreciated. Part of the counselor's job is to have each spouse articulate things they like and times that the other spouse has surprised them in some way. The types of things I've seen people reveal range from gifts of flowers, candy, jewelry, tools; breakfast in bed; being allowed to "sleep in;" doing a house chore for the spouse (vacuuming, dishes, laundry); and a surprise outing. With these types of assignments, I see each spouse separately to plan the surprises, so it will really be a surprise.

Affection and intimacy. This is one of the areas that is usually the first to go when there are couple issues. It also naturally decreases when the couple gets focused on parent duties. Gradually, hugging, holding hands, kissing, and caressing just seem to slip away, and with it, sexual intimacy. This group of interventions focuses on helping the couple get back in touch with their honeymoon period. The assignments are simple but risky, and can have a powerful impact if the spouses' emotional connection is still intact. They include in order of intensity and risk:

- Holding hands or hugging while watching television or a movie.

- Hugging without being asked or shamed into it.

- Holding hands when walking together.

- Intentional, purposeful hugging and kissing goodnight and goodbye before going to work.

- Going parking.

- Giving each other massages.

- Sexual relations, elicited by the spouse who is more passive.

It is not unusual for one spouse to be more physically affectionate and the other to be more reserved. Part of the purpose of these interventions is to re-establish the physical bond that typically exists at the beginning of relationships, when the couple became intimately connected. In addition, these help to rebalance the complementarity between the spouses, so that one spouse is not always the one soliciting physical contact and affection. I frequently ask the more reserved, less affectionate spouse to take the role of initiator for this reason.

Providing Feedback

It is very important to provide couples with feedback on their progress, as they move through the counseling process. For me, this starts with the assessment of their strengths and the severity of their problems. I let couples know how I think they compare to the findings of research on couples, and to my own pool of experience with couples. When I do this, I try as much as possible to highlight the couple's strengths, even if these existed in the past and not currently. I see this as an important element of instilling hope.

As is true with the counselor position with families, part of the function of the couple counselor is to act as coach. Thus, as counseling continues and my relationship with the couple has developed, I provide concrete direction on how they need to do things that are planned as interventions. When they discuss how a homework assignment proceeded, I help them evaluate how they did things and make suggestions on how they might modify behaviors and activities to make them more useful in creating the changes the couple desires. In this way, I help them develop their own yardstick for evaluating their interactions.

The Ship is Sinking

There is a point at which I arrive with couples that are not making progress after a reasonable period of time and repeated attempts to stimulate change, when I have to "pull the plug" on counseling. This isn't easy for me, because I don't like giving up. But there are signs that I watch for that signal that either one or both spouses is not committed to repairing the relationship, or that I'm not the right counselor for them. One of my best rules of thumb is what I call "Cerio's Law." Simply stated, if I find myself working harder than the client to make things better for a long period of time, then it's time to back off and allow the client to take responsibility for their lack of action. I realize that this flies in the face of the basic strategic doctrine that the counselor is responsible for creating the conditions for change, but at some point, the couple needs to either ante up or walk away.

There are situations in which this is more obvious. For instance, I have seen couples where one spouse continually "hangs back," minimally involving themselves in the sessions, and not making strong commitments to homework assignments. It is not unusual that at some point, the spouse finally states that they "are done," and had been waiting for the other spouse to realize that, or to make the first move to separate. No one likes being the bad guy.

There are other couples that don't follow through on any strategies or interventions for improving their relationships. They remain in the same dysfunctional or conflict pattern that brought them to counseling and replay the same session over and over. Their one goal for counseling seems to be to prove that counseling cannot help and that they are doomed. While I understand that change is difficult and creates anxiety, if the couple continues to stagnate, it is usually time to "cut bait." I recommend that they can see a different counselor or take a break to "reset" and try again. As with the above situation, the intransigent behavior is often due to the fact that one spouse has already decided to end the relationship, and terminating the counseling facilitates the actual act of leaving.

The big thing to walk away with from this discussion is that, you can't help everyone or save every relationship. You are the coach and the couple is the team. If the team doesn't want to play to win, then it might be time to end the game.

Summary

This chapter has presented an introduction to couples counseling for novice counselors. This is a complex sub-category of family counseling and an important one. The functioning of the couple has a critical impact on the functioning of the family as a whole. Couples that are stable and functional tend to be more effective as parents, as it is easier for them to "be on the same page," and when they aren't, they are able to resolve differences and disagreements more effectively. Couples that are unstable and conflicted tend to transmit their conflict to the children through their dysfunctional parental interactions. In other words: happy couple, happy family.

If you are interested in developing expertise in this area, I strongly recommend that you familiarize yourself with the work of John Gottman (Gottman, 2012; Gottman & Silver, 2015; 2012) who has conducted seminal research on couple interactions. You should also review the work of Murray Bowen (1993), Frank Pittman (1987), and Gus Napier (2010), all of whom were pioneers in the couples counseling field. These will provide understanding of the context of couples issues and intervention frameworks and strategies. I find that working with couples is one of the most frustrating and rewarding activities of family counseling. There is nothing like helping a couple work through a situation that at first appears hopeless, and see them successfully repair their relationship and emerge as an even stronger and more stable couple than they previously had been in the best of times. It's hard work, but it's worth it.

References

Ackerman, N. (1966). *Treating the troubled family.* New York: Basic Books.

Adler, A. (1925/2011). *The practice and theory of individual psychotherapy.* Eastford, CT:

Martino Fine Books.

Baker, J. (2009). *50 Physics ideas you really need to know.* New York: Book Sales, Inc.

Baker Miller, J. (1987). *Toward a new psychology of women, 2nd ed.* Boston: Beacon Press.

Bateson, G. (1971). The cybernetics of self. Psychiatry, *34,* 1-18.

Bateson, G., Jackson, D., Haley, J., & Weakland, J. (1956). Toward a theory of schizophrenia.

Behavioral Science, 1, 251-264.

Becvar, D., & Becvar, R. (2000). *Family therapy: A systemic integration,* 2nd Ed. Boston:

Allyn & Bacon.

Bell, J.E. (1975). *Family therapy.* New York: Jason Aronson.

Berg, I., Nichols, K., & Pritchard, C. (1969). School phobia, its classification and relationship to

dependency. *Journal of Child Psychology and Psychiatry and Allied Disciplines, 10,*

123-141.

Boszormenyi-Nagy, I. (1987). *Foundations of contextual therapy.* New York: Brunner/Mazel.

Boszormenyi-Nagy, I., & Framo, J. (1965). *Intensive family therapy: Theoretical and practical*

aspects. New York: Harper & Row.

Bowen, M. (1993). *Family therapy in clinical practice.* New York: Jason Aronson.

Bowen, M. (2013). *The origins of family therapy: The NIMH family study project.* New York:

Jason Aronson.

Carlson, C. (1987). Resolving school problems with structural family therapy. *School*

Psychology Review, 16, 457-468.

Cerio, B. (2009). fnals09.blogspot.com.

Cerio, J. (1993). The family intervention action team: Putting family systems to work in the schools. *The Family Psychologist, 8* (3), 22/29.

Clarizio, H., & McCoy, G. (1976). *Behavior disorders in children.* New York: Crowell.

Christenson, S., & Conoley, J. (1992). *Home-school collaboration: Enhancing children's academic and social competence.* Silver Spring, MD: National Association of School Psychologists.

Conoley, J. (1987). Strategic family intervention: Three cases of school-aged children. *School Psychology Review, 16,* 469-486.

Dew, J., Britt, S., & Huston, S. (2012). Examining the relationship between financial issues and divorce. *Family Relations, 61,* 615-628.

Dush, D., & Brodsky, M. (1981). Effects and implications of the experimental double bind. *Psychological Reports, 48,* 895-900.

Ellis, J. (2000). *Founding brothers: The revolutionary generation.* New York: Random House.

Ellis, J. (2015). *The quartet: Orchestrating the second American Revolution 1783 – 1789.* New York: Knopf.

Erikson, E. (1950/1963*). Childhood and society.* New York: Norton.

Eysenck, H. (1952). The effects of psychotherapy: An evaluation. *Journal of Consulting Psychology, 16,* 319-324.

Fine, M., & Carlson, C., Ed. (1992). *The handbook of family-school intervention: A systems perspective.* Boston: Allyn and Bacon.

Fleming, A. (2015). Screen time v play time: what tech leaders won't let their own kids do. *The Guardian*, May 23, 2015. http://www.theguardian.com/technology/2015/may/23/screen-time-v-play-time-what-tech-leaders-wont-let-their-own-kids-do.

Freud, S. (1920/2016). *A general introduction to psychoanalysis*. CreateSpace

 Independent Publishing Platform: Pantianos Classics.

Freud, S., & Brill, A. (1995). *The basic writings of Sigmund Freud*. New York: Modern

 Library.

Fromm-Reichman, F. (1948). Notes on the development of schizophrenics by psychoanalytic

 psychiatry. *Psychiatry, 11*, 263-273.

Gilbert, R. (2004/2006). *Eight concepts of Bowen Therapy*. Lake Frederick, VA: Leading

 Systems Press.

Gottman, J. (2012). *Why marriages succeed or fail: And how you can make yours last*. New

 York: Simon & Schuster.

Gottman, J., & Silver, N. (2015). *The seven principles for making marriage work: A practical

 guide from the country's foremost relationship expert*. New York: Random House.

Gottman, J., & Silver, N. (2012). *Making love last: How to build trust and avoid betrayal*. New

 York: Simon & Schuster.

Gunn, W., & Fisher, B. (1989). Systemic approaches. In Brown, D. & Prout, H. T., Eds.,

 Counseling & psychotherapy with children and adolescents, 2nd Ed. Brandon, VT:

 Clinical Psychology Publishing.

Gunnison, H. (1990). Hypnocounseling: Ericksonian hypnosis for counselors. *Journal of

 Counseling and Development, 68,* 450-453.

Gurman, A. (1983). Family therapy research and the "new epistemology." *Journal of Marriage

 and Family Therapy, 9*, 227-234.

Haley, J. (1976). *Problem-solving therapy*. New York: Harper-Colophon Books.

Haley, J. (1991). Founders Interview with Jay Haley. AAMFT Founders Series.

Isaacson, W. (2007). *Einstein: His life and universe.* New York: Simon & Schuster.

Jackson, D. (1957). The question of family homeostasis. *Psychiatric Quarterly Supplement, 31,* 79-90.

Jackson, D. (1965). Family rules: Marital quid pro quo. *Archives of General Psychiatry, 12,* 589-594.

Jacobson, N. (1995). The overselling of therapy. *The Family Therapy Networker, 19* (2), 40-47.

Kahn, J., & Narsten, J. (1962). School refusal: A comprehensive view of school phobia and other failures of school attendance. *American Journal of Orthopsychiatry, 32,* 702-718.

Kelly, E. (1973). School phobia: A review of theory and treatment. *Psychology in the Schools, 10,* 33-42.

Kennedy, W. (1965). School phobia: Rapid treatment of 50 cases. *Journal of Abnormal Psychology, 70,* 285-289.

Lidz, R., & Lidz, T. (1949). The family environment of schizophrenic patients. *Journal of Psychiatry, 106,* 332-345.

Madanes, C. (1981). *Strategic family therapy.* San Francisco: Jossey-Bass.

McGoldrick, M., Gerson, R., & Shellenberger, S. (1999). *Genograms: Assessment and intervention, 2nd ed.* New York: Norton.

Minuchin, S., Lee, W., & Simon, G. (1996). *Mastering family therapy: Journeys of growth and transformation.* New York: Wiley.

Minuchin, S., & Nichols, M. (1993*). Family healing: Tales of hope and renewal from family therapy.* New York: Free Press.

Minuchin, S. (1991). "Founders Interview with Salvador Minuchin." AAMFT Founders Series.

Minuchin, S., & Fishman, C. (1981). *Family therapy techniques*. Cambridge, MA: Harvard University Press.

Minuchin. S., Rossman, B., & Baker, L. (1978). Psychosomatic families: Anorexia nervosa in context. Cambridge, MA; Harvard University Press.

Morris, R., & Kratochwill, T. (1991). *Childhood fears and phobias*. In T. Kratochwill & R. Morris (Eds.), *The practice of child therapy*. New York: Pergamon.

Napier, A. (2010). *The fragile bond: In search of an equal, intimate and enduring marriage*. New York: Harper Collins.

Nichols, M. & Schwartz, R. (1991). *Family therapy: Concepts and methods*, 2nd Ed. Boston: Allyn and Bacon.

Ohlsen, M. (1982). *Family counseling and therapy*. Itasca, IL: F.E. Peacock.

Papp, P., & Imber-Black, E. (1996). Family themes: Transmission and transformation. *Family Process, 35*, 5-20.

Pittman, F. (1987). *Turning points: Treating families in transition and crisis*. New York: Norton.

Power, T., & Bartholomew, K. (1987). Family-school relationship patterns: An ecological assessment. *School Psychology Review, 16*, 498-512.

Richtel, S. (2011). A Silicon Valley school that doesn't compute. *The New York Times*, October 22, 2011, http://www.nytimes.com/2011/10/23/technology/at-waldorf-school-in-silicon-valley-technology-can-wait.html?_r=0.

Rogers, C. (1942). *Counseling and psychotherapy*. Boston: Houghton Mifflin.

Rogers, C. (1961/1989). *On becoming a person: A therapists view of psychotherapy*. New York: Houghton Mifflin Harcourt.

Scott, J., Cully, M., & Weissberg, E. (1996). Helping the separation anxious school refuser.

    Elementary School Guidance & Counseling, 29, 289-296.

Skinner, B.F. (1974). *About behaviorism.* New York: 1974.

Satir, V. (1967). *Conjoint family therapy.* Palo Alto, CA: Science and Behavior Books.

Satir, V. (1991). Thinking aloud: Interview with Virgina Satir. New York: Spectrum

    Foundation.

Sullivan, H.S. (1968). *The interpersonal theory of psychiatry.* New York: W.W. Norton.

Tahmisian, J., & McReynolds, W. (1971). Use of parents as behavioral engineers in the

    treatment of a school phobic girl. *Journal of Counseling Psychology, 18*, 225-228.

Walters, M., Carter, B., Papp, P., & Silverstein, O. (1988). *The invisible web: Gender patterns*

    in family relationships. New York: Guilford.

Watzlawick, P. (1978). *The language of change.* New York: Basic Books.

Watzlawick, P., Weakland, J., & Fisch, R. (1974). *Change: Principles of problem formation and*

    problem resolution. New York: Norton.

Weinberg, G. (1975). *Introduction to general systems thinking.* New York: Wiley.

Whitaker, C. (1991). Founders Interview with Carl Whitaker. AAMFT Founders Series.

Whitaker, C., & Bumberry, W. (1988). *Dancing with the family: A symbolic-experiential*

    approach. New York: Brunner/Mazel.

Wiener, N. (1948). Cybernetics. *Scientific American, 179 (5)*, 14-18.

Wynne, L., Ryckoff, I., Day, J., & Hirsch, S. (1958). Pseudo-mutuality in the family relations of

schizophrenics. *Psychiatry, 21*, 205-220.

Yalom, I., (2005). The theory and practice of group psychotherapy. New York: Basic Books.

Appendix A

Answers
to
Chapter 2
Application Activities

Identifying Development Stages

1) Family Stage: Parent Separation from Children

   Issues: Redefining the couple
                          Intimacy

2) Family Stages: Couple Formation
                          Parents of Young Children

3) Family Stages: Adult Children with Aging Parents
                          Parent Separation from Children
                          Parents wth Tweens
                          Parents of Teens

World Views

1) Mother   They're just like their father.
                          I'm a victim of men.

   Boys   She's weak and we don't have to listen to her.

2) Mother   Circle the wagons.
                          The system is out to get us.

3) Tom   Spare the rod, spoil the child.
                          Mind your own business.

Subsystems and Boundaries

1) Subsystems: Parent and Child   Boundaries: Enmeshed

   Why   Mom is inappropriately looking to the child for comfort.

   Subsystem: Couple   Boundaries: Disengaged

   Why?   Husband is avoiding intimacy with wife.

2) Subsystems: Parent and Child   Boundaries: Disengaged

   Why?   Father is putting his own needs (drinking) ahead of the needs of the children and putting them at risk.

3) Subsystems: Parent and Child   Boundaries: Enmeshed

   Why?   Parents are "helicoptoring" when son needs to be independent.

4) Subsystems   Couple, Parent, and Child   Boundaries: Normal

   Why?   Parents can invite the oldest daughter into the Parent subsystem, appropriately, to babysit, and then have her return to the Child subsystem after their date. They are also making time for the Couple subsystem, appropriately.

5) Subsystems: Parent and Child   Boundaries: Disengaged

   Why?   Parents have no idea of what is appropriate regarding their child's needs and safety, so make a very selfish decision.

Family Hierarchy

Hierarchy	How might this affect the family?
1) Mom Dad Kids	Dad might not be listened to by the kids.
2) Emma Parents Siblings	Emma's siblings' needs might not be recognized by the parents.
3) Boys Parents	Parents feel incompetent regarding setting limits. Boys know that they don't have to follow rules because parents won't do anything.

Triangles

1)

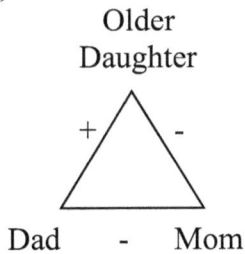

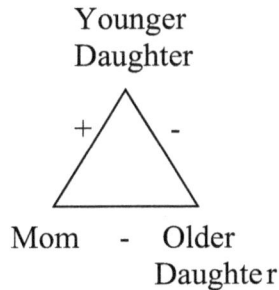

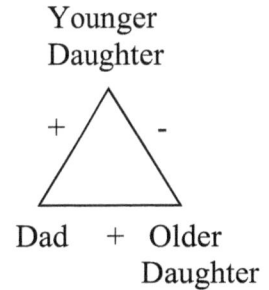

2)

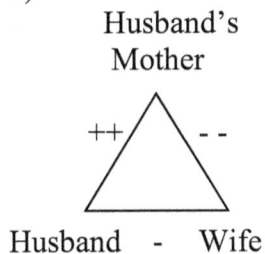

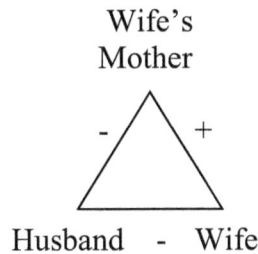

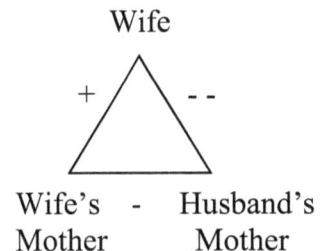

3)

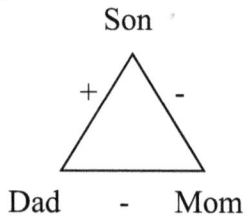

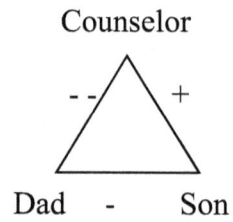

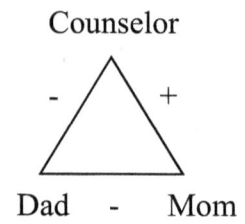

Appendix B

Answers
to
Chapters 3 and 4
Application Activities

Chapter Three

Reading the Genogram

1) What health patterns do you see?

   McPhersons: Heart disease

   Flanigans: Alzheimer's Disorder

2) What employment or education patterns are evident?

   McPhersons:
   - Employment   Teachers
   - Education   College degrees

   Flanigans:
   - Employment   First responders – Law enforcement, fire fighters, nurses
   - Education   High school diplomas.

3) Which individuals are divorced?
   - Sean and Agnes
   - Mary Elizabeth and Robert
   - Nancy and Anthony
   - Nancy and Tim

4) List 4 pairs of step-siblings.
   - Allison and Allison
   - Gabe and Allison
   - Mary and Allison
   - Allison and Nancy
   - Gabe and Nancy
   - Mary and Nancy

5) How many biological children does Nancy in the third generation have?   3

   How of them reside with her?   0

6) Are there any pregnancies shown?   Yes

   If so, which couple(s) are expecting?   Gabe and Jen

Chapter Four

Reframing

1) The lights are telling us that it's time to get some rest.

   The lights want us to get frisky.

   The lights are telling us to spend some quality time together.

2) She's reassuring us that she can live independently.

   She wants us to know that she can get along without us.

3) He wants to be close to his new sibling.

   He's so proud of his new sibling that he wants to be just like him.

   He is trying to teach his sibling how to be a baby.

4) She's trying to make sure that her mom gets her nourishment.

   She is so close to her mother that she wants to be just like her.

Index

D
DAFFI-DUCC, 88-95, 104-113, 139-149
Decomposition Law, 8
Defense mechanisms, 40
Denial, 40
Developmental stages, 56, 57-63
Differentiation, 29-32
Disengaged subsystems, 67
Disorganized complexity, 4
Divorce, 218-224
Double-bind, 36-39

E
Emotional cutoff, 31
Empathy, 46, 118
Enactments, 125-126, 133
Enmeshed subsystems, 67

F
Family developmental stages, 55-63, 90, 96, 107, 144, 223-225
Family emotional system, 30-32
Family fun time, 169-170
Family Group therapy, 28
Family of origin analysis, 96-101
Family-school system, 232-233
Family-school triangles, 205-210
Family therapy history of, 14-49
Feedback loops, 10-14
Feminist therapy, 48
FIAT, 208-211
First session, 126-133
Fromm-Reichman, Frieda, 20
Fry, William, 34
Fusion, 29-32

G
Games, 159, 166-168
General Systems Theory, 3-5
  amplifying feedback loops, 12
  attenuating feedback loops, 10
  boundaries, 5, 6
  circular causality, 4
  closed system, 6
  cybernetics, 3, 10-14

www.ingramcontent.com/pod-product-compliance
Lightning Source LLC
Chambersburg PA
CBHW050239290326
41929CB00048B/3006